Control and Protect

Control and Protect

Collaboration, Carceral Protection,
and Domestic Sex Trafficking in the
United States

Jennifer Musto

UNIVERSITY OF CALIFORNIA PRESS

University of California Press, one of the most
distinguished university presses in the United States,
enriches lives around the world by advancing scholarship
in the humanities, social sciences, and natural sciences.
Its activities are supported by the UC Press Foundation
and by philanthropic contributions from individuals
and institutions. For more information, visit
www.ucpress.edu.

University of California Press
Oakland, California

Library of Congress Cataloging-in-Publication Data

Names: Musto, Jennifer, author.
Title: Control and protect : collaboration, carceral
    protection, and domestic sex trafficking in the United
    States / Jennifer Musto.
Description: Oakland, California : University of
    California Press, [2016] | Includes bibliographical
    references and index.
Identifiers: LCCN 2016015690| ISBN 9780520281950
    (cloth : alk. paper) | ISBN 9780520281967 (pbk. : alk.
    paper) | ISBN 9780520957749 (electronic)
Subjects: LCSH: Human trafficking victims—United
    States—Case studies. | Human trafficking—United
    States—Prevention—Case studies.
Classification: LCC HQ281 .M87 2016 | DDC
    306.3/620973—dc23
LC record available at https://lccn.loc.gov/2016015690

Manufactured in the United States of America

25 24 23 22 21 20 19 18 17 16
10 9 8 7 6 5 4 3 2 1

Contents

Illustrations

Tables

Preface

On August 31, 2015, a news app on my iPhone alerted me to a story that had just come out in Texas. It was about a new state law—H.B. 418—broadly aimed at enhancing protections for youth who have been in sex-trafficking situations, including a mandate for a speedy, non-court-ordered response to "rush a rescued sex trafficking survivor into 'a safe refuge' ideally a secure foster home."[1]

The story detailed the challenges faced in implementing the law, including limited resources and a general lack of secure (i.e., restrictive) housing options, something deemed integral to keeping kids safe. Yet it was what a district judge featured in the story said that grabbed my attention. In responding to concerns about what happens when a child is placed in an unsecure foster home, she told reporters at KXAN: "The question: Is that child being further traumatized by being treated as a criminal? Do I want to lock them up? No I don't. . . . We've got to get them the services that meet their needs. Until we build the services that meet their needs we can count on, the traffickers are already ahead of us."[2]

Some books are born out of a particular place, a memorable scene. This news story and the judge's comment took me back to the more abstract origins of this project, reminding me of a recurring message I heard from a few law enforcement agents back in the late 2000s when I first started to learn about domestic sex trafficking in the United States: underage youth involved in prostitution—whom we now refer to as victims of domestic sex trafficking—are sometimes arrested or locked up to get help. It was a message I couldn't fully shake. What's more, around the time I heard it, the paradigmatic victim they were referring to—a young girl presumed to be in love with the pimp exploiting her (now reimagined by law enforcement as a trafficker)—met the U.S. federal government's definition of a victim of sex trafficking.

In 2000, the U.S. Congress passed the Trafficking Victims Protection Act (TVPA),[3] a law that treats human trafficking as modern-day slavery.[4] This benchmark federal antitrafficking legislation covers a broad range of trafficking situations that are both sexual and nonsexual in nature, but which contain elements of force, fraud, or coercion. It defines trafficking as follows:

1. sex trafficking in which a commercial sex act is induced by force, fraud, or coercion, *or* in which the person induced to perform such act has not attained 18 years of age; or

2. the recruitment, harboring, transportation, provision, or obtaining of a person for labor or services, through the use of force, fraud, or coercion for the purpose of subjection to involuntary servitude, peonage, debt bondage, or slavery.[5]

Notably, under the TVPA, there are no coercion requirements for minors. This means that youth involved in the sex trade are de facto defined as victims of sex trafficking whether or not they frame their experiences as such. "Trafficking" is, as political scientist Joel Quirk notes, an ill-fitting aggregate category to describe myriad forms of exploitation.[6] It is unruly, but capacious, and has proved quite adaptive in extending in new directions. The expansion of trafficking to include "domestic" sex trafficking situations in the United States is one of its more curious developments.[7] And with respect to youth in general, and cisgender[8] girls in particular, the TVPA performed a notable discursive feat: it rebranded an established trend—underage children and teens' forced involvement with commercial sex—and reframed it as sex trafficking and a form of modern-day slavery.[9]

The TVPA's definitional attention to youth under 18, coupled with subsequent reauthorizations, has had other effects too. For instance, it expanded[10] and implicitly prioritized a two-pronged ideological agenda: First, that trafficking for sex is of greater importance than forced labor cases that are nonsexual in nature, a finding that runs counter to scholars' suggestion that nonsexual forms of labor exploitation are as pressing of a problem as sex trafficking.[11] Second, that antiprostitution or what some scholars refer to as neoabolitionist interventions are best equipped to orient antitrafficking advocacy.[12] Following the TVPA's reauthorizations in 2005 and 2008 and during the second term of the Bush Administration, there was a concerted policy push to prioritize sex trafficking over other forms of nonsexual abuse. As anthropologist Denise Brennan has described, the policy and advocacy effects of these trends translated into more funds and attention dedicated to the "part of the TVPA that grants protections to U.S. citizen youth in the sex sector."[13] So although the TVPA clearly recognizes nonsexual forms of exploitation, the perception that sex trafficking in general and sex trafficking of youth in particular is a more pressing problem than nonsexual forms of labor trafficking has focused some frontline law enforcement activities on this specific part of the law.

As the legal boundaries of trafficking have expanded, so have perceptions about victims. Once figured in mainstream media as a girl or woman forcibly trafficked into prostitution and invariably hailing from third world origins, the image of a trafficked person has shifted to include American girls and women trafficked for sex, now assumed to be modern-day slaves and "hiding in plain sight."[14] With a newfound focus on domestic sex trafficking cases taking place in the United States, perceptions of suspected sex traffickers changed too. Once typically perceived as non-U.S. citizens with ties to organized crime, prototypical traffickers may now be seen as gang-affiliated pimps who exploitatively profit from selling the sexual services of people they exploit on the street and online. A focus on domestic trafficking in the United States has thus moved trafficking discussions away from an exclusive focus on borders, migrants, and coercive labor practices that are nonsexual in nature and towards discussions about pimps, gang members, and local crime.[15] We can situate the growth in attention to domestic sex trafficking in the United States as both the result of federal and state legislative changes and broader trends taking place within the criminal-justice system, where communities of color in general and black men in particular have been disproportionally exposed to police oversight and incarceration.[16]

Heightened attention to domestic sex trafficking also emerges within a national context where the carceral state[17] has been leveraged to respond to gendered crimes and violence against women.[18] It is not that migration is no longer central to how trafficking is understood in a U.S. context or that "movement across borders" and the forced labor of non-U.S. citizens are no longer constitutive definitional attributes.[19] Rather, what the decidedly American invention of domestic sex trafficking offers is a companion story of sorts, one with plotlines centered on domestic "at risk" victims, the carceral state as protector, and different kinds of state-oriented, non-state-assisted responses where the boundaries between punishment and protection, victim and offender, and state and nonstate authority are not always clear.[20]

This brings me back to the Texas news story and the idea that youth now viewed as domestic victims sometimes need to be treated like offenders in order to receive assistance. Federal law recognizes that teens and kids under eighteen are victims of trafficking not criminal offenders. However, state laws on underage prostitution vary, which means that young people in some states still face criminal sanctions or other types of intervention ranging from criminal prosecution to diversion, rehabilitation, intervention, decriminalization, or some combination.[21] The promising news is that more states have passed laws that recognize youth involved in the sex trade as victims and have advanced different coordinated, collaborative, and multidisciplinary response systems aimed at treating them as such.[22] The range of victim-centered, collaborative responses to domestic sex trafficking now in development further suggests that the "arrest-to-assist" model I've previously discussed, and which I describe throughout this book, has shifted somewhat, or more precisely, it isn't the only model out there.[23] Yet like adults and migrants seen as vulnerable to sex trafficking irrespective of age, some "domestic" youth may nonetheless face a twofold risk, both from individuals who may exploit them and from a collaborative anti-trafficking response system in development that utilizes criminal justice tactics of rescue and recovery as a way to protect them.

The reason for this is plain: prostitution is widely criminalized in the United States. Because people now deemed "at risk" of domestic sex trafficking—generally assumed to be youth—may be mistaken for adults engaged in illegal activity, they, like adults may endure varied types of carceral oversight.[24] Moreover, as law-enforcement agencies have become attuned to the domestic sex-trafficking problem in their own corners of the country, efforts to identify victims of trafficking have given rise to policing strategies that authorize the arrest of sex-trade-involved women and girls of different ages as a way to identify them. As one Houston Police Department captain explained in a September 2015 *Houston Chronicle* story on prostitution busts in the city, "Here's the conundrum for law enforcement. . . . You want to help people but you have to make the arrest to get them the help they need." He went on. "We really do care about the women. Even though we're arresting them, we don't want them to go back to that life."[25] The story noted that of the 114 prostitution arrests the department made in July 2015, three juveniles and seven adults were identified as human trafficking victims.[26] Utilizing trafficking discourses to show care for prospective victims while simultaneously authorizing stepped-up anti-prostitution efforts by law enforcement is nothing new.[27] But what is noteworthy are the reasons why some frontline police officers and their nonstate partners may view an arrest and jail time, or, to put it in more victim-centered antitrafficking terms, a court-ordered diversion program, a secure (sometimes locked) placement, or protracted judicial oversight as the best way to help. Against the backdrop of mounting discussion—bolstered by government funding—that fighting sex trafficking demands cooperation between different law enforcement agencies and nonstate partners,[28] a central question emerges: do collaboratively focused, victim-centered antitrafficking interventions truly mark a wholesale departure from the more punitive methods of the past? That is the main question this book explores.

To answer it, I have travelled throughout the United States and spent hundreds of hours engaged in interviews, informal meetings, and on- and offline observations to learn more about people whose lives or work has been touched by antitrafficking efforts in some way. Between 2011 and 2015, I conducted interviews with law-enforcement agents, advocates, social workers, and professionals who have participated in a range of antitrafficking activities as well as youth and adults who had been identified as victims of sex trafficking by law enforcement, nonstate actors, or others. In addition to drawing upon around forty formal interviews, this book is shaped by observations and in some instances, direct participation in meetings, conferences, trainings and various antitrafficking events held throughout the United States. These activities provided the opportunity to informally converse with a broad range of actors, including but not limited to law enforcement agents, social service and legal advocates, analysts, technology researchers, a legislative staffer, and sex worker–rights advocates.[29] Observations and informal conversations also helped me to understand what goes into coordinating on-the-ground "antitrafficking interventions," a term I use throughout the book to describe formal and improvised state and nonstate responses to sex trafficking.

This research project was difficult from the start, but it became even more challenging as I learned about interventions framed as protective but that led to explicit and, in some cases, more subtle forms of punishment, surveillance, and social control of adults and youth seen as vulnerable to domestic sex trafficking. Fueling my confusion was a message I heard some law enforcement and nonstate actors relay to make sense of this work: "domestic" victims (particularly, though not exclusively underage youth) sold for sex and exploited by "trafficker-pimps" may look like victims, and may be legally defined as such, but may not see themselves that way. Because of this self-perception, and because some "at risk" victims are thought to act more like offenders, criminal justice tools are required to protect them. Arrests, detention, diversion, court supervision, and electronic monitoring are thus needed to keep them safe. Moreover, different actors made the case for why law enforcement cannot do this work alone. What is needed, some suggested, are ways for nonprofit, nongovernmental, faith-based, and corporate actors to become partners to law enforcement and help augment its work in this area. This book offers a partial explanation about some of the reasons and motivations behind some of these collaborations.

CAUTIONS AND CAVEATS

I offer a few additional caveats about what this book does and does not address. To begin with, this book does not, in any comprehensive way, describe the violence, exploitation, trauma, or suffering that people vulnerable to what is now called "domestic" sex trafficking experience at the hands of individuals presumed to exploit them (e.g., pimps and traffickers) or whom they interact with while in these situations (e.g., johns and clients or, in some antitrafficking actors' preferred terms, buyers and exploiters). Ideas about choice, coercion, and exploitation are complex and fall outside the realm of a book focused instead on explaining antitrafficking responses where the boundaries between what qualifies as protection and what constitutes punishment are difficult to define. All too often, descriptions about people's experiences with sex-trade involvement are reduced to morally panicked caricatures or melodramas that reflect the ideological persuasions and projections of the narrators rather than the perceptions of those who experience it most directly.[30] It is therefore out of an appreciation for the complexity of individuals' experiences with what we now call "domestic" trafficking and out of a commitment *not* to misinterpret their experiences, that this book does not delve deeply into the interpersonal dynamics between victims and those accused of exploiting them. The only exception to this rule involves specific instances where youth and adults I met mentioned these relationships in answering questions about the interventions to which they were exposed to. These stories were important to them, and I have therefore included their descriptions.

This book also does not go into detail about experiences with family members or adult caregivers. Some antitrafficking and child advocates have focused on the interpersonal struggles and familial disruptions that can set exploitation in motion. Others focus on the exploitative influence of trafficker-pimps or seek to construct corrective interventions to reform victims' relationships to those accused of exploiting them. These are valid areas of study. However, my "starting point"[31] is different. Rather than describing the contours of interpersonal relationships or analyzing what factors contributed to different youth and adults becoming involved in the sex trade, my primary point of departure is the point at which state and nonstate actors seek to intervene to assist persons assumed to be exploited. My aim is thus to examine antitrafficking interventions and better understand their discursive and practical effects.

With respect to language, the "at risk" trafficked youth, teen, or adult I refer to throughout the book generally refers to cisgender girls and women designated female at birth whose gender identities and chosen presentation aligns with that designation. When I began this project, I used the non-gender-specific term "trafficked person" to explain my project to prospective participants. Yet in interviews, observations, and informal conversations, talk of "trafficked" persons or a "trafficking victim" tended to function as a "shorthand" for talking about the experiences of underage girls, though adult women and migrants sometimes figured in discussions too.[32] That this book discusses "gendered" protection and gendered "punitive protection" without talking about the experiences of cisgender boys and transgender youth who also meet the TVPA definitions of trafficking victims is a limitation of it, and of research on trafficking more generally. Yet although underage girls are neither the only population who meet the TVPA's severe definition of trafficking nor the only population of youth who engage in survival sex or forced into sex-trafficking situations, in this book, the "at risk" victims alluded to are cisgender girls or women (hereafter referred to as girls and women respectively).[33]

I offer one final note of clarification by way of personal anecdote. In December 2012, I delivered a talk on aspects of this project before members of the Justice Studies Program at Eastern Kentucky University. Surrounded by keen observers of crime and justice, a member of the audience asked: "If pimps and traffickers aren't at the center of the domestic trafficking story you're trying to tell, then who is the 'bad guy?' Is it the case that neoliberalism is the real pimp daddy?" My interpretation of this question was that it was not meant as an incendiary or a racially insensitive comment about pimps. Rather, it was a way to flip the script on an antitrafficking response system I had described that positions individual perpetrators—here "trafficker-pimps"—as the sole source of the problem. After years of reflection, the short answer to is yes. The story I aim to tell in *Control and Protect* is that neoliberalism,[34] or more specifically, the carceral protectionist cures it authorizes, is the biggest pimp daddy of them all. Acknowledging this does not condone violence of any sort, nor does it minimize the real violence that people experience at the hands of individuals who harm and exploit them. Nor am I suggesting that state and nonstate assistance are not sometimes warranted or that collaborations cannot, at times, be helpful to victims in need. What I am proposing, however, is that collaboration can inspire state-orchestrated, non-state-assisted responses that sometimes come with punitive strings attached to them. No matter how much protective language is used to describe it, it is shaped by system whose structure is punitive by design.

Acknowledgments

Once and what now seems like a lifetime ago, I was a student of Women's Studies at DePaul University. During my undergraduate studies I had the chance to meet with and learn from some young women involved in the sex trade who were organizing on behalf of their own lives, needs, and well-being. I have tried to carry with me a few lessons I learned back then, namely: to listen deeply, to question my assumptions, and to never forget that people are their own best experts when it comes to their lives. I offer my heartfelt gratitude to them and to all of the people who daily live and passionately fight for the rights of sex workers and survivors of exploitation. You have been my greatest teachers. Thanks, too, to all those who took the time to explain what sex trafficking, sex work, and anti-trafficking practices look like from their perspective. I am unable to thank you by name, but I am grateful to have had the chance to learn from you.

The ideas in this book conceptually grew out of a dissertation project at UCLA. I owe a debt of gratitude to my dissertation advisor, Gail Kligman, who saw promise in me and potential in the project. She pushed me to delve into the law-enforcement piece of the anti-trafficking puzzle. From Gail I have learned to be clearer in word, to embrace the joy of rewriting, and to pick myself up and keep moving "onwards!" when faced with setbacks. I also want to thank the members of my dissertation committee, and Katie Oliviero, Saru Matambanadzo, Evangeline Heiliger, Loran Marsan, Laura Foster, Tina Beyene, and Anna Ward who critically engaged with my work in its earliest form. A few years into my graduate studies at UCLA, I had the great fortune to meet Elena Shih. Elena's brilliance as a scholar-ethnographer is matched by her infectious energy and kindness. I thank her for her friendship.

I am grateful as well to the many scholars whose research on human trafficking, anti-trafficking, sex work, and sexuality has contributed to my own understanding. I offer a special note of thanks to Elizabeth Bernstein for myriad scholarly contributions. The scholarly insights and research contributions of Carole Vance, Sine Plambech, Elena Shih, Crystal Jackson, Ronald Weitzer, Denise Brennan, Sealing Cheng, Kimberly Hoang, Gregory Mitchell, Joel Quirk, Paul Amar, and many others have also helped me to understand these topics.

The Women's and Gender Studies Department at Wellesley College has provided a supportive intellectual home for me to pursue this work. To my colleagues Elena Creef, Charlene Galarneau, Rosanna Hertz, Nancy Marshall, Irene Mata, Dulce Natividad, Susan Reverby, and Sima Shaksari, I thank you for the guidance you offered at different stages of the writing process. Working with Betty Tiro is a joy, and she helped me stay focused and get organized when I needed it most. I also want to thank colleagues Michael Jeffries and Hahrie Han for supporting public-facing research and providing an opportunity to present aspects of this work at a Project on Public Leadership & Action event in spring 2015.

Shannon Ward, Beth Feldstein, and Cristina Ferlauto provided impressive research assistance at different stages of the project. I also want to thank my colleague and neighbor extraordinaire Corri Taylor for helping me make sense of some important quantitative data. To my students, whose curiosity, critical insights, and brilliance daily challenge and inspire me to grow in new ways, thank you!

The support and friendship of many colleagues sustained me over the years. Katie Oliviero, Leslie Wang, and Saher Selod helped me to keep going and keep writing when I was in the thick of revisions. It was love at first friendship sight when I met Sara Hendren and Brian Funck in the Netherlands all those many years ago. For their friendship I am and shall forever be grateful. I also want to thank K. Surkan, Linda Blum, Olivia Banner, Kerry Ward, Avi Brisman, Judah Schept, Inela Selimovic, Erika Kates, Nick Knouf, Kimberly Hoang, and Henry Pontell for their support and generous advice.

While working on this book, I made a few cross-country moves, geographical relocations that brought with them enriching opportunities to connect with different scholarly communities. I thank the Women's,

Gender, and Sexuality Studies program at Northeastern University and especially Linda Blum and Lihua Wang for welcoming me to the program as a Visiting Scholar during the 2011–12 academic year. In 2012, I had the opportunity to join the USC Annenberg Center on Communication Leadership & Policy as a postdoctoral fellow. I am beyond grateful to Mark Latonero for bringing me onto his research team and sharpening my thinking about trafficking, technology, and data. My time at USC would not have been possible without Mark, funding support from Microsoft Research, and the visionary thinking of danah boyd, who together with Mark have created a dynamic and intellectually diverse community of technology and trafficking researchers. I would also like to thank Mitali Thakor and Rane Johnson, from whom I have learned so much. During the 2012–13 academic year, I was an external faculty fellow in the Humanities Research Center's inaugural Human Trafficking Seminar at Rice University. I want to extend my thanks to seminar participants and especially to the seminar leaders, Kerry Ward and James Sidbury, for seeing promise in my project and providing the time, space, and opportunity to move my research in new directions.

Over the years I have had the privilege of presenting aspects of this work at institutions including Eastern Kentucky University, the University of Colorado, Boulder, Yale University, Smith College, Rice University, New York University, and UCLA. I am grateful to the organizers, co-panelists, and audience members for their critical feedback and engagement with my work. I would especially like to thank Avi Brisman, Judah Schept, Victor Kappeler, and the faculty and students at the School of Justice Studies at EKU. I count my visit to EKU as a transformative experience, and I am so grateful to have had the chance to meet and learn from faculty and students during my stay.

Thanks especially as well to Wellesley College, the Humanities Research Center at Rice University, the Women's, Gender, & Sexuality Studies Program at Northeastern University, USC Annenberg Center on Communication Leadership & Policy, Microsoft Research and the Microsoft Digital Crimes Unit, and the UCLA Center for the Study of Women for providing generous financial and institutional support.

At the University of California Press, my deepest thanks go to my editor, Maura Roessner, whose belief in this project and guidance at every stage of the book-writing process means more to me than words can adequately express. I also want to thank Jack Young, the Editorial Board, and all of the staff at the University of California Press for their time and support.

This book has undergone multiple revisions and transformations. I thank my writing group– Leslie Wang and Saher Selod—for providing critical feedback on different chapters. I am also grateful to Rosanna Hertz, Gail Kligman, K. Surkan, Avi Brisman, and Jessica Cobb for reading and providing feedback on specific chapters. I especially want to thank Samantha Majic, Edith Kinney, and the anonymous reviewers for digging into the manuscript, drawing attention to structural issues, and offering concrete and detailed advice for how to improve it. And I thank John and Sue Morris for their help in preparing the manuscript for publication.

Different ideas and parts of the book originally appeared in other publications. I would like to acknowledge the following as original sources of publication: "Domestic Minor Sex Trafficking and the Detention-to-Protection Pipeline," *Dialectical Anthropology,* (2013) 37:2: 257–276. Reproduced as part of CC-BY license. "The Trafficking-Technology Nexus" (with danah boyd). *Social Politics: International Studies in Gender, State & Society* (2014): 21:3: 461–483. Reproduced with permission from danah boyd and through an Open Access license. "The Post Human Anti-Trafficking Turn: Technology, DMST, and Augmented Human-Machine Alliances." In K. Hoang and R. Parreñas, *Human Trafficking Reconsidered: Rethinking the Problem, Envisioning New Solutions* (2014). Reproduced with permission. "Carceral Protectionism and Multi-Professional Anti-Trafficking Human Rights Work in the Netherlands," *International Feminist Journal of Politics,* 12:3–4, 381–400 (www.tandfonline.com). Reproduced with permission.

I have been sustained and supported in this work through the love of my family. I thank my Mom, who has supported me in all things. It is she who taught me to keep my heart open and my dreams of justice grounded, and who showed me that love and grace and hope can always be found in the most adverse of circumstances. To the Musto family: Dad, Karen, Steven, Belinda, Lily, and Clara, thank you for believing in me. Dad, you have instilled in me a love of words, an interest in the law, and an obsession with all things newsworthy, for which I am very appreciative.

To Anthony and Noah, my family, my guys, my heart. Noah, your humor, wit, and shared love of bad television lifted my spirits on many a day when writing was slow-going and my focus adrift. Anthony, I thank you for your support of this work and your unwavering belief that I would someday finish. In between cross-country moves and bicoastal treks, we've managed to co-create a most beautiful life, and I thank you for the love, laughter, and delight you bring to my life each and every day.

Introduction

More than just the site of the Seattle Seahawks' upset win against the
Denver Broncos, the 2014 Super Bowl emerged as the symbolic epicen-
ter of the United States' supposed sex trafficking problem. In advance of
Super Bowl Sunday, a slew of media reports surfaced alerting the American public to the heightened risk of sex trafficking assumed to accompany the event. Law-enforcement agencies like the New York City
Police Department prepared for the anticipated uptick in trafficking
cases by orchestrating pregame crackdowns that resulted in two hundred arrests, mostly of "johns and sex traffickers."[1] Meanwhile, in a
show of multiagency cooperation, fifty different entities partnered to
recover underage sex trafficking victims. "Operation Super Bowl," as it
was called, involved local police departments, the Department of Homeland Security, nongovernmental organizations, and a technology firm,
IST International. After the sting, an FBI press release stated that "sixteen juveniles between the ages of fourteen and seventeen were rescued."[2] The press release did not mention whether adults voluntarily
engaged in the commercial sex trade were also identified or arrested as
part of the operation, a curious omission.

The media coverage that followed generally rehashed law enforcement press releases on the operations,[3] depicting the Super Bowl–
inspired stings as illustrative of law enforcement's proactive approach

to rescuing victims of trafficking—a term that broadly refers to coercive labor practices yet typically connotes exploitation linked to sexual labor.[4] Yet an op-ed piece that appeared in the January 31, 2014, edition of the *New York Times* offered a more critical and insightful take on the anti-sex-trafficking activities surrounding the event. In this piece, Kate Mogulescu—founder and supervising attorney of the Exploitation Intervention Project, formerly known as the Trafficking Victims Advocacy Project at the Legal Aid Society—suggested that mainstream discussions of sex trafficking were characterized by "hype, fear-mongering, and oversimplification" and called out law enforcement and policymakers for perpetuating myths about it.[5] Referencing analysis from the Global Alliance Against Traffic in Women—a leading nongovernmental organization well versed in the contradictory aims of global antitrafficking policies—Mogulescu pointed out that little empirical research exists that links sporting events like the Super Bowl to heightened sex trafficking, a finding supported in the scholarly literature.[6]

She also used the occasion of the Super Bowl and the hype surrounding it to alert readers to another crucial, yet seldom discussed, fact: individuals "officially" identified as victims of trafficking and people voluntarily involved in the sex trade face heightened risk of victimization from the very antitrafficking response system created to help them. "Turning them [the 'rescued'] into defendants," she wrote, "and pushing them through the criminal-justice system contradicts any claim of assistance." She concluded the piece by asking: "If the goal is to address human trafficking, why is law enforcement targeting those believed to be victims?"[7] Mogulescu's article was insightful, and the comments and responses that poured in afterward proved additionally instructive.

In a response letter to the editor of the *New York Times* on February 4, 2014, New York's attorney general, Eric Schneiderman, took issue with Mogulescu for having failed to mention "a major shift" in law enforcement's approach to trafficking. This "shift"— what some police I interviewed referred to, in turns, as a "culture shift" and "paradigm shift"—is an approach where "American law enforcement treat prostitutes as crime victims, not criminals."[8] Citing cooperative agreements his office established with nonprofit agencies,[9] Schneiderman underscored his office's prioritization of victim services[10] and commitment to a "victim-centered" response—a term used in antitrafficking circles that generally refers to a model of intervention that provides trafficked persons with access to social services and that affirms their status as victims rather than criminal offenders.

On one side, we have an approach that advocates for people in sex trafficking situations to be recognized as victims and to avoid justice-involvement that mirrors the treatment of criminal offenders. On the other side, we have a misguided criminal-justice system that unfairly treats trafficked persons like criminals, yet frames its work as "victim-centered" because of its cooperative arrangements with selected non-state partners. Yet despite their seemingly opposing goals, these approaches are not mutually exclusive. Instead, they represent interconnected truths I have tracked over several years, research based on documenting the blurred lines between protection and punishment for people deemed "at risk" of domestic sex trafficking in the United States and the overlapping and sometimes "fluid"[11] interplay between state and non-state actors' cooperative efforts to identify and protect them.

ARGUMENT

This book examines different initiatives that have been designed to respond to domestic sex trafficking in the United States. In it, I seek to explain what motivates anti-sex-trafficking interventions that target at-risk domestic victims (i.e., U.S. citizens and permanent residents) and to highlight how and why well-intentioned interventions designed to intervene on victims' behalves may subject them to different kinds of social control. For instance, girls and women deemed at-risk of domestic sex trafficking in the United States may experience a combination of punishment in the form of arrest, detention, and mobile and networked surveillance, as well as protective interventions such as victim-centered identification techniques, court supervision, and social-service referrals. Whether through cooperative state and nonstate efforts to identify and assist victims of domestic sex trafficking or through prostitution-diversion programs,[12] individuals now entangled in the anti-sex-trafficking net in the United States—who may include not only youth and adults in exploitative sex trafficking situations but voluntary adult sex workers—are increasingly subjected to a burgeoning, though largely unscrutinized, combination of law-enforcement punishment combined with psychosocial, social-service, and technologically mediated efforts to assist them.

The enmeshment of law enforcement, social-service, and sociotechnical efforts to address domestic sex trafficking raises two central questions this book explores: first, when different actors come together to intervene on trafficked persons' behalves and when collaborative efforts have the capacity to blur the boundaries between protection and punishment, what are the effects of this system on people deemed "at risk"? Second, how and in what ways have domestic anti-sex-trafficking efforts, commonly framed in victim-centered terms, concealed the protectionist *and* punitive role of the carceral state on at-risk victims lives? To answer these questions, I draw upon interviews and observations of selected on-the-ground anti-sex-trafficking interventions in the United States to draw attention to a carcerally oriented,[13] collaboratively inspired system of protection in development. The merger of these approaches reflects an orientation to antitrafficking efforts I call *carceral protectionism.*[14]

This process can be understood as enforcement with a protective bent or carcerality inflected with care. Because individuals vulnerable to domestic sex trafficking are discursively caught between competing notions of how victims and offenders ought to behave, the tools and interventions developed to assist them reflect similarly bifurcated goals. The legal status of at-risk victims, who occupy a precarious subject position, is complicated by the fact that they are not viewed as "typical" victims of gendered crimes like sexual assault or domestic violence, nor are they always viewed as criminal offenders under the law like voluntary sex workers or undocumented migrants. Carceral protectionism offers a framework for making sense of interventions where "at risk" victims of sex trafficking may in actuality be treated more like "victim–offenders."[15] It also provides a conceptual blueprint to account for collaborative state and nonstate initiatives where the lines between protection and punishment are less than clear.

Sometimes the punishment that at-risk victims experience is unambiguous, for instance, when a girl under eighteen trades sex for money. Though she legally meets the federal definition of a victim of domestic sex trafficking, in some jurisdictions, she may nevertheless still be arrested and detained. Among police officers I met who described the use of what I would call an "arrest to assist" model, the reason for doing so ultimately came down to seeing an arrest or detention as a tool to keep youth safe. Without the use of an arrest or the legal ability to detain youth, some saw this as translating into a broader inability to keep an underage girl safe from returning to the person(s) presumed to be exploiting them and safe from a life that involves trading or exchanging sex for money. In other cases, youth may experience other forms of control in the form of social-service oversight augmented by technologies with surveillance capacities.

Cara, an infectiously energetic Christian turned antitrafficking advocate, summed up the logic behind this type of carceral protection. Our 2013 Skype interview began with a broad discussion of the competing frameworks that exist for protecting youth and took a more focused, brass tacks turn when Cara described what protection looks like on the ground at Sunny Dawn—the shelter she runs.[16] Cara acknowledged the contradictory logic of an anti-sex-trafficking system that purports to protect victims of sex trafficking but invariably ends up punishing them. Yet she surprised me with her candid reflection on methods that are useful to her in her work with youth and teen residents placed at Sunny Dawn, techniques that seem to blur how we might understand punishment and protection. She explained that if all of the residents at her shelter were on probation, she and fellow staff members would welcome the ankle monitor bracelets that would accompany their placement. That is because for Cara, ankle monitor bracelets are useful, like the use of arrest or detention. They are tools with the capacity to ensure the safety of girls and teens in her care. Registering my discomfort with her disclosure that subjecting girls to punitive interventions like ankle monitor bracelets is one of the methods she thinks helps to keep them safe, Cara offered the following rejoinder:

> That piece of technology is huge in keeping them safe. . . . All I can share with you is my experiences of the thirty-six or forty kids that we've dealt with. . . . I can tell you right now that what they need, [is] to be treated as if they are a victim of a crime. However, we can't treat them like typical victims of a crime who come to you wanting help. I have to convince them that they're a victim of a crime. . . . So they don't necessarily even want to stop what they're doing. . . . If we don't have a way to keep them safe, they're just going to be back on the streets. So right now, that's juvenile hall and ankle monitors. If we take that away from law enforcement, if we say, "Okay, we're going to do safe harbor law, and that means none of these children can be taken to juvenile hall or ankle monitored for prosecution at all," then the question is, what are we going to do? . . . And that's hard because what right do I have to do that, because they're not a probation kid? These are hard questions that we've got to wrestle with, but in the end, it comes down to keeping the kids safe, and how are we going to do that?

Cara's question about how to keep vulnerable people safe—in this case, girls that meet the legal definition of a victim of domestic sex trafficking, but who do not see themselves as such—illuminates some of the tensions surrounding carceral responses to domestic sex trafficking. It was clear to me that Cara cares deeply for Sunny Dawn residents and wants to do everything she can for them. From what she shared with me, she has also dedicated extensive time, resources, and energy to providing youth with as much support and as many services as she can. Yet different tools—in this case, surveillance technology in the form of ankle monitor bracelets—is a method she sees as useful in protecting a girl who has traded sex, been identified as a victim of domestic sex trafficking, and placed at a shelter like Sunny Dawn. It is useful for her because it is a tool that takes away their impulse to run away or "AWOL," as some advocates, police officers, and judges sometimes refer to it. For Cara, passing Safe Harbor laws—policies that are broadly aimed at decriminalizing prostitution for underage persons and that limit law enforcement's ability to use punitive tactics of arrest, detention, and probation—makes it more difficult for her to protect youth at her shelter. Without the threat of arrest or an outstanding bench warrant, some youth in her care have the option to walk away, which Cara sees as compromising their well-being, because it carries the risk of sending them right back to the trafficker-pimps and dangerous situations that exposed them to exploitation in the first place. Cara is not alone. I heard variations of this theme from law enforcement and social-service providers during interviews and informal conversations.[17]

Since I first embarked on this project in the late 2000s, interest in domestic sex trafficking has exploded, with more attention focused on how to revamp the foster-care system and more fully engage schools, the medical and public health systems, local communities, and other systems of support. There is also mounting recognition that calling victims of domestic sex trafficking in name but treating them like offenders is deeply flawed. Many states have moved to[18] implement some version of Safe Harbor laws that recognize teens and youth as victims and to bring state laws "into line"[19] with the United States' benchmark Victims of Trafficking Victim Protection Act. In May 2015, another federal antitrafficking bill, the Justice for Victims of Trafficking Act, was signed into law, which includes, among other provisions, expanded benefits for trafficking survivors and a process whereby "a human trafficking survivor can move to vacate any arrest or conviction records for a nonviolent offense committed as a direct result of human trafficking, including prostitution or lewdness."[20] The fact that Congress has mandated remedies for domestic sex-trafficked persons who have been treated more like offenders than victims highlights the persistence of punishing youth as a pathway to protecting them, a theme developed in this book and described by other researchers.[21]

To some, these developments may suggest an important shift, one where arresting youth under the framework of protection or subjecting sex-trade involved adults and youth to punitive punishment may be an unfortunate relic of the anti-domestic-sex-trafficking past but that we have ultimately moved beyond the use of punitive methods of protection. My response? Not necessarily. A close reading of the social and political history of twenty-first-century anti-sex-trafficking efforts focused on migrants is instructive here and challenges this assessment for two reasons. First, gaps exist between antitrafficking laws on the books and activities on the ground. Carole Vance notes that although contemporary antitrafficking efforts have proven successful in shoring up a two-century-old melodrama based on narratives of women and girls' "sexual danger, drama, sensation, furious action, wild applause, and . . . identifiable victims, villains, and heroes," the laws designed to respond to it have been "disappointing in their implementation."[22] What researchers have additionally learned in the sixteen years following the passage of the Victims of Trafficking and Violence Protection Act,[23] and the adoption of the United Nations Convention Against Transnational Organized Crime, or Palermo Protocol, in 2000[24] is that distinguishing between "deserving" victims of trafficking and criminal offenders is a complicated endeavor. Consequently, at-risk victims of sex trafficking may still endure punitive treatment despite or perhaps in light of laws aimed at protecting them.[25]

Second, antitrafficking efforts that now focus on U.S. citizens and permanent residents—just like those developed for migrants—remain law-enforcement-centric[26] and prosecution-focused.[27] What this means in practice is that people affiliated with the carceral state in general and local and federal law-enforcement agents in particular occupy a central role in coordinating antitrafficking interventions. Though police and federal agents are now instructed, and in some jurisdictions specifically trained to refer to and treat people involved in the sex trade, especially girls and women, as victims now, adopting the language of victim-centeredness does not a paradigm shift make. Neither does it change the fact that law-enforcement agents are in the business of criminal enforcement, investigations, prosecutions, and punishment.[28] That is their mandate. The premise that carceral actors could rebrand and transform themselves into victim-centered (i.e., nonpunitive) actors through more training,[29] but without overhauling the tools of policing and enforcement that have helped grow the U.S. carceral state to "breathtaking" proportions[30] —proves limited. Such a vision of training as remedy, for instance, fails to acknowledge that law-enforcement agents—deemed the primary protectors of at-risk domestic-sex trafficking victims—may themselves perpetrate sexual assault and violence against the very groups they are now charged with protecting, as a report by the Young Women's Empowerment Project argued.[31] Yet in addition to questions surrounding what role, if any, law enforcement plays in perpetrating violence against individuals involved in the sex trade, it ignores the fact that in the United States, where sex work is still broadly criminalized, law-enforcement agents ultimately have the discretionary power to decide whether a person involved in the sex trade is a victim of sex trafficking or a criminal offender, and whether criminalization or some form of carceral protection is appropriate.[32]

Sociologist Elizabeth Bernstein has suggested that antitrafficking's "social justice as criminal justice" model has helped install multiple actors to the cause of human trafficking and congealed a neoliberal carceral agenda reliant upon "punitive systems of control."[33] Her research has been groundbreaking on multiple fronts, including her analysis about the ways in which increased attention to domestic underage trafficking in the United States has prompted "an unprecedented police crackdown on people of color who are involved in the street-based sexual economy—including pimps, clients, and sex workers alike."[34] Building upon Bernstein's work, I find that the "crackdown" on commercial sex—both on the street and online—has not only stepped up "traditional" law-enforcement activities—with, for instance, an uptick in online stings, street sweeps, and police raids—but has also helped inspire different forms of cooperation between state and nonstate actors that are framed as alternatives to punitive efforts of the past. In actuality, however, these developments reflect the reorganization of the carceral state in protective dimensions.[35]

Nonstate actors come into the equation when they collaborate with carceral actors like police and federal agents to identify victims. Or when they step in to protect and help "manage" victims, as some police put it. This type of victim management can in turn help support law-enforcement investigations and prosecutions. When nonprofit, corporate, or faith-based actors seek to help identify or protect trafficking victims—whether through official antitrafficking task force work or unofficial collaborations—some may hold as their ultimate goal the prosecution of traffickers. This sometimes requires cooperative trafficking victims, who may not see themselves as victims and therefore have no interest in prosecuting the people accused of trafficking them. That is why for all of the focus on law-enforcement paradigm shifts, the passage of Safe Harbor laws, and the creation of new kinds of victim-centered services for the trafficked victims among the broader population of people involved in the sex trade, one crucial detail has gotten lost in the fever pitch: namely, that antitrafficking interventions, even those that appear more supportive or protective in name have not supplanted criminal justice efforts per se. Instead, in some cases, they have augmented them and stretched them in new directions, as, for instance, when a girl is identified as a victim of domestic sex trafficking and her arrest serves as a referral to social services.[36] Or when law enforcement and nonstate actors monitor social media accounts, mobile phones, and online classified ads to identify or protect a victim. These technologies and the information gleaned from them have legal import as well; sometimes they are used to keep at-risk victims under observation or under the supervision of the carceral state.

In each case, the technology of collaboration blends with punitive and surveillant tools to secure trafficked persons' protection, which may also expose them to different forms of social control. In addition to facing criminal justice sanctions or being arrested or detained for offenses like prostitution, individuals involved in the sex trade may also experience other kinds of rehabilitative, psychosocial, neurological, and technologically mediated forms of control, have their movements monitored, their psychological well-being tracked, and their online and mobile activities followed or restricted all under the guise of protecting them.[37]

THE DEFINITIONAL COLLAPSE OF SEX TRAFFICKING AND SEX WORK

Researchers who study trafficking have consistently pointed out that not all human trafficking is sex trafficking, and that sex work is distinct from sex trafficking. Sketchy data[38] and panics about irregular border crossing[39] and women's sexual labor and agency in the commercial sex trade[40] have also led many observers to presuppose that sex trafficking is a more egregious problem than other forms of labor exploitation. A substantial body of legal, social science, and feminist scholarship traces the effects of discursively conflating human trafficking with sex trafficking and the problematic nature of assuming that all prostitution is sex trafficking.[41] Yet debates about these topics persist and are animated by contention as to whether legalized, decriminalized, or regulated sex work increases instances of sex trafficking and which legal model is ultimately most protective of those involved, whether voluntarily or not. A response to these debates has been the rise of two distinct frameworks for understanding these issues: the antiprostitution and pro–sex-work, or prorights, positions. The debate "revolves around the question of whether sex work constitutes a form of voluntary sexual labor or involuntary sexual objectification," Juline Koken observes.[42] The antiprostitution, or "neoabolitionist," perspective[43] treats prostitution as a form of violence against women.[44] This view defines those involved in various types of sexual labor—commonly presumed to be girls and women—as exploited victims devoid of choice and agency.[45] Conversely, the prorights position views prostitution as voluntary in some cases, and when consensually chosen, as a form of labor comparable to other service work, for instance what Eileen Boris and Rhacel Salazar Parreñas call "intimate labors."[46]

It is important to point out that feminist and social science literature on prostitution and commercial and transactional sex varies extensively, reflecting far more analytic diversity and nuance than is adequately captured by references to "antiprostitution" or "prorights" perspectives.[47] Moreover, some feminist and social science research has sought to link various types of gendered sexual labor to broader economic processes and migration patterns.[48] Yet despite the existence of scholarly work that challenges the ideological conflation of prostitution with sex trafficking,[49] and that disputes claims that *all* forms of sex work are "inherently traumatizing,"[50] neoabolitionist perspectives and antiprostitution sentiments have "gone mainstream" in the United States.[51] This mainstreaming has been made possible, in part, by focusing attention on the gender and age of sex trafficking victims. Focusing on victims' age is strategic in that it sidesteps debate about the voluntary nature of prostitution. Even if, as other research suggests, youth do not necessarily describe their experiences in exploitative terms, few people would agree that underage individuals are in a position to consent to trading sex.[52] Yet sustained and singular focus on the age of those involved or the moral reprehensibility surrounding all types of sexual labor is important because it can short-circuit examination of what Julia O'Connell-Davidson has described as the "multi-layered conditions of confinement"[53] that shape people's experiences and fails to explain why they may ultimately reject help from the antitrafficking "rescue industry," as Laura Agustín calls it,[54] including situations where exploitation has occurred.

Ronald Weitzer has analyzed the effects of neoabolitionism in a U.S. context, finding that through their "consultative access," neoabolitionists have "shaped the terms" and direction of antitrafficking policy.[55] Neoabolitionist consultative access has also solidified particular sentiments about prostitution and commercial sex, ideas that have brought police, advocates, and a host of nonstate actors together in salient new ways around the shared contention that prostitution is always harmful, exploitative, and traumatizing, and that the criminal-justice system coupled with social-service reinforcement offer the most efficacious tools for responding to the problem and rescuing girls and women in need.

When prostitution is understood as a form of violence against women and when researchers assume that anyone who trades sex is a victim, it makes the experiences of people who do not view their experiences as coercive, traumatic, or psychologically damaging "impossible" and "unknowable." This analytic move strikes the experiences of adult sex workers and sex-trade–involved youth from the empirical record by denying the validity of their experiences if and when such experiences do not conform with dominant understandings. Efforts by antitrafficking groups and some members of Congress to eradicate terms like "sex work"[56] and "child prostitute"[57] take this one step further. In January 2015, selected advocacy groups in the United States along with members of Congress launched the "No Such Thing"[58] campaign, which seeks to change the treatment of victims of child sex trafficking by calling for the eradication of the term "child prostitute." The campaign links a shift in language to changes in how youth are legally treated, implicitly suggesting that referring to young persons as "trafficked" or exploited rather than as child or teen prostitutes will lead to their being treated as victims rather than offenders.

Efforts to do away with certain vernacular terms may give weight to anti-sex-trafficking campaigns. It may also help self-identified survivors feel fully validated in their experiences as survivors of exploitation.[59] While I welcome a change in how we talk about people's experiences with exploitation, no matter its form, doing away with words alone does little to help us understand how individuals account for their experiences with various kinds of commercial and transactional sex arrangements and what interventions ultimately prove most effective in assisting those who want help.[60] It is worth noting that a carceral model of assistance may "work" and be welcomed by some youth and adults who self-identify as victim–survivors of sex trafficking and see assistance from the criminal-justice system and social-service providers as helpful and necessary. But for those who neither see themselves as victims nor view the police or nonstate actors as protectors, they have to be convinced of their victim-survivor status, which sometimes includes being exposed to different carceral and/or social-service interventions that assert the exploitative nature of prostitution.

UNIMAGINABLE DATA

Data on human trafficking in general and sex trafficking in particular are unreliable, and disparities exist between the estimated number of victims and the number actually identified.[61] Estimates about the prevalence of domestic minor sex trafficking (DMST) and commercial sexual exploitation of children (CSEC), a term more commonly used before the issue attracted heightened attention in the late 2000s, also vary.[62] In an important study that sought to gauge the size of the CSEC population in New York City and address gaps in CSEC estimates more generally, Ric Curtis and his coauthors used respondent driven sampling (RDS) to estimate CSEC prevalence rates.[63] Despite the innovative methods they employed, they found only a handful of minors who were domestically sex trafficked, underscoring the persistent gap between estimated rates of trafficking and the number of cases officially identified.

I would add another deficit to the long list of data problems that attend the issue of human trafficking: that it is difficult quantitatively to assess the number of people who interface with the criminal-justice system through antitrafficking interventions that seem protective but may also be punitive. These techniques and activities may include detention, including secure detention where mobility is constrained, court supervision, prostitution-diversion programs, GPS monitoring, and mobile and networked surveillance or services tied to placement in a juvenile or criminal justice facility. This number is so difficult to assess because the idea that protective interventions cause harm is mired in paradox. Data on the punitive dimensions of antitrafficking interventions are additionally difficult to locate because local and federal law-enforcement agencies report crime statistics differently, and because crime records assume neat distinctions between victims and offenders, or between categories of victimization and criminality. To use youth arrest data as an example, in 2011, the Bureau of Justice Statistics reported that 974 minors were arrested for prostitution and commercialized vice offenses, a relatively insignificant number. But the Bureau states that it "does not collect data regarding police contact with a juvenile who has not committed an offense, nor does it collect data on situations in which police take a juvenile into custody for his or her own protection."[64] Thus, youth stopped by law enforcement as part of an antitrafficking recovery effort may be questioned, searched, handcuffed, or held at a police station "for their own protection" without ever being "counted" in formal crime reports. Adults voluntarily engaged in sex work also endure criminalizing tactics that are harmful. But because prostitution is illegal in most U.S. states, these punitive tactics are legal, no matter how deplorable.

Yet for those who find themselves in coercive situations, enduring any type of punitive state intervention grates against commonsense expectations about what ought to happen to people legally classified as victims of crimes. Case in point: the FBI press release from Operation Super Bowl tells us that "sixteen juveniles between the ages of fourteen and seventeen were rescued, forty-five pimps and their associates were arrested," and "seventy women and children [were offered] services such as food, clothing, and referrals to health care facilities, shelters, and other programs."[65] On the face of it, we may see this rescue effort as a success bolstered by concrete numbers and shaped by the message that as a result of the sting, kids got rescued, "bad guy" trafficker-pimps got busted, and a bunch of other people gained access to services.

Yet there are a few details that the Department of Justice does not provide. First, the FBI does not state where the juveniles were placed after recovery. Were they arrested? Placed in an unlocked shelter where they were free to leave? Taken to jail? Did they run away and if so, why did they run? Second, we are told that seventy unidentified women and children were offered access to programs and referrals to services, presumed to be separate from the criminal-justice system. But we do not know what happened to any of them—the press releases do not provide this information—because there is scant mainstream attention paid to this other shadow side of antitrafficking efforts in the United States.[66] The dominant law-enforcement and social-service narratives about anti-trafficking tend not to offer a full account or full report of the impact—protective, punitive, or otherwise—on the people who bear the brunt of such interventions.[67]

It is only by learning about antitrafficking interventions and meeting a select group of people who have been involved with what we now call domestic sex trafficking situations that I have begun to piece together, or to use a law-enforcement term, *corroborate* some of what happens.[68] And what I have been curious to learn is that these interventions are generally assumed to be helpful and preferable to trading sex and/or interfacing with pimps, who are now referred to as sex traffickers. While individuals who have been in exploitative situations, including domestic sex trafficking, may indeed prefer to leave such situations, what is important here is the logic that authorizes state and nonstate efforts and an implicit presumption that any antitrafficking intervention is a helpful intervention, irrespective of its results. But people who have been in situations we now call "domestic sex trafficking" and exposed to different interventions have a lot to teach us. When I interviewed Shayla, a sixteen year-old black teenager in 2013 and asked her about the two months she spent in juvenile hall on a prostitution-related charge before she arrived at the shelter where we met, she spoke unambiguously about her experience: "It was hell, worse than I expected." Arresting, detaining, and rehabilitating at-risk victims in order to protect them is filled with complex contradictions not lost on Shayla, some of the girls I interviewed as part of this research, or the organizations and groups that have worked hard to mitigate the "collateral damage"[69] of antitrafficking interventions since the late 1990s.

Scholars have begun to document the harmful effects of antitrafficking operations intended as victim protection[70] and to track some of the punitive effects they produce.[71] What little empirical research exists paints an unpromising picture. As Anne Gallagher and Elaine Pearson's research suggests, globally, "victims of trafficking, the majority of whom are women and girls, are routinely detained in jails, immigration centers, and different types of 'shelter detention.'"[72] Other researchers have underscored the limitations of charitable antitrafficking interventions[73] and the sundry "rehabilitation complexes" it has produced.[74] These studies highlight the troubling effects of antitrafficking. For migrants at risk of labor and sex trafficking, this may mean enduring harsh detention and reintegration programs,[75] punitive immigration crime control tactics, and border management mechanisms.[76] For U.S. citizens and permanent residents, these kinds of unintended yet still punitive effects may spring from the very laws designed to help victims, as recent research on the harmful effects of safe harbor laws in New York and elsewhere suggests.[77] And just as antitrafficking efforts have contributed to the criminalization of immigration,[78] so is it arguably now also the case that antitrafficking efforts have fueled the growth of the U.S. prison-industrial complex[79] and stretched the bounds of the carceral state in new gendered and punitive-protective directions.[80]

For feminist scholars and social justice advocates who have long drawn attention to the oppression that undocumented, racially marginalized, and gender-nonconforming individuals experience—at the hands both of individual perpetrators of violence and of "state systems of oppressions"[81]—it will come as no great surprise that antitrafficking efforts orchestrated by the state and augmented by nonstate partners also bear the imprint of punishment. Yet for activists and global leaders who, to cite President Obama, frame trafficking as "a great human rights cause of our time"[82] such trends should give pause and ought to prompt scrutiny of a model of protection where "at risk" domestic victims of sex trafficking - or other vulnerable populations - are exposed to protective interventions that reassert the centrality of the carceral state.[83]

NEOLIBERALISM AND THE CARCERAL STATE

The connections between neoliberalism, carceral politics and antitrafficking advocacy are well established and have been cogently analyzed by Elizabeth Bernstein.[84] For readers less familiar with the connection between these topics, neoliberalism is important to research on anti-sex-trafficking efforts in the United States in general and responses to domestic sex trafficking in particular because, under it, we have witnessed the rise of the carceral state and heightened reliance on punitive law-enforcement efforts as an antiviolence strategy, whether to respond to sexual violence or to sex trafficking.[85]

Equal parts ideology and a "package of politics," neoliberalism lauds goals like "low taxes, macroeconomic stabilization, financial and trade deregulation, privatization of public assets and services and the retrenchment of the welfare state."[86] Commonly associated with a shift away from Keynesian-styled policies that emphasize state intervention, in practice, neoliberal policy signals the "financialization of everything."[87] Beyond the specific policy outcomes proponents of neoliberalism cleave to, and however contradictory its effects,[88] neoliberalism is an ideology steeped in aspiration, in which a host of social and political issues are framed as problems best solved by the market[89] and public-private partnerships.[90]

Discussions about the carceral state have mounted as scholars have sought to reconcile the epic expansion of the American criminal-justice system in general[91] and mass incarceration in particular. In the United States, there are approximately "2.2 million people in jail or prison today" (i.e., in 2015), with millions more subject to court supervision, probation, parole, or some other form of state oversight, numbers that do not take into account the countless families and communities that are also impacted.[92] Following Michel Foucault's description of the carceral archipelago in *Discipline and Punish*,[93] Marie Gottschalk shows in her 2015 book *Caught: The Prison State and the Lockdown of American Politics* just how porous, pervasive, and extensive its reach has become in twenty-first-century America: "A tenacious carceral state has sprouted in the shadows of mass incarceration and has been extending far beyond the prison gate. It includes not only the country's vast archipelago of jails and prisons but also the far-reaching and growing range of penal punishments and controls that lies in the never-never land between the prison gate and full citizenship."[94]

Since the 1970s, neoliberal policies have resulted in growing economic and political insecurities, shifts that have in turn helped to propagate punitive criminal justice responses to manage inequalities.[95] Yet not only has mass incarceration become a "strategy to deal with problems arising from discarded workers and marginalized populations,"[96] it has also emerged as an economic stabilizing force par excellence, what Gottschalk describes as a kind of "penal Keynesism."[97] In this model, punishment is financially lucrative and mass incarceration a source of jobs for law-enforcement agents, correction officers, and those who stand to profit from the "multi-billion dollar private corrections industry."[98]

The rise of the carceral state under neoliberalism has also fostered sundry tough-on-crime policies that have disproportionately and devastatingly impacted people of color in general and black men in particular.[99] Legal scholar Michelle Alexander describes a criminal-justice system fueled by a war on drugs and inflected by "color-blind racism." This is a system of injustice that has carcerally captured and politically disenfranchised countless black men.[100] Scholars generally agree that the U.S. carceral state is shaped by "racial disparities, racial discrimination, and institutional racism."[101] However, as much as race is central in accounting for the growth of the carceral state and in understanding how the United States' experiment with neoliberalism has been shaped by it, the story of the carceral state includes other intersections too. Indeed, its expansion is a story about a failed war on drugs and legacies of racism as well as a tale about the growing carceral control of women, girls and other vulnerable populations and criminalization of phenomena like migration and sex crimes, all of which have surged in the wake of growing economic and political insecurity.[102] Carceral responses to the case study I explore, domestic sex trafficking, are part of this story too.[103]

Yet neoliberalism is relevant to a discussion of carceral protectionism for another reason: It gives us a framework for accounting for the public–private partnerships that have become more commonplace in matters of American governance.[104] The advent of punitive forms of protection and growth of cooperative antitrafficking alliances between state, nongovernmental, faith-based, and corporate networks[105] follow neoliberal incursions into the "privatization of social welfare and marketization of political and social life,"[106] what Amy Lind aptly describes as "neoliberal governmentalities."[107] The emergence of neoliberal governmentalities is not just a response to a crumbling welfare system, the privatization of public systems, and the outsourcing of public safety to a diffuse network of for-profit and nonprofit actors. While it is all those things, it is also a collaborative triage model assembled to deal with the heightened social instability and economic precarity that has occurred as a result of neoliberal economic restructuring.[108] Neoliberal policies contribute to economic and social instability, "roll out"[109] carceral interventions as a "strategy" to manage vulnerable populations,[110] and then look to public–private partnerships[111] and particular nonstate collaborators to clean up the mess. In the case of anti-sex-trafficking efforts, this is a trend where identifying a victim of domestic sex trafficking or coordinating a trafficked person's postidentification protection becomes an occasion for a strange-bedfellow[112] crew of local police officers, social-service providers, federal agents, probation officers, nongovernmental advocates, persons of faith, judges, technology innovators, and concerned citizens to come together to address it. An ever-expanding network of actors have attached themselves to the trafficking cause and formed partnerships foregrounded in the belief that human trafficking is everyone's mutual problem, and that state and nonstate partnerships are most efficacious ways to respond.[113] In principle, expanding the constellation of actors who can help a victim in need is a way of enhancing their protections. Yet at a deeper level, it also represents a distinct model of governance based on outsourcing the management of vulnerable populations, in this case, victims at risk of domestic sex trafficking, to different state and nonstate actors. What we have here is a blending of criminal justice efforts with non-state assistance, efforts that put a collaborative spin on efforts aimed at protection yet which sometimes controls.

When social-service providers, faith-based actors, and nongovernmental advocates become formal or loosely allied partners to the state, we also see a paradigmatic feature of neoliberalism transformed into a collaborative form of governance that may protect through punishment and assist populations "at risk" through the technology of state and nonstate cooperation. And significantly, collaboration between selected state and nonstate actors to identify and protect at-risk victims of domestic sex trafficking does not necessarily reduce state power and control. Rather, neoliberal ideologies and the attendant carceral strategies they engender expand the power and control of the state in new directions.[114]

DIFFERENT MANIFESTATIONS OF THE "CARCERAL": CARCERAL FEMINISM, THE CARCERAL ASSISTENTIAL NET, AND CARCERAL PROTECTIONISM

The carceral protectionist practices I detail in this book are part of a larger scholarly conversation about the growth of the carceral and neoliberal governance.[115] Elizabeth Bernstein's research on the carceral dimensions of antitrafficking efforts is once again instructive and has been pathbreaking in the field. Her work has drawn attention to the overlap between antiprostitution feminist and law-enforcement approaches to the issue. Like the antirape and battered-women movements preceding antitrafficking activism, "carceral feminism," a term she coined, is a model that fastens contemporary antitrafficking efforts to a "law and order agenda."

For Bernstein, carceral feminism has emerged as the dominant epistemic paradigm in organized antitrafficking efforts and feminist theorizing about trafficking and prostitution more generally.[116] Bernstein's findings help account for why the care and protection of trafficked persons—goals that have historically been considered as disparate from those of the criminal-justice system[117]—have nevertheless been integrated into the United States' arsenal of carceral and juridical interventions. In much the same way that feminist activist struggles have been increasingly replaced by individualized empowerment projects and "neoliberal postfeminist professionalism that remains inattentive and oblivious to structural injustices,"[118] so too have feminist visions of redistributive justice largely been upstaged by this brand of carceral feminism.[119]

Bernstein's research focuses on how carceral feminist attachments overlap with a law-and-order agenda and are bound to a "broad agenda of criminalization and incarceration."[120] Notably, there are now also a wide array of actors who participate in formal and informal antitrafficking initiatives focused on "at risk" domestic sex trafficking populations that have no explicit commitment to feminism or gender justice, aside from gestures towards sex trafficking victim–survivors' "empowerment." Some nonstate actors who help law enforcement identify at-risk victims of domestic sex trafficking and manage their postrescue protection do so, not in the name of feminism per se, but under the auspices of protection, safety, and a commitment to fight modern-day slavery assumed to be taking place in the United States' own backyard.

Although carceral feminist goals have helped foster an antitrafficking agenda informed by antiprostitution politics that prioritizes state and nonstate cooperation, the terms of collaboration have evolved to include multiple nonstate actors and multiple agendas. So while carceral feminism in general and carceral feminist politics in particular undoubtedly inform the process and practices I refer to as carceral protectionism, the latter explores interventions designed to intervene on behalf of "at-risk" domestic victims and describes how such efforts utilize state habits of punishment, control, and surveillance,[121] as well as discourses of safety and protection. The carceral protectionist practices I detail throughout this book may therefore be understood as an expression of carceral feminist ideologies made manifest when at-risk victims are identified and their protection is overseen by law enforcement and different nonstate actors. Not only do these trends highlight how antitrafficking activities have moved beyond their expressly feminist origins to an institutionalized and expert-oriented field of work and activity,[122] they also show how domestic sex trafficking's framing as a form of modern-day slavery has authorized exceptional "anti-slavery projects,"[123] including new, albeit not wholly unprecedented, collaborations between state and nonstate actors.

Carceral protectionism also bears a theoretical and bureaucratic likeness to the "carceral assistential net" sociologist Loïc Wacquant describes,[124] yet carries its own distinct features and meanings. For Wacquant, the growth of the carceral state[125] now characteristic of advanced liberal nations like the United States corresponds with ever-more-sophisticated social-service techniques, tactics, and ideologies deployed to criminalize poverty and to manage "so-called problem populations."[126] Moves to protect, rehabilitate, and intervene on behalf of domestic trafficked victims similarly support the expansion of the carceral apparatus and reaffirm broader law-enforcement goals. Carceral protectionism offers what I think is a complementary yet slightly mutated variation of Wacquant's carceral assistential net. Both reflect a "new penal material and symbolic" order[127] where state and nonstate actors and criminal justice and social-service techniques fuse together in the creation of a new hybridized state.[128] Carceral protectionism differs most significantly, however, in its theoretical treatment of rehabilitation and the symbolic purchase it carries. Whereas Wacquant suggests "that the therapeutic philosophy of 'rehabilitation' has been more or less supplanted by a managerialist approach," I find that calls for the rescue, rehabilitation, and empowerment of trafficked persons, especially sex-trade–involved youth, serve as the pretext and provide an "alibi" for their carceral protection.[129] Individuals subject to protective forms of punishment may still be managed, sorted, and controlled by the managerialist approach Wacquant describes. But what I am suggesting is that what gets people deemed "at risk" known to the state in the first place is the perception that protection and safety are primarily, though not always exclusively, arrived at through carceral pathways.

WHAT IS CARCERAL PROTECTIONISM?

Extending the Carceral State in Protective and Collaboration Directions

Carceral protectionism is a state-oriented framework, and as such, all trafficking victims or potential victims are routed primarily through the carceral *enforcement apparatus*[130] in order to be officially recognized by the state. In the past, trafficked persons interfaced with the enforcement apparatus expressly through interactions with law-enforcement officials, including local police officers and federal agents charged with enforcing local, state, or national antitrafficking laws. Their official identification and subsequent protection was contingent upon successfully conveying to law-enforcement agents that they were victims of trafficking rather than willful lawbreakers. This proved difficult, in part because few people in forced labor situations self-identify as "trafficked" victims.[131] However, the law-enforcement apparatus is broader than the name suggests, and the actors that play a role in supporting the carceral state extend beyond sworn officers and specific law-enforcement agencies. Nonstate actors such as victim advocates, social workers, service providers, and technology advocates may be consulted before, during, or directly following police raids to assist in the identification and protection of potential victims. The expansion of the enforcement apparatus is not limited to nongovernmental advocates and social-service providers, either; judges, probation officers, technology experts, and community volunteers, among others, are also included. Specialized collaborative courts have been created in different U.S. cities to offer more victim-centered alternatives to typical adjudication processes designed for more "typical" (read: nontrafficked) offender populations. Technology companies have funded research and come up with collaborative initiatives in order to better understand the sociotechnical dimensions of the trafficking problem.[132] Private citizens have engaged in their own rescue operations. These are only a few examples pulled from the variety of actions and collection of actors who now constitute the antitrafficking multiverse. Yet in some cases—not all, but enough to merit attention—the underlying goals are consistent: to leverage the technology of collaboration and include nonstate actors who can help the state by supporting its antitrafficking agenda and broader enforcement goals.

A Flexible/Portable System

The expansion of the enforcement apparatus to include nonstate actors and the integration of victim-centered tactics illustrates an important characteristic of carceral protectionism, and neoliberalism more generally, specifically, that it is a *flexible* and portable system.[133] Flexibility is key here because, in addition to expanding the actors who may act as proxy partners to the state, the flexible nature of carceral protectionism also allows for the tactics and goals defined by a nongovernmental, social-service, or sociotechnical paradigm to be integrated into the state's law-enforcement approach. Whether or not such a paradigm reflects human-rights, faith-based, corporate, or gender/sexual justice–oriented goals, an implicit requirement of combining a nonstate agenda with that of law enforcement is adherence to the United States' main antitrafficking agenda, which includes prosecuting traffickers, criminalizing the buyers of sex, and coordinating victims' protection, primarily though not always exclusively, through the criminal-justice system.

Technological Mediation of Protective Surveillance

Efforts to respond to domestic sex trafficking in the United States demonstrate that the lines between protection and punishment and the boundaries between carceral and rehabilitative spaces are commonly transgressed. Sociologist Lynne Haney's research on gender and mass incarceration offers a theoretically insightful framework for accounting for these trends.[134] She observes that in our current neoliberal penal order, social scientists and feminist scholars ought to look not only "behind bars" but also "beyond" them to understand the diffusion of state authority and the transposition of state-based punishment into localized "semicarceral institutions"—areas in which women are especially concentrated.[135] Applying insights from Haney's research to the case study of domestic sex trafficking helps explain why efforts to identify and assist victims have stimulated the creation of semicarceral gray zones, spaces like shelters that may be attached to but not geospatially confined by prisons, jails, juvenile camps, or rehabilitative detention facilities. This kind of carceral protectionist oversight may be taken up or facilitated by state and nonstate actors. And, crucially, semicarceral spaces need not be bound to a particular geographic location. Nor do carceral activities necessarily lead to forms of punishment like an arrest or detention. Instead, carceral oversight can be extended and augmented by a variety of surveillance technology in the name of protection. For instance, youth on probation or house arrest for prostitution-related charges may have their movements tracked by GPS ankle-bracelet monitoring technologies.[136] Or, sex-trade involved individuals who post ads to online classified advertising sites may be algorithmically evaluated as "at risk" of sex trafficking and approached by nonstate actors seeking to help law enforcement with their efforts.[137] That these are some of the same surveillance techniques used to monitor sex offenders[138] and identify terrorists, respectively, is notable. Yet it also underscores how technology and technical innovation expand the spatial and geographic boundaries in which the identification and protection of trafficked persons is imagined and that tools developed for more "typical" offenders may be adapted to manage at-risk victims.

The Protective End Justifies the Punitive Means

Another distinguishing feature of carceral protectionism is that it relies upon law-enforcement methods to protect at-risk victims. Whatever its origins, the proposed remedies typically include expanded carceral or carceral protectionist interventions. When law enforcement and social-service providers suggest that sometimes the only way to keep youth and teens safe is through some kind of arrest, secure detention, or carceral oversight, they draw attention to a controversial but still noteworthy insight: In some situations, precious few options exist outside or beyond the carceral state to assist them. Notably, some of the people I met who advocated for the use of arrest or detention did not view what I refer to as carceral protectionist responses as ideal. Rather, it was born out of a recognition that in some situations, the criminal-justice system is one of the only available safety nets, an unfortunate reality, yet still a practical way to provide victims with some modicum of support—whether services or shelter—and help get them out of exploitative situations.

Curative Harms and Balms That Burn

On one level, carceral protectionism may be understood as a set of interventions cultivated to respond to the particular "problem" of trafficking—a model of intervention aimed at mitigating future harm.[139] But situated alongside a broader U.S. history of punishment, what emerges is that, like jails, prisons, and other punitive systems that perpetuate racial and class inequalities, carceral protectionism is a cure with the capacity to generate additional harms. In 2007, renowned scholar and prison abolitionist Angela Davis delivered a speech at the University of California, Santa Cruz, titled, "Prison: A Sign of Democracy?" where she agreed with Michael Tonry's point in *The Future of Imprisonment* that the prison is "indisputably iatrogenic, that is to say its putative cure creates even more disorders."[140] For his part, Tonry likens the iatrogenicity of the prison to "a medicine that cures one ailment while causing another."[141] While Tonry concedes that prisons "damage people," he also proposes various reforms that might reconfigure prisons and repurpose their everyday operations into humane and constructive sites for prisoner self-improvement.[142] Davis disagreed with his suggestion that the problematic cure can be reformed. In her speech, she likened his call to humanely reimagine prisons as a "reenactment of a 200 year drama to which Michel Foucault turned our attention of proposing the prison as the only solution to problems that have never managed to be solved. Indeed they have been consistently exacerbated by the prisons. Bigger and better prisons have always created more crises, the solution of which are even better prisons, which in turn produce more crises."[143]

Carceral protectionist responses similarly reflect an *iatrogenic* system, a carceral cure aimed at addressing the problem of trafficking but which may create new problems and demands new expert solutions to undo the damage of punitive interventions. Consider one such cure involved in carceral protectionism: arresting youth and adults engaged in prostitution in order to assist them, which leaves them with criminal records, limiting their future housing and employment opportunities.[144] Once harmed by the curative system, it is difficult for victims of trafficking to find a solution to their new problems that does not require additional carceral or legal solutions. *Control and Protect* is ultimately a story about protectionist cures with the *potential* to harm. Here I think it important to clarify that I am not suggesting that state and nonstate assistance are not sometimes warranted or that collaboration between state and non-state actors necessarily leads to punitive interventions. This is not my argument. Instead what I am proposing is that carceral protectionism reflects a state-orchestrated, non-state-assisted response system with the capacity to control even as it aims to protect.

THE ORGANIZATION OF THE BOOK

The chapters in this book follow a chronological flow chart that resembles antitrafficking investigations. In addition to highlighting the role that collaboration plays in authorizing state and nonstate efforts to identify, protect, and manage "at risk" victims, each chapter also includes a discussion of the sociotechnical dimensions of antitrafficking efforts and how various technologies shape cooperative efforts to identify victims, pursue investigations, and protect and control "at-risk" victims.

Chapter 1, "Collaboration Meets Carceral Protection," explores how antitrafficking responses geared to identifying and protecting minors "at risk" of domestic sex trafficking has fostered cooperative alliances between law-enforcement agents and nonstate actors such as social workers and nongovernmental advocates. This chapter suggests that when nonstate actors contribute to the identification, protection, and management of prospective trafficking victims and voluntary sex workers, this does not reduce the latter group's exposure to law enforcement control, but instead renders them vulnerable to a law-enforcement-orchestrated, non-state-assisted form of punitive protection.

Chapter 2, "Investigations" explores how heightened dependence on technology to build sex trafficking investigations has created a new kind of antitrafficking collaborative partner, this time in the form of digital evidence and corroborating data amassed to gather intelligence into suspected trafficker-pimps' activities and to keep surveillant watch over individuals deemed vulnerable to domestic sex trafficking. Chapter 3, "Trafficking, Technology, and 'Data-Driven' Justice," follows the technological turn of anti-sex-trafficking efforts further still by examining how selected technical innovations in development, including machine learning, predictive analytics, and big data are being leveraged to respond to domestic sex trafficking. Like chapter 2, this chapter highlights the risks and liabilities that accompany the use of technologies with inbuilt surveillance capacities and additionally demonstrates how these tools stretch the boundaries of protective punishment into new juridical, geographic, and sociotechnical directions. This chapter further suggests that when domestic sex trafficking is framed as a technological problem, it authorizes the creation of extraordinary tools for its disruption.

I then move on to discuss the effects of carceral protectionism on the people who have experienced it most directly; namely, individuals involved in the sex trade who have been targets of antitrafficking identification and protection efforts. Chapter 4, "The Switch Up," documents the legal and emotional toll that carceral protectionist strategies have had on youth and teens placed at one unlocked residential facility, Dreams & Destiny. This chapter follows residents' experiences leading up to their placement at the shelter and questions whether bringing youth into closer contact with carceral systems is indeed the best way to protect them. Chapter 5, "Curative Harms and the 'Revolving Door' of the Criminal Justice System," argues that antitrafficking interventions aimed at assisting those seen as "at risk" of being sex trafficked through arrest and carceral encounters leaves a digital trail that limits life opportunities for years afterwards.

1

Collaboration Meets Carceral Protection

I met fourteen-year-old Che, a brilliantly witty, fast-talking Latina teenager, in June 2013, at a private shelter for youth who have been involved in domestic sex trafficking situations. In 2012, one year before I met her, Che had been identified by federal agents in a sting operation. On the day of the raid, the agents banged on the door and swiftly entered the hotel room where Che was staying with the adults she referred to as "her people." The man accused of pimping Che was also in the room, as were two other women, one African American woman and one white woman, both of whom were also involved in prostitution and later charged. When the agents found her, they handcuffed and questioned her. Later she told me she was placed in juvenile detention.

A year after the raid, Che's anger and frustration were still palpable, but not for the reasons I anticipated. She was not upset about being briefly detained, which she matter-of-factly compared to being put in a daycare facility, albeit one where the girls were separated from the boys. Instead, she was mad that the agents had tricked her into giving them information about the man accused of being her pimp, and she harbored feelings of guilt about the unwitting role she had played in sending him to prison, a sentence that would make it difficult for him to see his daughter and require him to register as a sex offender upon release.

Che's story is notable, not only because or her critical take on the raid that led to her recovery, which is to say the law-enforcement effort that led to her removal from a situation in which sex trafficking was alleged and later legally confirmed to be taking place. What is additionally important about her story is what she experienced *after* she was identified in the raid and *after* she was placed at and then subsequently ran away from a placement designed to assist her. When Che ran away—from what in antitrafficking terms may be referred to as the protection phase of her recovery—a local police unit that works on domestic sex trafficking cases was called. Members of the unit exchanged text messages with Che and set up a date with her to catch her in the act of soliciting sex. It worked. Che was arrested and then taken back to the shelter.

Che's post-federal-raid trajectory reads like a zigzagging maze punctuated by moments of protection interspersed with instances of punishment. To recap: following her identification in the raid, she was handcuffed and detained. Later she was offered assistance in the form of shelter placement. Then, after running away from the shelter, she was arrested and returned to it. What Che's story signals is that when the carceral state is situated as one of the main systems of first response to intervene on at-risk victims' behalves, law enforcement and some nonstate partners sometimes play a role in exposing them to various types of control and punishment, even if their main intention is squarely focused on securing victims' protection and keeping them safe.

. . .

Notable changes are afoot with respect to individuals, particularly sex trade-involved girls in the United States. Where once they might have been profiled by police as juvenile offenders, they are now, thanks to widespread national public attention to human trafficking and the passage of federal and state antitrafficking and safe harbor legislation, provisionally viewed by local law-enforcement agents and their nonstate partners as victims of domestic sex trafficking, not offenders, replete with traumatic pasts, turbulent family histories, and violent pimps controlling them, factors that authorize state intervention. Not only have "at-risk" domestic victims received heightened state and nonstate attention aimed at securing their protection, they have also been the targets of law-enforcement coordinated, social-service assisted interventions that may include arrest, detention, or technological surveillance—all under the auspices of helping them.

The idea that sex-trade involved individuals, especially girls may be classified as victims of domestic sex trafficking yet encounter interventions that can include punishment grates against mainstream expectations about what ought to happen to a group of people legally defined as vic-

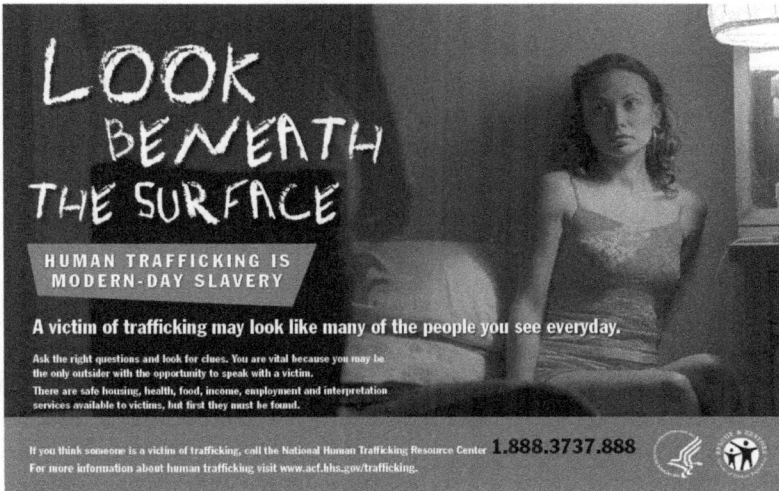

FIGURE 1. Look beneath the Surface Campaign. Image Courtesy of the U.S. Department of Health and Human Services (HHS).

FIGURE 2. Metro trafficking billboard. Image courtesy of Metro Los Angeles. ©LACMTA 2015.

tims of crimes, both in international protocols such as the Palermo Protocol and to domestic statutes like state and federal antitrafficking laws.[1] That some youth meet the federal definition of sex trafficking but may nonetheless be arrested, detained, or diverted to specialized courts or programs also clashes with campaigns instructing the public that services are available to victims once identified, and that members of the American public need to "look beneath the surface" to facilitate their protection.

My suggestion is not that efforts to identify and protect at-risk victims universally translate into punitive results. There aren't sufficient data on punitive or protective interventions targeting domestic sex trafficking victims to make this claim, and neither are some forms of punishment ever counted as such, issues discussed in greater depth in chapter 4. Yet what I want to complicate is the premise that finding at-risk victims "hiding in plain sight" will automatically lead to efforts that are protective, narrowly defined here as activities not reliant on punishment, criminalization, or control in the form of handcuffs, arrest, detention, probation, or court-monitored supervision. A more nuanced assessment is needed, because coordinated state and nonstate efforts to assist vulnerable groups—for the purposes of this chapter, youth trafficked for sex—are sometimes assumed to have broken with the more punitive methods of the past.[2] Yet interventions in the name of domestic sex trafficking victims' protection at times merge with broader efforts to control, discipline, and punish them.[3]

This chapter explores how efforts to identify and protect "at-risk" victims of domestic sex trafficking have given rise to interventions that blur carceral control with protection. In it, I examine how and why arresting girls in order to help them or detaining them for their safety are not always viewed by frontline antitrafficking actors as diametrically opposed goals. On the contrary, some of the law-enforcement orchestrated, nonstate-assisted antitrafficking efforts I have learned about subject people deemed "at risk" of domestic sex trafficking to different situations where assistance is secured through encounters and the use of carceral methods that bear a closer likeness to punishment.[4] That punitive techniques may be leveraged in the service of protection is itself worthy of attention. Yet equally significant is that collaboration—a much-vaunted ideal in formal antitrafficking circles—allows overlapping forms of control and protection to occur. Indeed, though cooperation between state and nonstate actors is commonly framed as a way to achieve more responsive, victim-centered anti-sex-trafficking efforts, my suggestion is that collaboration holds the potential to outsource the protection *and* control of at-risk victims to state and nonstate actors alike.[5]

COLLABORATION WITHIN ANTITRAFFICKING NETWORKS

Researchers Mitali Thakor and danah boyd have likened antitrafficking activities in the United States to a networked enterprise, a model where different actors are situated at "various nodes of the network relative to one another"[6] Whether one describes interactions between different antitrafficking actors as collaborative or networked, what both of these frameworks suggest is that on-the-ground activities to respond to sex trafficking can include bringing different actors from disparate backgrounds together to respond.

The specific sliver of the antitrafficking universe I observed most closely centered on localized law-enforcement activities in general and interviews and observations of a few officers and police units whose work includes investigating domestic sex trafficking in particular. Yet equally instructive to learning about a select few local police efforts to respond to domestic sex trafficking was having the chance to learn about some of the other actors they partner with—social-service providers, nongovernmental advocates, faith-based actors, and technology experts among them—whose own antitrafficking work loosely constellates around local and federal law-enforcement activities. What research on a few highly localized collaborative networks impressed upon me is that it is misleading to view anti-sex-trafficking efforts focused on domestic victims as something solely undertaken by sworn local police officers or federal agents. In reality, social-service providers, victim advocates, representatives of for-profit companies, technology experts, and enterprising researchers together with police, prosecutors, federal agents, probation officers, judges, public defenders, and members of the public play a hand, even if limited, in supporting, supplementing, and in some instances supplanting activities typically associated frontline police activity.[7] Sometimes those pushing for carceral interventions are nonstate actors, rather than individual law-enforcement agents or their agencies.

The idea that nonstate actors may work in support of rather than in opposition to law-enforcement efforts complicates earlier research pointing to the tensions between law-enforcement and social-service responses to trafficking. Amy Farrell and Stephanie Fahy have observed, for instance, that service providers are often "unwilling to alert law enforcement about human trafficking victims they are assisting out of fear that the victims will be harmed by the criminal-justice system."[8] Table 1 presents a breakdown of NGO and state-based approaches to human trafficking and their corresponding aims.[9] This list is not exhaustive. Rather, it is aimed at showing these two approaches and the different goals they are assumed to produce.

The premise that the criminal-justice system's de facto agenda of "identifying and punishing offenders" is at odds with service providers' goal of assisting trafficked persons and providing them with restorative

TABLE I   ANTITRAFFICKING INTERVENTIONS

Nonstate Approach Advocacy, Social Service, Victim/Survivor-Centered	State Approach Law Enforcement, Criminal Justice, Carceral
Victim-centered Goal: Empowerment of Victim–Survivors	Prosecution-oriented Goal: Witness Cultivation and Prosecution of Traffickers
Victims supported through biomedical, mental health, restorative, or trauma-informed services and through job training and education	Victims managed to serve as witnesses
Trafficked persons are victim-survivors in need of justice	Trafficked persons are victims of individual crimes law-enforcement intervention
Change envisioned through training, social services, and altered consumption habits (i.e., participation in "redemptive capitalism"[a] or end-demand strategies)	Change imagined as pursuing more criminal cases against traffickers-pimps and buyers-johns

[a] Bernstein, "Introduction."

services needs updating, or least ought to be tempered. That is because it does not account for the collaborative partnerships that have been formed between state and nonstate actors since the passage of the Trafficking Victims Protection Act in the United States and as attention to trafficking has expanded to include victims of domestic sex trafficking who are U.S. citizens and permanent residents.

In a U.S. context, state and nonstate activities sometimes converge, some of which can be traced to the U.S. government's efforts since the early 2000s to facilitate cooperative arrangements between different actors to deal with trafficking through federally funded task forces.[10] For instance, Department of Justice, Office for Victims of Crime (OVC), and the Bureau of Justice Assistance (BJA) task forces have been formed to address human trafficking involving migrants and domestic trafficking situations involving children. In addition to creating a formal structure for bringing different actors together, task forces have also aimed to strengthen coordination and information sharing between local and federal law-enforcement agents and selected nongovernmental task force members.[11]

A few people I interviewed participated in the OVC, BJA, and the Department of Justice's Innocence Lost task force.[12] Zack, a federal prosecutor and member of one of the collaborative Bureau of Justice human trafficking task forces explained the twofold mission of the work of his task force this way: "to rescue victims of human trafficking and restore them and prosecute the traffickers. . . . We worked [at] those two things hand-in-hand with our NGO community. . . . We have coordination on every case." Zack was direct about the initial tensions that surrounded his task force's activities. "We certainly did start off somewhat misaligned . . . law enforcement has a mission, and that's to get the bad guy. Social-service organizations have a mission, and that's to help the poor victim." It took a big case and a sizeable federal grant, equally divided between the law-enforcement and social-service sides, to bridge some of the cultural divide in the task force.

Though it is difficult to quantify the scale and impact of collaborative interventions in the United States, Zack's note about the grant money attached to human-trafficking task forces offers cursory insight into the federal government's commitment to collaboration in monetary terms.[13] Fiscal spending aside, formal human-trafficking task forces (e.g., those funded by the federal or state governments) are important to my discussion of less well-known collaborations in the domestic anti-sex-trafficking field for two main reasons. First, task forces have advanced a model of governance predicated on state and nonstate cooperation.[14] Second, task forces are geared toward bringing different constituencies together to find victims and prosecute traffickers, yet also aim to raise public awareness of "the menace of trafficking and the plight of victims."[15] In this way, task forces are significant in more widely promoting the message that trafficking is taking place in the United States and that coordination between different actors and groups is an important way to eradicate it.

The local collaborations I learned about typically weren't the public-facing versions. However, one collaboration did emerge from a federally funded task force where the impetus for one police detective to go off the task force script was the result of feeling like it wasn't sufficiently focused on activities he thought were most important. Grady, a detective in a unit that handles runaway and domestic minor sex trafficking cases offered insight into his own transition from participating on a formal task force to a local arrangement. Though he once sat on an Office for Victim of Crimes Human Trafficking task force, he felt isolated on it and found the politics overwhelming.[16] He attributed some of the tensions to what he thought were some NGO members' myopic focus on victim rescues, with less attention paid to criminal prosecutions. Despite his misgivings, the task force was useful to him in one way; it gave him the opportunity to connect with Tina, an advocate who also sat on the task force. Together, they came up with their own local collaboration based on separate but mutually supportive goals. As he explained: "Her and I kinda felt like we were all alone. We were trying to do some things that the task force wasn't necessarily doing. . . . She wanted to get much more intimate with the victims, and I wanted to get much more intimate with the crooks, with the perpetrators. So that's why her and I fit together in the beginning. We fit together like a perfect puzzle."

Grady's narrative offers insight as to how different professionals with seemingly different goals can find common ground cooperating in antitrafficking activities. For instance, the relationship Grady developed with Tina's nonprofit organization helped his unit figure out what to do with potential victims from the moment they are picked up to the time they are placed either in juvenile hall or some other placement. Grady said Tina is instrumental in helping manage victims so that he can focus his work and attention on investigating pimps, who he describes as the bad guys and "true criminals."

Social-service providers may help police figure out what to do with a victim or may help police identify a victim in the first place. Other types of cooperation between law enforcement and nonstate actors include promoting victim cooperation in interviews and criminal investigations, coordinating postidentification victim support in the form of housing (locked or unlocked), or working together in the context of specialized courts. Collaborations can be, but are not necessarily, formal, nor do they need be long-term arrangements. Some occur as a limited occasion to work together on a specific case or in helping a particular victim. Yet, no matter the scope or specific timeline of more local forms of cooperation, what is important is what law enforcement and social-service providers stand to gain from cooperation in the following ways:

- Identification: nonstate actors (NA) share tips with law enforcement (LE)
- Interviews/Investigations: NA accompany LE before, during, and/or after interviews, help to establish trust between victims and LE, and stabilize victims, encouraging them to cooperate with LE

- Protection: NA help LE find housing and placement options after or in lieu of arrest (i.e., the "2 A.M. problem")

Some police described specific social-service agencies and particular advocates who accompany their units on street runs or hotel operations, which generally center on identifying at-risk victims. It can be beneficial for local police, for instance, to partner with nonstate actors so that the latter can provide prospective victims with stability and support after they are identified. This supports criminal investigators especially in situations where they need victims to be available to them to serve as witnesses in prosecutions against trafficker-pimps. And whether in interviews, court proceedings against trafficker-pimps, or during or immediately following street runs and antitrafficking "rescue" operations, the rationale for allowing victim advocates to participate in law-enforcement-centered efforts is based on the premise that they can help facilitate communication and encourage victims' cooperation with police, facilitating

- Referrals: LE grants NA access to victims, which in turn may translate to victim referrals
- Legitimacy: LE carries out sting operations, victim recoveries, and similar operations that would be challenging, if not legally risky, if executed by NA alone
- Enforcement: NA can call upon LE to help find victims who have run away, arresting them if necessary

Nonstate actors such as NGO advocates and social-service providers benefit from collaboration too. Some partner with police as a way to "get intimate with victims." Others seek out law enforcement's help if and when victims run away from shelters. The "perfect puzzle" of cooperation Grady describes thus appears to work—even in situations where tensions emerge between state and nonstate actors—because different parties who comprise a short-term or more deeply established antitrafficking constellation, or "node," to use Thakor and boyd's term, stand to gain something from the arrangement.

Scholars have previously established that state and nongovernmental actors have played a crucial role in shaping the political terms of trafficking, both by myopically focusing attention on sex trafficking,[17] and foregrounding all forms of commercial sex as innately exploitative, dangerous and traumatic.[18] Years of NGO advocacy, lobbying, and messaging linking antitrafficking to antiprostitution politics[19] have similarly shaped what Elizabeth Bernstein describes as "carceral feminism," a dominant antitrafficking ethos that sutures state and nonstate responses to trafficking with stepped-up criminal-justice responses.[20] Understanding the mechanics of carceral feminism helps to account for the cooperative arrangements between state and nonstate actors and the "NGO-ization"[21] of antitrafficking efforts more generally. Yet these trends are also crucial for unpacking how and why collaboration is a technology of neoliberal governance and a technique that fosters public–private partnerships.[22] Collaboration is a way to patch up, in piecemeal form, a state in decline.[23] Importantly, a declining "redistributive welfare state"[24] does not signal the retreat of the state altogether, as scholars Marie Gottschalk and Lynne Haney have separately argued in their research on the carceral state.[25] Rather, the state is revivified through carceral projects and public-private partnerships between state and nonstate actors to address different social problems.[26]

Domestic sex trafficking—like state and nonstate efforts to respond to sexual violence—is now one of those problems.[27] If we follow the flow of grant funds and technical assistance efforts from federal to local law-enforcement agencies and grant solicitations like the FY 2015 Enhanced Collaborative Model to Combat Human Trafficking, where grantee eligibility is contingent on bringing together law-enforcement agencies and providers of victim services operating in the same "community, jurisdiction, or geographic area of the human trafficking task force," we get a glimpse of the money that is available to combat trafficking and how state and nonstate collaborations are prioritized.[28]

These trends are also crucial to unpacking how and why collaboration is a defining feature of the anti-sex-trafficking response system I call carceral protectionism. Why? Because selected law-enforcement agents and their nonstate allies wield "interpretive power,"[29] not only in distilling what counts as coercive or consensual third-party facilitated sex, but in determining what kinds of interventions are best equipped to assist victims deemed "at-risk." Select localized efforts to respond to domestic sex trafficking offer a partial window through which to observe a collaborative model of governance in development, a framework where individuals assumed to be in sex trafficking situations experience different forms of protection and punishment by the state and its noncarceral partners (e.g., nonstate actors), sometimes within but also beyond the physical confines of juvenile hall, jail, locked mental health facilities, and unlocked shelters.[30] What a closer look at selected anti-sex-trafficking activities targeting domestic victims further reveals is that state and nonstate responses sometimes constitutively overlap in important ways:

- Nonprofit and social-service techniques are sometimes harnessed to "soften" law-enforcement activities.
- Carceral techniques like handcuffing, arrest, detention, and/or court supervision may be used to find victims and/or refer them to services.[31]

"IT'S NOT PUNISHMENT": WHEN IDEAS ABOUT PROTECTION AND PUNISHMENT OVERLAP

How do you help a girl who is in love with the trafficker-pimp alleged to exploit her? How do you get this girl to see that she's a victim of sex trafficking even when she doesn't view herself as such? And what do you do when she runs away from the shelter she's been placed at to help her? These questions vex some police and victim advocates who fear that a placement in an unlocked shelter will put a kid or teen right back into an unsafe situation.

The contention that youth, particularly girls, are variously brainwashed, in love with, and exploited by trafficker-pimps is a theme that emerged in interviews and informal conversations and is a topic other researchers have drawn attention to it in order to understand its legal, social-service, and perceptual ramifications.[32] Law enforcement, like social-service providers in anti-sex-trafficking circles, is arguably becoming more fluent in speaking the language of underage victims' exploitation and trauma at the hands of trafficker-pimps. However, youth trafficked for sex—like migrants who have been in forced-labor situations—pose a challenge to law enforcement in that many do not self-identify as victims,[33] at least while they are still in the situations assumed to be exploitative.[34] Police and their nonstate partners may therefore look for examples of exploitation offline by frequenting geographically well-known "strolls" where street-based prostitution is known to take place. Or they may go online to monitor general and sex-specific classified ad sites such as Backpage.com or the Facebook pages and social-media accounts of prospective victims or suspected traffickers. If and when at-risk youth don't identify as victims, officers may look for signs of psychological duress, physical scarring, or tattoo branding and question youth about pimps to gauge whether they are being victimized.

Discourses about trafficked youth's trauma and victimization also authorize legal and rehabilitation interventions, evidenced, for instance, through the passage of state safe harbor laws. Legal researcher Brendan Conner notes that though there is no single definition of safe harbor laws, they are broadly understood as "rely[ing] on custodial arrests to prosecute or divert youth arrested for or charged with prostitution-related offenses under the criminal law to court supervision under state child welfare, foster care, or dependency statutes."[35] Laws in as many as twenty-five states meet this criterion, Conner finds, and the Stop Exploitation Through Trafficking Act of 2015 "require[s] that states have a safe harbor law as a condition for receiving federal grants."[36]

Safe harbor laws, like "trauma concepts," offer important contextual details for my analysis of state and nonstate collaborations.[37] When laws are passed that recognize youth involved in the sex trade as severe victims in need of services,[38] law enforcement and social-service providers begin to imagine what alternative options should consist of. Relatedly, when the federal government and states pass laws to treat youth as victims, not offenders, it sets the stage for more criminal-justice-orchestrated, non-state-assisted collaborative interventions. Not only does the circulation of discourses about youths' trauma signal its move "from clinical psychiatry"[39] to anti-sex-trafficking activities, it also creates a language of intelligibility between state and nonstate actors where the arrest, detention or protracted supervision of a victim "at-risk" isn't seen as punishment but rather as a mechanism for helping them access rehabilitative and social-service assistance.[40]

Becca, an advocate for commercially sexually exploited girls, thought that sometimes youth needed to be arrested and put in juvenile hall in order to "figure out where to place them." But for her, temporarily putting a kid in juvenile hall doesn't qualify as punishment per se. Rather it functions more like a short stay and point of contact that sets into motion subsequent access to services. As she explained:

> They [youth] are not in there [juvenile hall] as criminals. It's really just a holding place for them. And so they see a judge and a judge determines where they're supposed to be placed. Now, juvenile halls are supposed to have mental health services. . . . I don't know if it's the best services. That's a whole different discussion. But they have those services and they get evaluated. They get . . . a rape kit, a psych evaluation, go through that and see a judge to place them in an appropriate placement . . . the services within juvenile hall may need to get a little polished. . . . If I see a kid and they're involved in prostitution. I'm gonna arrest them and put them in juvenile hall, but not keep them—it's not punishment. I'm holding them in there.[41]

That sex-trade-involved girls sometimes experience a combination of state control and rehabilitation "for their own protection" hews to a twenty-first-century neoliberal vision of justice where the carceral state provides triage in dealing with problems other systems of support like child welfare, public health, and educational systems are ill-equipped, underfunded, or not fully prepared to handle.[42] And though interventions designed to intervene on behalf of at-risk victims of domestic sex trafficking is suggestive of the carceral state's diversification into new kinds of *protective* punishment, it is not altogether new.[43] A cursory examination of the history of juvenile justice in the United States suggests that saving girls from prostitution and their perceived morally troubled lot dates back to the late nineteenth and early twentieth centuries and the earliest days of juvenile justice. Arresting to assist or detaining girls to rehabilitate them is thus part of a longer history of gendered protective punishment, or if readers prefer, punitive protection.

While not new, what is novel is the rationale offered by some police, service providers, and victims' advocates to explain why arrest or detention are useful tools for getting youth away from trafficker-pimps assumed to be exploiting them and to help them gain access to the services they need.[44] For her part, Becca was clear that she was not in favor of the extended confinement of youth in juvenile hall. But her baseline assumption that arrests and detention don't count as punishment is instructive. Bracketing a discussion about whether or not the experience of an arrest qualifies as punishment, and whether arrests or detention carry minimal risks for those subject to them, questions I return to in chapters 4 and 5, what her narrative draws attention to is an important trend—a theme reiterated in different form by others—which is that antitrafficking efforts require retooled criminal justice solutions rather than an end to carcerally orchestrated antitrafficking interventions altogether. Put another way, rather than stopping arrests or detention for sex trafficking, some victims' advocates and their law-enforcement partners have sought to reimagine the criminal and juvenile justice systems, whether in order to provide victims with services or to inspire their cooperation with the police in the prosecution of trafficker-pimps.

RETOOLING CARCERAL PROCESSES

There are three general areas in which antitrafficking collaborations may occur between state and nonstate actors where identification and protection are concerned: finding at-risk victims, figuring out how to assist them without an arrest after they have been identified, and managing them after they have been identified with an arrest. In the sections that follow, I describe some of the collaborations I learned about and how both enforcement-centered and social-service-oriented activities have been reconfigured as a result of cooperation.

Soft Rooms and Softening Carceral Processes

Some law-enforcement agents used the language of softening otherwise punitive carceral processes, talking about *soft* lockdown or *soft* rooms.[45] Chris, a police officer who works on domestic sex trafficking cases, said detectives in his unit had enlisted the help of nonprofit victims' advocates to teach detectives how to communicate with trafficked youth in a victim-centered manner. He told me that victims' advocates might also accompany his unit before, during, and after an antitrafficking operation took place. Chris mentioned three different nonprofit agencies that his unit cooperated with, agencies whose work I was familiar with from public presentations they gave.[46]

If the unit is doing undercover work at a hotel, for instance, a nonprofit agency might send one or more counselors to the operation. Here they wait in a room next to where police are staked out. Immediately following the officers' initial contact with prospective victims, Chris said, they "hand over the girl" to the counselor. If the unit isn't running a hotel operation, but what Chris referred to as a "street run," focused on identifying underage victims of sex trafficking on the street, a counselor will wait in surveillance vehicles while an officer from the unit makes contact with a person on the street. After that, and assuming the team finds an underage youth they believe is a victim of sex trafficking, the victim (assumed to be a girl) is taken back to the police station, where a counselor waits for her in what Chris described as a "soft room" his vice unit had created. The counselor then stays with her during the interview with police.

Although the softened tactics Chris's unit uses to identify and interview at-risk youth may be seen as an alternative to more typical forms of punishment, they have their limits. When I asked Chris if his unit ever had any conflicts with nonprofit partners as a result of these types of cooperative antitrafficking operations, he recalled one time when a new member of the team "didn't play along." The walls separating their hotel rooms were paper-thin, Chris said, and his team could overhear things the counselor was saying to the girl. According to him, the counselor had offered advice about what information to share and withhold from police. Thus, by acting like a defense attorney, the counselor had, according to Chris "subverted the process." This was a problem for him because when a counselor starts giving youth legal advice, there is a risk that they'll decide not to talk with police. For Chris, the only way this kind of collaborative intervention works is if "everyone is on the same page," by which I think he meant that cooperation between police and a nonprofit agency is only successful to the extent that counselors and victims' advocates are willing to assist police. For Chris, nonstate actors' cooperation with police thus depends upon their efficacy in getting youth to talk to police and helping him and fellow officers gather as much information as possible in order to build cases against traffickers.

The 2 A.M. Problem

In addition to accompanying police on street-sweeps and during interviews, nonprofit and other noncarceral partners may be called upon to offer postidentification support in the form of housing and other social services that frontline police officers are incapable of providing themselves. Some police officers I interviewed referred to this as the "2 A.M. problem," a way to describe challenges police face when they come across youth and teens at 2 A.M. and are unsure what to do with them.

When a police officer finds a youth engaged in prostitution on the street, in a hotel room, or in some other location, the immediate challenge—assuming no counselor, social worker, or victims' advocate is present—is to determine where to place them. There aren't a lot of placement options, or many people to call upon for help, at 2 A.M., a detective remarked.[47] Other officers referenced both the 2 A.M. problem and 2 A.M. solution in the form of an NGO advocate, employee of a Christian organization, social worker, or probation officer with a proven track record of showing up at random places at unseemly hours of the morning when police make the call. In designating someone as the go-to "2 A.M. person," the police not only highlighted the person's commitment to helping victims in need, but identified them—and by extension the supporting organization—as a preferred partner who would assist them in managing victims.

Victim Management

Since the earliest days of contemporary antitrafficking efforts in the United States, scholars and advocates have drawn attention to the fact that the protection of victims is often problematically tied to their cooperation with law enforcement.[48] Understood as antithetical to the goals of a "victim" or "survivor-centered" approach, requiring victims of trafficking to cooperate with law enforcement has additionally been critiqued on the grounds that it ties protection—and, for migrants, immigration relief—to the prosecution of traffickers.[49] Yet in an antitrafficking environment primarily organized around the criminal-justice system, victims of domestic trafficking may be encouraged to cooperate with law enforcement by testifying against those suspected of trafficking them. This can prove challenging for U.S.-born youth for the same reasons as for adult U.S. citizens permanent residents, and migrants: they may fear for their own and their family's safety,[50] or they may not want to participate in a process that punishes someone with whom they feel a connection, whatever the terms of their relationship. Yet without youth's cooperation and willingness to testify, state and federal prosecutors may be reluctant to file a case, or, if a case is filed, they may have little chance of success without their testimony. Enter nonstate collaborators.[51]

The H.E.A.T. Watch Unit in Alameda County, California, is a program that assists youth who have been sexually trafficked. On its web site, Deputy District Attorney Sharmin Bock describes the challenges of getting underage victims to testify this way: "One of the greatest challenges of prosecuting a trafficking case is making sure the victim is on the train when the train pulls into the courtroom. Without the victim's participation in the prosecution, we don't have a case."[52] The H.E.A.T. Watch program looks to social-service providers and other first-responder collaborators to help manage youth and to ensure that they get on the "antitrafficking train" to testify. The H.E.A.T. Watch Unit is one example of what may be described as a victim-management strategy. Providing services is also a way of encouraging youths' participation in criminal trials as witnesses against suspected trafficker-pimps.

Victim management sounds quite formal though. Sometimes advocates play a role by showing up to court with youth or encouraging them to cooperate with law enforcement, a decision that comes with risks for both youth and advocates. For Cara, encouraging youth to testify has put her own and her staff's safety on the line. As she explained, "It is real. It is organized crime. They [traffickers] don't want to get caught. What we do is dangerous especially when we encourage our girls to testify. With the new laws, these guys go away for a really long time. No one seems to bother us unless we can participate in a very real way in putting them away." In chapter 4, I return to a discussion about how some youth talk about the risks they face when deciding whether or not to testify. For now, what is important to stress is that when the postidentification management of victims is dispersed among selected state and nonstate actors, whether to encourage victims to testify and/ or to help them access services, the process holds the real potential to create a feedback loop in which criminal justice tools designed to punish are the same tools used to foster victim cooperation and protection. When I asked Grady in 2013 whether we had evolved beyond thinking that we need to arrest victims first in order to provide them with protection, here is how he responded:

> At this point, I just wanna speak for me, and I'll speak for my partner too, when I say this. It's been our experience, or my experience, that if we have a victim who is in custody with charges pending against them for their involvement, those are the cases where we're able to prosecute the true criminal, the exploiter. We have had cases where the victim is not in custody, but I would put that—from a percentage, I would put that as a single-digit number . . . unfortunately, the success rate [for prosecutions] is way low if the girls aren't somehow legally detained.

Law enforcement is sometimes called upon to help service providers protect and manage victims too. Cara, for instance, asks sheriffs to find girls who have run away from the unlocked shelter she runs. Sometimes, she said, responding officers don't know what to make out of what they're being asked to do: go out and arrest and charge a girl who hasn't actually committed a crime? Cara acknowledged the fraught nature of this request. "What right do any of us have to pick up a girl and charge her with prostitution?" Yet when girls run away and are assumed to return to unsafe situations, she pressed me to consider: "How do we keep girls safe when locking them up isn't an option?"

It is not unprecedented for advocates to assist victims of other types of gender-based violence, such as sexual assault, in negotiating the criminal-justice system. Nevertheless, because youths' relationship to the justice system holds the potential to be punitive, this creates particular challenges for advocates who remain closely allied to it. Whether offered services or not, "once captured by the system, many youth may feel distrustful toward the adults protecting them . . . and . . . the use of threats of prosecution against them to encourage them to provide evidence . . . against trafficker pimps" can backfire, Linda Williams observes.[53] As Williams further points out, threats of prosecution are not only ineffective but may actually heighten victims' emotional vulnerability and reliance on pimps, perceived by youth to be "the one person who can protect her from the system, incarceration."[54] What this suggests is that even with programs aimed at empowering youth and providing them with comprehensive services—services that are desperately needed and ought to be adequately funded— youth sometimes only gain access to such services after they have been arrested, detained, or placed on probation for prostitution or other offenses. And because youth may be channeled through multiple systems—including the foster care and juvenile justice systems— before they are identified as sexually trafficked by law enforcement, they may be distrustful of adults and not see cooperation with law enforcement or participation in collaborative anti-sex-trafficking efforts as a fair or full expression of justice.[55]

Collaborative Courts

"There's a huge resistance to identifying the criminal-justice system as harmful," Tory explains. She would know. She bears witness to it every day in the context of her work as a public defender in a human trafficking court. In the specialized court where she works, clients aged sixteen and older come to her by way of a prostitution charge or related offenses. An arrest serves as a "referral"[56] that places them in a human trafficking court designed to assist them. From there, criminal defendant clients-cum-trafficking victims are assigned to Tory by the state so she can mount a legal defense on their behalf.

Though she doesn't think the police set out to arrest survivors of sex trafficking on a daily basis, the frequent and repeated arrests her clients experience make it difficult for her to imagine situations where they aren't arrested, whether for prostitution or other offenses. After arrest, Tory's clients are subjected to court-monitored supervision that prolongs their involvement with the criminal-justice system, which she views as another harm in itself.

Few specialized courts existed for victims of human trafficking and sexually exploited girls in the late 2000s when I started this project. Now there are collaborative, girl-centered, human-trafficking courts scattered throughout New York, California, and Hawaii.[57] Yet the fact that criminal courts even exist to assist victims of sex trafficking lends support to Tory's observation and my larger argument that the carceral state has emerged as a system that is imagined as helping at-risk victims secure some form of protection. Tory articulated the fraught dimensions of court by posing a two-part question to me:

I think there's two things you have to figure out. One is, do you support the idea that prostitution should be handled differently by the criminal-justice system. I do. Because as long as prostitution is a crime and people are arrested for prostitution, I think the criminal justice response should be moving away from incarceration and a punitive focus. It is critical to reduce the harms, to the extent we can, caused by criminalization. The second question you have to answer is whether you are comfortable calling these initiatives human trafficking courts? That seems to be a real problem and I'm not comfortable with that. And I'm not sure we should be comfortable with that . . . what you're saying is that the person you're prosecuting for a prostitution violation is a victim of trafficking and that's why we're going to coordinate this different response in court. . . . The first question out of anyone's mouth should be, "Why are we prosecuting this person? Why is this happening in criminal court?

Tory's analysis not only points to the slippage between prostitution and human trafficking that occurs in a court where people aged sixteen and over (the age of consent in her state) are charged with prostitution and then routed to a criminal court where they are called trafficking victims but effectively treated like criminals. She also provokes us to ask the obvious: why is a criminal court, even one with services attached, used to help victims?

Kevin, a public defender who is part of a different court in another state, and works with commercially sexually exploited youth eighteen and younger, asked a similar question. When I spoke with him, he was overwhelmingly positive about the court he works in. He praised the judge, social workers, and prosecutors in equal measure and said that the girls referred to the court—the majority of whom are black—volunteered to be a part of it. For Kevin, the innovative court was an unequivocal success. Yet despite his positive experiences, he wondered why the court is part of the criminal-justice system—a dependency court would be a better option, he thought. "None of these girls should ever be charged for prostitution," he said. Though more laws have passed in his state to curb arresting youth involved in prostitution, Kevin told me that arrests still happen. That is because, in some jurisdictions, before "at-risk" victims can access services, an arrest is needed to "trigger" their diversion.[58]

It may be the case that participants placed in specialized court and diversion programs may be helped, get rehabilitated, and feel empowered for having gone through them. My data on these programs are limited, and I therefore cannot speculate on their efficacy. More research is needed. What I do want to call into question, however, is something far more basic, and which expands upon Tory's questions: should collaborations between state and nonstate actors—to identify, assist, divert, or court-supervise people assumed to be victims—really qualify as alternatives to the more punitive interventions of the past? Some nonstate actors accompany law enforcement agents during antitrafficking rescue operations. Others play a direct advocacy role for youth placed in juvenile hall at the behest of judges who oversee specialized courts in which they are processed. Still others share tips gathered from online classified-ad sites or through algorithms specially designed for law enforcement, topics I return to in chapters 2 and 3. Though collaborative efforts may be discursively framed as "victim and survivor-centered," those I have described are implicitly designed to encourage at-risk victims to become known to law enforcement. In some instances, to get them into the system. Nonstate actors play a role in this.

That is why I think it important to point out another underappreciated fact: it is inaccurate to suggest that we have moved completely away from treating at-risk victims of domestic sex trafficking either as offenders or completely as victims either. Instead, state and nonstate actors that rely on a combination of protection and punishment mean that some legally–defined victims in actuality aren't treated either as victims or as offenders. Some occupy an entirely different category altogether, a subject position of "victim–offenders," which some local anti-sex-trafficking activities support rather than challenge.[59]

CONCLUSION

If we concede that sexually trafficked youth may be called victims in name but that in practice, some are treated more like "victim–offenders," than we can situate collaborative alliances and the development of coordinated efforts between police and actors as an effort to sensitize and soften otherwise punitive carceral systems and processes. Yet the softened approach and stereotypically feminized procedures offered by nonprofit advocates and actors (most of whom are women) and instrumentalized by law enforcement agents (a great many of whom are men) aren't just suggestive of a gendered form of punishment or an antitrafficking gendered division of labor—both noteworthy trends.[60] In addition to that, these trends shed some light on what happens when protective logics fuse with carceral systems, the culminating result of which is a carceral protectionist system augmented by collaboration.

Talk of collaboration—like discussions of rescuing victims—implies a move away from punitive law-enforcement-centered activities.[61] Yet the inclusion of different nonstate actors and seemingly noncarceral activities into identification and protection efforts has arguably expanded the criminal-justice approach to antitrafficking efforts beyond what some of the earliest critics of it might have envisaged.[62] Rather than being illustrative of a state in retreat, collaborative antitrafficking interventions reflect a state and its sundry habits of punishment, social control,[63] and protection "redeployed."[64] If antitrafficking is a network,[65] and a carceral one at that, and if carceral systems are by design diffuse and archipelagic, as Michel Foucault suggests,[66] then we can see nonstate actors as the bridge-builders that link "at-risk" trafficked persons' identification and protection to systems with the capacity to control them. Nonstate actors and individual law-enforcement officers may not see their role as such, and many may wholly disagree that that is what they are doing. Yet if the ultimate goal of collaboration is to get trafficked persons identified and known to a system predisposed to discipline, control, manage, and punish, it is difficult to ignore the role they play in maintaining a protectionist twenty-first-century version of the carceral archipelago.

2

Investigations

I am on a ride-along with a vice unit whose enforcement activities include prostitution and sex trafficking as well as non-sex-related vice crimes. The unit covers approximately ten square miles of a densely populated area presumed to be a hotbed of prostitution and gang activity. The station where the unit is located is just a few blocks away from a few well-known "strolls" where street-based prostitution is known to take place. For a mid-June, early week ridealong, it proves to be a whirlwind night. In the first two hours of observation, officers in the unit execute a search warrant at the apartment of a suspected trafficker-pimp's girlfriend. Ten of us arrive at the apartment—eight officers from the vice unit, one investigator from the District Attorney's office, and me. Before entering the apartment, we're told that Tara, an eighteen-year-old "Catholic girl from a good family and decent background," had been kidnapped by Tru, a black pimp suspected of having gang affiliations.[1] The officers tell me that Tru laid claim to Tara by branding her with a tattoo of his name—a move they say is common—and then put her out on the street to prostitute. There are three other victims mentioned by police, all of whom are underage. One of the victims, Cassie, is now seventeen, but she first came to their attention when she was arrested for prostitution at the age of sixteen.

Tru had already been arrested and was in jail on the night we arrived at his girlfriend's apartment. The police obtained his cell phone and upon analyzing its contents, positively ID'd another victim. They also found a bunch of self-produced videos, some of which I later viewed at the station. Tru liked to turn the camera on himself and created these short video vignettes to document life as a pimp. Sixty videos were recovered in total along with six or so still images. He also had cameras installed in his car to document parts of his everyday life. In one video, he sits in the driver seat of the car and says, "These hos ho real hard for a pimp. They want to sock it hard for a pimp." Nicole, an officer from a different unit that also works on domestic sex trafficking told me that it is not uncommon for suspects she's encountered to "memorialize" their activities by keeping detailed text, video, and photo records on their cell phones and social media accounts. Tru's accumulation of such a large trove of digital evidence gives weight to Nicole's claim. It also demonstrates Tru's prowess in keeping careful track of his activities.

Back at Tru's girlfriend's apartment, the officers and investigator wade through its jam-packed rooms, one if which is a dedicated marijuana grow room. They are in search of two main pieces of evidence—a computer and another cell phone—though they don't have much luck. I'm later informed that Tru had called his girlfriend from jail before the police arrived at her apartment. Even though when making calls from jail, users are informed that their calls will be recorded, Tru did not self-censor what he said on the phone and told his girlfriend to go to the apartment with trash bags and to get rid of the computers and pictures. Despite his instructions, the police are still able to gather some evidence at his girlfriend's house. Once collected, we return to the station to debrief.

Brody is the officer in charge of the unit. At the station, he tells his team of assembled police officers and detectives that the operation went smoothly. In the course of discussing the evidence that was gathered, Brody warns about cell phones confiscated as evidence: "We sit with these phones and we eat snacks at our desks. These girls are out there with twenty, thirty people per day and we know what kind of money they make. Exchanging all those bodily fluids and all the things they're touching. Remember to wash your hands." Though viscerally evocative, Brody's message gestures toward the critical importance that cell phones and commercially available technologies play in law enforcement's investigation of domestic sex trafficking cases. And just as the unit's investigation into Tru's alleged kidnapping and sex trafficking activities focus on locating his computers and mobile devices, so does his production of self-generated content—evidence veering on the archival—help Brody's unit strike an "evidentiary goldmine" in pursuing a criminal case against him.[2]

. . .

The idea that technology needs to be leveraged to combat human trafficking in general and domestic sex trafficking in particular has garnered
heightened attention in antitrafficking circles throughout the United
States.[3] In addition to its ability to render trafficking more visible, technology is understood as providing new tools for law enforcement to
respond. Discussions have focused on how law enforcement should
"exploit available technology to its investigative advantage," particularly with respect to cases involving sex.[4] A key theme framing these
discussions is that suspected traffickers, pimps, and clients, also referred
to as johns or buyers, unfairly benefit from the anonymity offered by
mobile and networked technologies. As a 2012 State of Human Trafficking Report released by the California Attorney General states:

> Traditional law enforcement tools should be supplemented with innovative
> investigative techniques . . . while technology is being used to perpetrate
> human trafficking, that same technology can provide a digital trail. This
> digital footprint offers greater potential opportunity for tracking traffickers'
> and johns' communications, movements, and transactions.[5]

The presumed visibility of trafficking offers new opportunities for
tracing suspected traffickers' digital footprints; the digital and data tracks
left by mobile phone calls, text messages, financial transactions, GPS patterns, automatic license plate readers, and geolocation data help law
enforcement track suspected traffickers and corroborate relationships
between them and those they are suspected of exploiting.[6] Assuming that
law enforcement had sufficient technological training and resources to
collect and analyze the digital traces left behind by individuals suspected
of trafficking, they could, in principle, gain access to a treasure trove of
material with which to build cases against them.[7] And whether cases are
filed under state or federal human-trafficking statutes or child pornogra-
phy possession or distribution charges, there has been increased focus on
how to collect digital evidence and a corresponding focus on the types of
tools that can augment law enforcement work in pursuing sex trafficking
investigations. There has not, however, been as much attention paid to
how technologies and innovative tools are being used to observe individuals perceived as potential victims. This omission is notable since law
enforcement may employ various strategies to gain access to evidentiary
material in the form of digital and mobile phone records, not only of
individuals suspected of crimes related to sex trafficking and pimping but
also of victims presumed to be exploited by them.

This chapter examines how law enforcement and nonstate actors look to technology to pursue domestic sex trafficking investigations, and why digital evidence is seen as so crucial in locating domestic sex trafficking victims and building investigations. That law enforcement rely on particular technologies lends support to theories about the decline of "self-help" policing, what legal scholar Paul Ohm describes as a shift where law enforcement increasingly become "passive consumers rather than active producers of surveillance."[8] Now, instead, law enforcement can build sex trafficking cases from the self-generated content produced by the people suspected of committing criminal acts rather than tools and technologies developed expressly for law enforcement agencies. Yet in law enforcement's efforts to build investigations, those deemed "at risk" may also experience carceral oversight. An examination of why digital evidence is helpful in building domestic sex trafficking investigations thus illuminates some of the sociotechnical dimensions of antitrafficking efforts and how efforts to identity and protect potential victims may rely upon different forms of surveillance.

TECHNOLOGICALLY MEDIATED SURVEILLANCE

Individuals engaged in trading or exchanging sex for money on the street in the United States have historically been subject to "traditional" police surveillance, including in-person observation of street-based "strolls," or "tracks," where prostitution and commercial sex are assumed to take place. With the issue framed as one of quality of life and nuisance abatement, such efforts have aimed to move commercial sex "out of public view" and away from schools and other public places.[9] When I have observed police in their antiprostitution and antitrafficking efforts, time is spent driving to various "strolls," where officers stop and question women and girls presumed to be engaged in prostitution.

In some cases, an officer approaches a woman but then lets her go with a warning to "get off the stroll." On other occasions, in the area I observed, girls and women—the majority of whom were black— were arrested, handcuffed, and taken to jail. It was not always clear to me how and why these decisions were made, which is to say, what accounted for the minute-by-minute decision making that went into separating a prospective victim of trafficking from a suspected criminal. What is somewhat clearer, however, is that when officers instruct people to move away from the stroll or track, they are following a long-standing vice practice of policing prostitution through its removal from the street and out of the public view.[10] In a unit tasked with both enforcing prostitution and identifying situations involving domestic sex trafficking, the techniques used to monitor both groups were indistinguishable, at least to my untrained eye.

And though the pretext for police attention may now be couched in protectionist terms, the two groups may experience comparable degrees of surveillance if anti-sex trafficking efforts employ antiprostitution practices. The introduction of federal and state antitrafficking legislation since the year 2000 offers a partial explanation of why law enforcement has bolstered antitrafficking and, by extension, antiprostitution surveillance tactics in recent years.[11] Meanwhile, technological innovations have also created unparalleled opportunities for law enforcement to extend its investigative tactics in all areas, including sex trafficking and prostitution. Commercial technologies with different surveillance capabilities and functions built into them provide law enforcement with the ability to access information, data, images, and intelligence that would previously have been unavailable.

Police and federal agents do not need to solely rely on court-ordered wiretaps[12] or their own "in-house" technologies to conduct surveillance of suspects' activities, as legal scholar Paul Ohm has presciently observed.[13] Police can now obtain intelligence from smartphones, computers, and the digital content generated by the very people who are the intended targets of surveillance.[14] To paraphrase and build off of Ohm's insights on these topics, we may ask: Why would a police officer or federal agent need to get a court-ordered wiretap to build a sex trafficking case when sending a "mere subpoena"[15] request to Google, Facebook, an online classified ad site like Backpage.com, or a telecommunications company might suffice, a tactic that does not carry the same requirements as court-ordered wiretaps. And notably, police may not need a subpoena, probable cause, or a warrant to gain access to information to pursue leads. Sometimes finding people they believe are being exploited is also a way to gain access to their cell phones, laptops, and online accounts, or to those of the people suspected of exploiting them.

AUGMENTATION OF ANTITRAFFICKING AND ANTIPROSTITUTION ACTIVITIES

"It's kind of funny," Nicole, a supervisor of a human trafficking unit opines. "When you look at our cases, at least the fundamental makeup of our cases, all are pretty much the same." For Nicole, the elemental makeup of cases and the investigative follow-up it sets into motion typ-ically starts with a tip about a possible victim, which may come from various sources: an anonymous source; the National Center for Missing and Exploited Children; an antitrafficking NGO; or even the classified-ad site Backpage.com. Once a tip is received and after law enforcement has made contact with an alleged trafficker-pimp and/or the potential victim, the next step, Nicole explained, is gaining access to their laptops or cell phones. "By the time we catch up with them," she continued, "on the stroll or if we've run into them on Backpage ads, we try to take custody of the cell phone. That is usually a first part of when you start talking about technology. It's usually with the cell phone." To gain access to information from cell phones, laptops, and online accounts and supplement traditional surveillance techniques like policing street-based tracks, police must make contact with people they think are vic-tims, implicitly assumed to be girls or women.

Online Sting Operations

Sometimes police monitor online classified-ad sites. After looking through ads, an officer may pose as a potential client or "buyer" and then reach out to the contact featured in the ad.[16] Nicole, for instance, worked on a case where her unit responded to a Backpage ad they thought featured a young girl in the advertisement. Nicole said that a young girl did in fact show up at the hotel where they agreed to meet. "Obviously we take her into custody," she explained. "We look at her cell phone. We got those pictures and eventually, the pimp calls and he's looking for his girl." Nicole said that after police "egged" him on, he eventually showed up at the hotel, where, after realizing that he had been set up by police, he pretended to be at the wrong door. "So when he gets up here, obviously we take him into custody, we take his phone." After looking through his phone, they found a picture of the girl who was in the other room. This offered proof, Nicole explained, that "this was the guy"—meaning the guy they assumed was exploiting her.

Law enforcement may go to different online classified-ad sites to set up stings. However, it is hard to know if a person featured in the ad is an adult or underage. Mark, a police officer who has worked on both domestic sex trafficking and labor trafficking cases, described his process of manually combing through ads posted on the now defunct online classified ad-site MyRedBook.com. He looks at the text and images featured in each post, and sets up a date if someone looks under eighteen. According to Mark, this approach yields poor results. That is because unlike facial recognition technologies that are increasingly accurate in the identification of people, humans are unequivocally less precise at guessing an individual's age.[17] In 100 percent of the cases in which he has used this strategy, he told me, it wasn't an underage person who showed up for the sting but rather an adult voluntarily engaged in prostitution. While Mark's cherry-picking tactic of manually mining ads may have initially been intended to locate victims of domestic sex trafficking, it serves as an example of how antitrafficking efforts—even those narrowly focused on youth—can create a context for monitoring and possibly criminalizing both voluntary adult sex workers and victims of sex trafficking as well. Put another way, when law enforcement look to identify underage or adult victims of sex trafficking, they do so because child sex trafficking is presumed to "be hidden within prostitution" on and offline.[18] This means that a voluntary adult sex worker may experience some form of criminalization even if the point of the sting is to find, assist, and protect an underage person.

Search Incident to Arrest

In the case Nicole describes, a Backpage ad led her unit to set up a date with an underage girl. Once at the hotel, they looked through her phone to gain information and access to the person they suspected was exploiting her, which led them to him and his cell phone. Yet crucially, Nicole's description that both the girl and the man were "taken into custody," suggests that both were arrested, which allowed police to search both of their cell phones.

Making an arrest in order to seize and search the contents of a person's cell phone—what is known as "a search incident to lawful arrest"—is also a strategy Mark has used. In two separate interviews, he explained that an arrest allows him to search the contents of prospective victims' phones and locate a phone number for a suspected trafficker or pimp.

He looks through the individuals' cell phone where "Daddy" or "Big Money" may be listed as contacts. He also looks for text message exchanges in the phone like, "Daddy I got a date. I made $[amount]." For him, these kinds of text help provide corroborating evidence of youth's coercion by suspected trafficker-pimps and an arrest of the person believed to be a victim gives him access to the texts. In June 2014, the U.S. Supreme Court ruled unanimously that police are obliged to obtain a warrant before searching the contents of a cell phone, even after suspects have been placed under arrest.[19] Arresting a sex trade involved adult or youth —or the person(s) alleged to be exploiting them—in order to peruse the contents of their cell phones is thus now unconstitutional unless police get a warrant to search it. However, there are workarounds to this, including asking a person to consent to a search.

Show Me Your Phone

"Can I look at your text messages?" Brody asked a girl on the street who looked under eighteen. He then inquired how long she had "been in the game." She responded that she had been working for three months, worked alone, and that she didn't talk to pimps. Brody didn't believe her. Later he told me that pimps "are like magicians. They convince girls they love them. The girls never admit that they have a pimp," a sentiment some other police officers expressed. Brody had previously told me that he thinks that girls and women engaged in prostitution are victimized by pimps who prey on them. On the topic of cell phones, he offered a carefully considered legal argument regarding his ability to search the contents of cell phones held by the people he stops and questions, some of whom may meet state and federal definitions of sex trafficking. He said that if they give him their consent or if they are on probation, they have no reasonable expectation of privacy. And although individuals who were approached on the street by Brody seemed hesitant to hand over their cell phones, most complied, which I interpreted as a decision born out of fear of arrest.

It is unclear how widespread or common these show-me-your-phone tactics are in different units across local, state, federal, and tribal jurisdictions. However, in an interview with Araceli, a thirteen-year-old Latina girl who had left a sex trafficking situation in a different city and jurisdiction, I learned that at a minimum, it isn't isolated. Araceli experienced the dual dimensions of street-based and technologically–mediated carceral oversight firsthand. At twelve, she started trading sex for money and drugs. This was around the same time her single mom was struggling to pay rent and couldn't buy her things. She said her friend, a girl who is a member of a gang, had told her she could make money prostituting and introduced her to some people she knew. Araceli met a guy who told her, "If you do this with guys, you'll get money and half goes to me." She referred to him, a nineteen-year-old gang member, as her pimp. She was with for him for about a year, with a four-month break in between while she was in rehab. One night, she was wandering the streets with a friend when a cop stopped them and wanted to see her phone. "They seen my phone and they said, 'Oh, she has things right here. Like when they're calling her and sending messages about prostitution and stuff.'" They took her friend's cell phone too. "We're picking you up and taking you into the police station," they told her and her friend.[20]

Araceli said the police didn't explain why they were being taken to the station. But once they got there, the police told Araceli, "'Put all your belongings here,'" including her cell phone, and she complied. According to Araceli, they "put it [the cell phone] in the computer. And then all these things came out in the little computer." I asked her if the police had used a Cellebrite machine, which allows police to extract texts messages from cell phones.[21] She didn't know what it was called but affirmed that the machine put the text messages on the screen of the little computer. I asked her some follow-up questions about her cell phone:

Jennifer: They thought the text messages might have been about prostitution?

Araceli: Yeah.

Jennifer: So were they looking at text messages or were they looking at Facebook and other pictures?

Araceli: Well they were looking at pictures too.

Jennifer: They were looking at pictures too?

Araceli: Yeah.

Jennifer: Did they ask like, "Who is this?"

Araceli: Yeah.

Jennifer: What else did they ask you?

Araceli: Like they were asking me, "Who are these addresses from? Who are these numbers from?" Stuff like that.

. . .

Jennifer: How many phones did you have?

Araceli: Two.

Jennifer: You had two. And you tried to keep them separate? Like phones that you had to maybe call your mom and then a different phone?

Araceli: Yeah. 'Cause my pimp had a phone. He said it was only for work. And he wouldn't let me give that number to my family.

Jennifer: Did you ever have access to the phone he used?

Araceli: Oh no.

Jennifer: You couldn't text people yourself?

Araceli: No.

. . .

Jennifer: So you didn't have any of the numbers of the people you used to see [to trade sex]?

Araceli: No . . . when I would ask him why I couldn't talk to them and stuff, like he would say like, "No, because you don't need to know who they are" . . . and he would give me like fake names and stuff.

I also asked Araceli if the police who stopped her and her friend on the street placed her under arrest or if they asked her if she had a pimp. She answered no to both questions. Though she wasn't placed under arrest or told why they had seized her cell phone, the police gave her a choice between going to juvenile hall or calling her mom. They told her this after they discovered that she was underage and that the ID she had given them was fake. Though Araceli's story is multifaceted, a few themes emerge. First, the police who stopped her and her friend wanted access to their cell phones. Second, though Araceli was underage, not on probation, and not placed under arrest, they seized her cell phone at the station and analyzed its contents. Third, though her pimp had given her a cell phone, controlled her communication on it, and instructed her to lie about her real identity, based on what she shared with me, it didn't appear that the police asked her questions about having a pimp, why her communication was mainly with one person, or why she was trading sex. That these show-me-your-phone tactics don't necessarily lead to arrest is notable. Police are able to augment ongoing investigations by collecting information (e.g., text messages) or gathering intelligence (such as names, phone numbers, photo identities) that may differ from what the person being questioned chooses to disclose to them. What these tactics additionally suggest is that there are new types of "strolls" police patrol—the technologically-mediated, digital and mobile versions of street-based tracks where law enforcement gather different kinds of data in the form of corroborative evidence.[22] It is important to stress that police and non-state actors may employ any number of surveillance techniques with the express and well–intended purpose of finding victims of domestic sex trafficking and offering them protection. Yet in Araceli's case, the search of her cell phone did not result in any protective follow-up.

Fake Facebook Accounts

Law enforcement may also create fake social media accounts and online identities in order to befriend, identify, and monitor people suspected of engaging in criminal activities, as well as those who are presumed to be victims.[23] Brody, for instance, set up a fake Facebook account, where he poses as a pimp and tries to connect with pimps and prostitutes (terms he used). He built up his network by sending out friend requests to people he had previously picked up or booked, something he said was possible because pimps in particular tend not to be too selective about the friend requests they accept. Brody doesn't spend much time on Facebook. When he told me about it, he didn't have many Facebook friends and had never directly built a case against anyone on it. Nevertheless, his fake Facebook account had proved to be a useful tool, in that it has helped him figure out which other pimps his "friends" associate with, who post on each other's walls, and who appear in posted photos together (an investigative technique made easier thanks to Facebook's tagging feature).[24] His Facebook account also serves a kind of monitoring function where he can follow some of the girls he has previously arrested and then friended under his fictitious profile name.

Alice Marwick has observed that Web 2.0 technologies such as Facebook and Twitter foster new types of surveillance that enable "users to continually investigate digital traces left by the people they are connected to through social media."[25] In addition to providing a platform for known friends, family, and acquaintances to "friend" and keep tabs on one another, social networking platforms may also be used by law enforcement to "track the activities of suspected or even potential criminals (Strandburg 2011)."[26] People's participation on different social networking sites can lead to what Marwick and collaborator danah boyd refer to as "context collapse," a term meant to capture the ways in which divergent self-presentation strategies get "collapsed" and the diverse audiences they are intended to speak to get "flattened."[27] If context collapse is a common feature of social media, users who reveal too much or who don't fully vet the friend requests they receive, may essentially end up posting and sharing material with unknown lurkers, including law enforcement, who can use this material to keep track of their whereabouts even if they are not under criminal investigation but people of interest to law enforcement, even when the interest is to protect.[28]

Letting the Evidence Speak for Itself

Just as youth may become unknowing tipsters to law enforcement, so too can they become sources of intelligence that assist law enforcement gain access to pimps' social media and passwords and help them gather other types of corroborating evidence. Tate, a police officer who has investigated sex trafficking cases, told me that juveniles have helped him gain access to suspected trafficker-pimps' Facebook accounts. He cited two cases involving multiple underage victims of domestic trafficking where youth gave detectives their own Facebook passwords, enabling the police to access their accounts to find evidence that could confirm certain events they described in their interviews with police. Not only is digital evidence sometimes instrumental in corroborating victims' stories, but it may also make it easier for police to file cases with prosecutors. "The problem with our prosecutors and what causes the biggest heartburn with them are the inconsistencies of the [youth's] story," Nicole explained. "Where the defense attorney is just going to eat this child alive because she is not telling the truth. So that [digital evidence] helps the prosecutor. If there are any voids, it at least supports some of what she's saying is true. . . . Depending on what kinds of evidence you have, it's a lot easier to let the evidence speak for itself." Nicole's understanding of the importance of digital evidence is based on working with prosecutors and learning about the kinds of evidence needed to file a case with them successfully.[29]

What these narratives draw attention to is that augmented surveillance techniques can help police corroborate certain details about the cases they're investigating. The digital evidence that is collected as a result also helps transform investigations into suspected traffickers' alleged criminal activities into fileable prosecutions. But in order to gain access to other parts of the evidentiary puzzle, law enforcement sometimes needs potential victims of trafficking and voluntary sex workers. Or they get tips from nonstate actors who do some of their own investigative work and then pass information along to law enforcement.

Not on My Watch

I learned about Project Look 4 Me (PL4M) through Mark. I scheduled a phone interview with T, a representative of PL4M and it is the first interview—in person or via cell phone or Skype—where I have little information about the person on the other end of the conversation. Had I not learned about the details of their work from Mark—who outlined the nature of the work they do in separate interviews—I would have had little insight or confirmation about their work based on their website profile alone. That is because PL4M's efforts to monitor trafficking online, organize stings, coordinate rescue missions, and liaise with law enforcement seem to work because of the more undercover approach they take.

My interview with T began with me giving him a little background information about why I had contacted him. Mark had told me about a faith-based organization that performs its own investigations of online classified ad sites and then passes tips along to his unit. I told T I wanted to learn more about PL4M's online antitrafficking efforts and understand how they sought to cooperate with law enforcement. T kicked off our discussion by telling me a story about Kai, a young girl he knew personally. A few years earlier, when Kai was seventeen, she had been raped and taken to another city, where a pimp put her out on the street to sell sex. After T learned of this, PL4M spent months trying to find her. It wasn't until a woman from the group saw Kai walking down the street that T was reunited with her. When T saw Kai again, he was shocked to see her feet cut up and covered in blisters. Kai spoke of being shot at and, by T's account, "abused every way you could imagine." Months later, T also seemed shaken to recall the details, which disturbed me too.

After Kai was found, she was placed in a juvenile detention camp. For T, the camp wasn't the best place to send a girl who had been exploited. But he viewed it as preferable alternative to sending Kai back out on the streets with her pimp. But before Kai was found, T and members of PL4M had gone to look for her, first by frequenting Central Street, a well-known track in the area where street-based prostitution is known to take place. Later, they learned about online classified-ad sites where sexual services are advertised. PL4M's initial search efforts focused more widely on well-known classified ad sites like MyRedbook and Backpage, though in the months since, they had become familiar with another twelve or so lesser-known sites. They searched for Kai's phone number and made the more general observation that "nine times out of ten, you'll find the girl's online ads by searching in Google against her phone number." Finding the online ads gave PL4M proof that Kai was being commercially sexually exploited. Yet they also found other information through a search of Kai's online postings, which led to Kai's arrest. As T explained:

> We found the ads, which proved that she was being exploited. And there were some other illegal things that were going on, and finally because of the other illegal things the police arrested her. During this search we collaborated with a couple volunteer private investigators, the DA, law enforcement, and at one point I even had some off-duty officers that were volunteering their time. They're no longer able to do that, but . . . I developed a

methodology for looking for girls online. . . . That has been quite successful. We've done twenty rescues . . . over the course of the last two years. I would say about fifteen of them were found through online searching.

I asked T to clarify what he and PL4M meant by rescue. What follows is a discussion about the rescue efforts PL4M has initiated and T's thoughts about the role that communities play in addressing trafficking and helping to gather evidence about it by using technology:

Jennifer: You've developed a methodology . . . you use the methodology to get the information. . . . What do you do with the information?

T: So you mean once I locate the ads?

Jennifer: Yeah. Walk me through the next step. "Rescue" gets used a lot . . . is rescue like forwarding the information to a local police station? Is it talking to off-duty . . . private investigators?

T: Yeah. For example, in one instance we found the ads of another minor. We were working with the mom. The mom had come to us in distress. Her . . . daughter was being exploited and was in and out of the home. And so at one point her daughter completely left the home, and so we were able to locate her ads. She did not have any ads using her phone number. So there was a different methodology that we used to find her ads. And then, once we found her ads, we began to use those phone numbers to learn—harvest all the phone numbers from the different ads to learn who was working with [whom]—who she was working with and the different geographies that her—the other girls that she was working with lived in or were—had ads in . . . that can kinda tell you where the girl might be transported to. Because typically the pimps are gonna keep their girls in different places—the same places. You know?

I responded, "Right," since this was something other law enforcement had said. T elaborated.

T: Like they go to a certain hotel in City X and a certain hotel in City Y and [a] certain one in City Z, and they tend to like stick to a little bit of a routine. Even though they try to move around, they, there's always . . . 'cause it's human nature to try and . . .

Jennifer: Like a pattern to it?

T: We just follow . . . different areas where the girls are, and we say, "Well, if she's not here in this particular geography, then she's probably over here." And we harvest all the information: who's in the crew, what's the name of the crew, what the look and feel is of their girls. All that. And then we interact with law enforcement to try to get them to perform a sting to go [get] the girl. And so wherever there was a minor; minors we don't actually go and get ourselves . . . we refer to the police 'cause we don't want a minor saying we're kidnapping them.

> Then the police goes and gets them and brings them in using the intelligence that we provided.
>
> *Jennifer*: And so before you had learned this and cultivated on your own this methodology, had you ever done any work with law enforcement?
>
> *T*: Nope.
>
> *Jennifer*: Connecting with law enforcement or off-duty private investigators is a new thing for you?
>
> *T*: Yeah. I have no background in this at all.
>
> *Jennifer*: It's striking to me that you've got so many people working on this as well as your use of technology and partnership with law enforcement using technology. I'm interested in how that process works and how people . . . cultivate those relationships.
>
> *T*: No fault of the police, but they don't have enough resources to do all the things that need to be done. This is a very complex issue, and unfortunately it was just getting swept under the rug 'cause the girls wouldn't easily come out. . . . So it takes the community to say, "Not on my watch! . . . It's not okay that you're [the trafficking victim] being exploited and being held, and you don't even know that this is wrong because you've been brainwashed. So I'm gonna step in and intervene on your behalf—and make sure that I speak out for you to get you some help."

When T says, "Not on my watch!" he is expressing a heightened sense of urgency and state of localized emergency that demands an extraordinary response from groups like his. Armed with online intelligence and flanked by on- and off-duty law enforcement and private security contacts, T is part of a dedicated network of Christian volunteers whose antitrafficking efforts aren't just an extension of faith.[30] Rather, theirs is a mission of crisis intervention aimed at taking up the slack of a state seen as too resource-strapped to respond robustly. T's personal connection to Kai and concerns about the exploitation of youth and adults appear to spark his effort to intervene on behalf of victims who are "too brainwashed" by trafficker-pimps to speak for themselves. PL4M's efforts—a cross between "direct digital action"[31] and "participatory surveillance"[32]—are made possible in an antitrafficking landscape where the state makes use of nonstate collaborators like PL4M, provided that its carceral goals remain intact.

WHITHER EXPECTATIONS OF PRIVACY?

When people are stopped by police on the street, taken to police stations, or arrested on prostitution or other charges and refuse to disclose certain details, cell phones, text messages, and pictures hold particular salience: they provide police with more information as to whether the person being questioned is affiliated with a pimp or "trafficker." And when police create fake social media accounts, mine online classified advertisements, or ask prospective trafficked victims to show them their phones and give them their social media passwords, or those of the people who are assumed to be exploiting them, they aren't just letting the evidence speak for itself. They are augmenting surveillance techniques and gathering digital evidence from people assumed to be victims. It is difficult to gauge the full extent to which law enforcement augments its antitrafficking investigative techniques, since, as federal prosecutor Zack pointed out, investigators want to "protect our secrets." For his part, T was careful not to relay too much information to me, especially about their online methodology.

The techniques described in this chapter may be initiated with the broader goal of making prospective sex trafficking victims known to law enforcement and to help find victims in order to put them on a pathway to assistance. Yet what selected observations and interviews illuminate is that these methods may still expose possible victims to surveillance and carceral oversight that corresponds with the treatment of suspects. I gleaned a few other takeaways from learning about how law enforcement and PL4M seek to augment antitrafficking investigations. First, even in an area known for street-based crimes like prostitution, technologies in-built with surveillance functions, including cell phones, computers, license-plate readers, cameras, and private security footage, are sources of intelligence that can prove helpful to law enforcement in building investigation of sex trafficking, prostitution, and other criminal cases. Technology doesn't disrupt the boots-on-the-ground, foot-patrol tactics employed by frontline officers so much as supplement it and give police access to bits of corroborating data and digital evidence to pursue leads and build criminal cases. If street-based "strolls" are the "low hanging fruit" of domestic sex trafficking investigations, we can also situate show-me-your-phone tactics, cops on Facebook, and police monitoring of online classified ad sites as the online and mobile equivalents of investigative low-hanging fruit, particularly since they require little, if any, judicial oversight and require little technical expertise.[33]

Second, the ubiquity of commercial technologies raise a number of questions about how they enable law enforcement to surveil and "socially sort"[34] different groups. If ours is a time defined by surveillance technologies verging on the postpanoptic,[35] and if one concedes that the United States has emerged as the surveillance state incarnate,[36] it behooves us to grapple with the enhanced surveillance and socially sorting powers that innovative technologies wield in all of our lives, but especially for groups who are already subject to criminalization and state surveillance, including voluntary sex workers and people who are in exploitative situations. Privacy may be all but dead in a late modern moment marked by its absence,[37] but a closer look at some of the anti-sex-trafficking investigative efforts I have described suggests that some groups' privacy, including that of youth and adults at-risk of sex trafficking, may be even more precarious than others.

Arguably, people vulnerable to law enforcement surveillance on the street are also those most vulnerable to it online. For instance, sociologist Sharon Oselin observes that because of its visibility, people involved in street-based prostitution are more likely to be arrested and comprise a higher proportion of sex workers arrested for prostitution.[38] Likewise, people involved in the sex trade who can pay their way to some modicum of privacy or managed invisibility, for instance, through encrypted e-mail or secure data services, may also be those who can limit or avoid the effects of technologically mediated carceral and, by extension, criminalized interventions, whether they are trafficked or not.[39]

Third, the fact that text messages, Facebook updates, and assorted types of digital evidence may be gathered without the knowledge of a group of people presumed to be victims of exploitation gives pause, particularly if "victim centeredness" is based on giving people some degree of control over their lives. In her analysis of law enforcement's online undercover activity, legal scholar Katherine Strandburg finds that it is "cheaper, safer, and the deception much greater" than activities that take place offline. Some undercover activities may still be legal, for instance, where "certain types of criminal activity" are thought to occur. Yet Strandburg suggests that online undercover activities do raise Fourth Amendment questions,[40] a constitutional right meant to protect against unreasonable searches and seizures by the government.[41]

If we live in a world devoid of privacy, as Paul Ohm suggests, determining what qualifies as a legitimate search or a reasonable expectation of privacy is tricky at best.[42] In situations where people suspected of being involved in criminal activity are able to exercise choice over their behavior, perhaps it is an easier distinction to draw. But what counts as reasonable, I wonder, when a person who is engaged in illegal activities is both viewed as a potential victim and at the same time being watched by state and nonstate actors using surveillance methods that mimic tactics used to monitor more "typical" offenders? For the sake of clarity, let me state plainly here that my aim is not to make a normative statement about whether certain behaviors *should* be criminalized or that Fourth Amendment protections shouldn't apply to everyone. Consensual adult sex work is criminalized in most parts of the United States, for instance, even if it shouldn't be. But my point is that if underage youth or adults are thought to be at-risk of domestic sex trafficking and legally deemed incapable of giving consent to the exploitative situations they're in, than any illegal activity they commit in the context of that exploitative situation should presumably render them immune from arrest and prosecution. Relatedly, shouldn't they be free from certain kinds of surveillance—even if the form it takes is based on promoting their safety and well-being? For the sake of argument, certain surveillance techniques may be warranted when a person is in immediate need of help. Others may argue that extraordinary efforts are justified to help get a person out of a violent and what is believed to be a life-threatening situation. I am sympathetic to these arguments. Yet my concern with such techniques is when an emergency situation or an assistive occasion to intervene on at-risk victims' behalves leads to arrest, detention, and protracted court supervision. Kai, for instance, was put in a juvenile camp following her identification. In a follow-up interview in early May 2014, T told me that Kai had completed the camp program but remained on probation.

In addition to more well-established forms of carceral control (e.g., arrest, incarceration) different types of augmented investigative techniques may further extend the harms that accompany the criminalization of sex work. The harms of criminalizing sex work are well documented on human rights, health, and occupational safety grounds.[43] But what if harms don't just arise out of criminalization or the pursuit of criminal investigations, but take on new "networked" dimensions,[44] particularly in instances where it's not just police but nonstate actors who make use of different tools and methods to fill in what are perceived as gaps in enforcement. In early 2014, some posters of ads on the Edmonton adult-services section of Backpage experienced nonstate antitrafficking interventions firsthand. Some posters received SMS (i.e., text messages) from Project Backpage—a collaboration between academic researchers and a few advocacy groups—with text messages like "Want out? There is hope!"[45] The collaborative partners behind Project Backpage devised the project by scraping data off of the non-password-protected site and then used the data to connect with posters—whom they viewed as potential victims of trafficking.[46] Yet some voluntary sex workers who spoke out publicly about it didn't see this SMS outreach as helpful, but rather as a form of work-based harassment. On one hand, the dissonance between the creators of the project and those subject to it reflect ongoing contestation about the differences between voluntary sex work and forced sex trafficking. On the other hand, the fact that the ad posters who received SMS messages about being rescued lacked control over the context in which information about them was gathered, analyzed, and then acted upon—a feature of networked harm that Karen Levy and danah boyd develop[47]—suggests that augmented enforcement or technologically mediated surveillance activities by police or their non-state partners not only have the potential to punish, harass, or harm some of the people they aim to help but may also contribute to new types of networked harm for sex workers and sex trafficking victims alike.

THE FUTURE: POSTHUMAN WITNESS STAND-INS?

To find potential victims or build sex trafficking investigations, law enforcement and nonstate actors rely on sex trade involved youth and adults, some of whom are in situations that meet legal definitions of sex trafficking, to gather intelligence and collect digital evidence. Or they may get different kinds of investigative assistance, some of it in the form of assistance from third-party networks and selected for-profit and non-profit actors willing to help police augment and piece together parts of the investigative puzzle they're trying to solve.

Some antitrafficking actors recognize the challenge of law enforcement investigations, which, among other things, includes the problem of "requiring a victim to testify against her trafficker can cause additional trauma."[48] In 2015, in an attempt to address this, the New York State Assembly unanimously passed the Trafficking Victims Protection and Justice Act (TVPJA),[49] which authorizes law enforcement to collect digital evidence via wiretaps.[50] This could transform digital evidence into a proxy witness and posthuman stand-in for people presumed to be victims of sex trafficking. Prioritizing evidence collected via wiretaps would thus blunt the need for victims' cooperation, testimony, and participation in criminal proceedings against those suspected of trafficking them. At first glance, this seems like a promising development. By allowing the digital evidence to speak for itself, it could potentially reduce reliance on youths' cooperation with law enforcement or testimony against the people suspected of exploiting them. Yet it is instructive to compare this idea to another gender-based crime that is criminalized—domestic violence.[51] Drawing insight from the impact that mandatory arrests and prosecutions have had on domestic-violence victims, such a move could take away the one thing youth and adults deemed "at risk" of domestic sex trafficking currently have any degree of agency over: that is, their ability to refuse to participate in a criminal justice process that does not serve their broader needs and interests.[52] As reliance on digital and corroborative evidence grows, dependence on trafficked victims as witnesses in prosecutions may wane, giving rise to questions about how this will impact their ability to exercise some degree of input and choice over the terms of future antitrafficking criminal justice interventions designed to protect them.

Trafficking, Technology, and "Data-Driven" Justice

Summer 2013 may come to be defined as the season of surveillance or rather the moment in which mainstream America woke up to an expansive array of surveillance tactics advanced in the name of national security. A comprehensive public account of the National Security Agency's spying programs is still being sorted out. And although questions about whether the NSA's programs compromised Americans' privacy and civil liberties remains a source of rich debate, disclosures about them couldn't be more timely, offering new insights into surveillance techniques and their widespread implications.

Several of the technologically mediated antitrafficking efforts I have been tracking over the past few years bear a symbolic likeness to some of the surveillance claims that lie at the heart of the Spy Gate scandal. Leaked PowerPoint slides detailing some of the NSA's activities, such as the PRISM program,[1] and the Snowden disclosures that drew U.S. and international attention to the NSA more generally are noteworthy for a host of reasons, chief among them being its illustration of a security-focused, state and nonstate collaborative model of governance in action, a term I use to describe the ways in which nonstate actors cooperate with the state to augment, expand, and extend its surveillance and security agenda.

While the NSA may have orchestrated the massive collection of metadata of citizens and noncitizens alike in an effort to prevent future terrorist attacks, it relied upon different third-party actors who, some argue unknowingly collected, sorted, and stored the data and an ancillary cohort of actors who analyzed it, efforts that enabled the U.S. government to actualize some of its security goals.[2] Though the terms of cooperation between the NSA and technology and telecommunication companies have been discussed, much is still unknown.[3] However, one unambiguous insight can be gleaned from it all—namely, that technologies with surveillance and predictive capacities have become important tools in the U.S. government's efforts to fight terror. Moreover, in the post-9/11 environment, the U.S. government depends upon data, analytics, and networks administered by nonstate actors to follow up on intelligence leads regarding suspected terrorists' activities, whether via subpoena requests, FISA-court orders, or through more covert means.

A seemingly analogous yet distinct trend is under way with respect to antitrafficking efforts where the U.S. government may make use of technology from third-party sources or networks to gather data about suspected traffickers' activities, assist in the identification of trafficked persons, and create tools to search and assess the mobile, networked, and hidden dark-web sources of the problem more effectively.[4] The co-constitutive dimensions of the trafficking and terror paradigms have elsewhere been observed,[5] as have the ways in which trafficking politics are animated by an overarching security and crime-control agenda.[6] Anthropologist Pardis Mahdavi's comparative examination of trafficking and terror is particularly salient here. "Discourses on trafficking and terror," she observes, are "infused with morality," and "have been socially constructed to create ideas about deviance . . . in the case of both the wars on terror and trafficking, discourse and policy continue to reinforce one another . . . with policy slippages between the two wars."[7] Mahdavi provides examples of discursive sites where race and sexuality, trafficking and terror cohere, for instance, in the antitrafficking initiative called Stop Child Sex Trafficking Now, a project advanced by Ashton Kutcher, Microsoft, and Facebook, the film *Taken,* and the work of columnist Nicholas Kristof and his wife, Sheryl WuDunn.[8]

My research takes up complementary yet distinct questions by exploring the collaborative, networked,[9] and expert-oriented[10] antitrafficking initiatives that have helped shape technical antitrafficking innovations. Consider a term like "collaboration." In antitrafficking activities, we can see collaboration at work by tracking how data gets collected and information shared across different institutions and networks. For instance, in April 2013, the Global Human Trafficking

Hotline Network was launched, an antislavery hotline initiative led by Google Ideas and which is part of a collaboration between Polaris, Palantir Technologies, La Strada International, and Liberty Asia.[11] The hotline grew out of the idea that "connecting anti-trafficking helplines in a global data sharing collaboration could help identify illicit patterns and provide victims anywhere in the world with more effective support."[12] Its launch followed the Illicit Networks Summit held in Summer 2012 and a Google Ideas roundtable in April 2012,[13] and it has emerged alongside broader conversations suggesting that technology can empower victims and assist antislavery actors through the development of new tools capable of disrupting the efforts of technologically savvy traffickers.[14]

Beyond what is self-reported, however, little is known about the effects of various technology initiatives focused on addressing sex trafficking either in the United States or globally. Yet what is somewhat clearer is that like antiterror efforts, intelligence that may be useful in pursuing victim identifications and law-enforcement investigations can arise from data and tools created or maintained by third-party actors and networks. Here state agents may look to non-state actors to access data believed potentially to help law enforcement pursue its antitrafficking goals. What conjoins seemingly disconnected phenomena such as antiterrorist programs and antitrafficking initiatives is that they represent different sides of a data-oriented "security-surveillance"[15] complex that has, in turn, brought together an assemblage of state and nonstate actors, blended state and non-state interests, and leveraged mobile, networked, and connective technological innovation in the service of national security and trafficking victims' safety, respectively. Antitrafficking efforts can be seen in this context as a "militarized humanitarian,"[16] securitized,[17] and I would add "data-valent" flip side of the antiterror coin.[18]

And just as the NSA surveillance programs raise questions about nonstate actors' cooperation with the government, antitrafficking collaborations raise questions as to whether programs geared to identifying and assessing the risk of vulnerable populations, including U.S. citizens and residents at-risk of domestic sex trafficking, subject them to heightened scrutiny and control. It is important to clarify this chapter's intent: my aim is *not* to suggest that efforts mounted to respond to trafficking, and particularly domestic sex trafficking, mimic government-orchestrated U.S. antiterrorism efforts. Nor is my claim that collaborative antitrafficking tech initiatives directly contribute to, correlate with, or cause punitive treatment of domestic sex trafficking victims. Even though there is evidence to suggest that antitrafficking investigations have emerged out of intelligence gathered to fight terrorism, and even as this book and other research draws attention to anti-sex-trafficking activities that have contributed to subjecting at-risk victims to carceral oversight, my interest is not on the empirical congruence of antitrafficking and antiterror programs, nor is my aim to speculate about the effects of particular technology initiatives about which my knowledge remains limited. With respect to the latter point, we—researchers and the public more generally—simply do not know enough about what is being done in the name of fighting sex trafficking through technology.

Despite these caveats, what I think prompts some degree of examination is that antitrafficking programs, like selected antiterrorism programs, raise questions about how social problems deemed extraordinary[19] end up authorizing systems of response and promoting formal and informal collaborations between state and non-state actors with the capacity to overwrite more typical forms of intervention. In both cases, collaborative modes of governance coupled with particular technical tools in the form of big data, predictive analytics, and predictive policing[20] have the capacity to extend the powers of the state and create new ways for state and nonstate actors to interface on law-enforcement and security issues. It is this *potential* to crowdsource matters of governance and the capacity for collaboration to create new paradigms of protection as well as control that I think warrants reflection.

In chapter 2, I examined how some law-enforcement agents make use of technologies in corroborating evidence and augmenting antitrafficking investigations. In this chapter, I extend the discussion of data and technology further still by considering how and why technology has become part of anti-sex-trafficking conversations in the United States and how a focus on technology in the anti-trafficking space has facilitated cooperation between different actors.[21]

TRAFFICKING AS A PROBLEM OF TECHNOLOGY

Technology is at once presumed to make sex trafficking visible and also understood as providing new tools for law enforcement to respond to it.[22] Different nongovernmental actors, governmental officials, and technological innovators have entered the antitrafficking space and foregrounded trafficking as a problem that invites technological solutions. Consider the U.S. Department of State's 2014 Trafficking in Persons Report, which states: "innovation and technology are essential in the fight against human trafficking. The private sector, antitrafficking advocates, law-enforcement officials, academics, and governments are working together to develop innovative solutions to address the complexities involved in both fighting this crime and supporting victims as they strive to restore their lives."[23] In addition to promoting innovative technologies, collaborative partnerships are vaunted for their crime-fighting and victim-centered potential.

The origins of the technology and trafficking story are, however, decidedly more deterministic, its sociolegal history punctuated by fears that some technologies, particularly online classified-ad sites, are vectors of sexual exploitation. In the United States, the linkages between trafficking and technology came out of debates centered on the role that online classified-ad sites like Craigslist and Backpage play in giving rise to trafficking, specifically domestic minor sex trafficking. Starting around 2008, a broad coalition of child-safety and antitrafficking advocates started rallying against Backpage (and Craigslist prior to the closure of its Adult Services Section in 2010), arguing that the mediated technologies these sites support make it far too easy to advertise the services of exploited individuals, with some commentators suggesting that going online to pay for sex with minors is as easy as "ordering a pizza."[24]

Various attorneys general followed suit, linking domestic trafficking to certain technologies,[25] particularly online classified-ad sites. A 2012 report released by the California attorney general and the California Department of Justice demonstrates the assumed connections between trafficking and online classified-ad sites that are typical in mainstream discussions. The authors write: "nowhere is the growth of sex trafficking on the Internet more apparent than on classified advertisements sites."[26] The perception that such sites exacerbate sex trafficking of youth prompted forty-nine attorneys general to call for sweeping policy changes to Section 230 of the 1996 Communications Decency Act (CDA). On July 23, 2013, members of the National Association of Attorneys General sent a letter to senators and representatives sitting on the Committee on Commerce, Science, and Transportation and the Committee on Energy and Commerce. The letter states, "every day, children in the United States are sold for sex. In instance after instance, State and local authorities discover that the vehicles for advertising the victims of the child sex trade are online classified ad services, such as Backpage.com."[27] The forty-nine undersigned attorneys general further suggested that law enforcement's ability to prosecute third-party entities like Backpage is curtailed because of the current framing of CDA

Section 230, and cited three law-enforcement cases where the sexual services of youth were advertised on Backpage. What the letter did not describe, however, is the process by which law enforcement obtained data and information about these three child sex trafficking cases. This omission is noteworthy considering that law enforcement have used information from Backpage such as through subpoena requests for investigations and tips Backpage forwards to the National Center for Missing and Exploited Children (NCMEC).

Backpage began its moderation process in 2008, around the time when public attention focused on the role of online ad sites in domestic sex trafficking cases. Backpage's moderation protocols have evolved and the company states that it has implemented a "triple-tier" moderation system that combines automated filtering and "hand-reviewed" procedures.[28] Even as Backpage has drawn the ire of various attorneys general, as an "onshore site," it is, in principle, legally obliged to comply with subpoena requests. Following selected NSA disclosures, there has been a deluge of media reporting on law-enforcement surveillance tactics. One important insight that has gained some mainstream media attention is the relative ease with which law enforcement and officers of the court can subpoena information from a host of sources.[29] This insight is important because for all of the attention focused on online classified ad sites as vectors of sex trafficking, it is curious that more attention has not been paid to the low threshold or legal scrutiny in which law enforcement can access records and digital content from nonstate, third-party companies without a search warrant or probable cause.[30]

While various attorneys general have regarded the involvement of online classified-ad sites in the trafficking of children for sex as a possible reason to rewrite CDA policy, what often goes unacknowledged is that a site like Backpage provides data, information, and evidence that may prove useful in building cases, even as some law-enforcement agents and others seek its closure.[31] And although it is plausible to assume that any number of technologies may be used by individuals in any number of activities defined as criminal, sites like Backpage provide antitrafficking actors with an accessible platform through which to make their antitrafficking claims. The non-password-protected accessibility of online classified-ad sites additionally enables law enforcement, technology innovators, nonstate actors, and researchers to occupy, trawl, mine data, and monitor individuals seen as at risk of being trafficked, as well as those suspected of trafficking and pimping. That is because when an online site or web page is "open"—that is, not password-protected or behind a pay wall—any person or group can scrape data off the site itself or via technological resources like the Internet Archive's Wayback Machine.[32]

What's more, third-party platforms may not be passive responders to law-enforcement requests for information; instead, they may also actively engage them outside of responding to a subpoena request, for instance, by training law enforcement about how to use the data. I had the occasion observe this firsthand when I attended a training session in which Backpage employees demonstrated to law enforcement agents how they might make use of its data in support of investigations. Some may write off Backpage's activities as an attempt to stave off criticism or litigation.[33] Still others, like members of the Senate's Permanent Subcommittee on Investigations have questioned Backpage's moderation claims and efforts to combat trafficking more generally.[34] Yet even as Backpage's contribution to antitrafficking efforts is disputed, the fact that its data has been used by law enforcement and non-state actors underscores my broader point; namely that third-party actors, companies, networks, and data play an important role in addressing human trafficking, even as different companies' position and activities in the antitrafficking space are afforded different degrees of acceptance and status.

For his part, John Ryan, the former CEO of the National Center for Missing & Exploited Children (NCMEC), has noted that technology companies are uniquely poised to address the problem: "What these companies in Silicon Valley are doing with their technology goes way beyond what you see on any crime show on television. This is ground zero, and the solutions to get ahead of the curve are here in these companies."[35] Irrespective of what each company hopes to get out of putting its technical or network expertise behind antitrafficking, one thing is clear: rather than treating technology strictly as a medium of exploitation, some actors ranging from law enforcement and social-service providers to nongovernmental actors, engineers, and technology firms regard it as a means of obtaining better (and bigger) data on trafficking, to identify prospective victims, and to disrupt sex traffickers and pimps in their digital tracks.[36]

BACKPAGE 2.0: TECHNOLOGY AS A DISRUPTIVE FORCE OF TRAFFICKING

The social history of sociotechnical innovation in the antitrafficking space may be parsed into two distinct periods, which can heuristically be termed Backpage 1.0 and Backpage 2.0.[37] Backpage 1.0 is reflected in the push by state attorneys general and other actors to shutdown online classified-ad sites presumed to facilitate prostitution and/or sex trafficking. Features of Backpage 1.0 are still in play, for instance as reflected by the June 2014 move by the FBI, DOJ, and IRS to shut down MyRedBook.com, a sex-work forum, as part of a prostitution and money-laundering case.[38] Yet whereas some actors view particular technologies as directly contributing to exploitation, there has been increased focus on how law enforcement may proactively use technology to curb trafficking and heightened investment in collaboration and sociotechnical tools with the capacity to augment their work in this area.

Alex, a nonprofit professional who has worked on various technology initiatives focused on curbing the sexual exploitation of youth, sums up the logic of what I would describe as Backpage 2.0 and its use of data from online classified-ad sites, which she calls "escort pages:"

> We were looking at what was happening with the escort pages and this whole kind of push . . . to take down escort pages. And legally, that just doesn't fly. Right? . . . Then let's stop saying, "We have to take them down. That's the only solution." Start saying, "What can we do with them up? They provide a lot of data, and can that data help us address this issue?" This is a role for . . . machine learning.

The proposition that data from such publicly available web sites can be mined, analyzed, and used to create algorithms capable of strengthening law-enforcement efforts to combat sex trafficking is novel. It signals an anticipatory direction in the antitrafficking space, one where publicly available data can be amassed and analyzed using machine learning and predictive analytics. Alex's organization isn't the only one working on technical innovations. Rather, she's among a growing group of nonstate actors who are building algorithms, mobile apps, and predictive analytic software and using machine-learning techniques to expand and enhance antitrafficking responses. Some of these initiatives have been publicized, such as those orchestrated in the lead-up to the 2014 Super Bowl (fig. 3).

An online news story titled "Super Bowl Prostitution Tracked Digitally by Terrorist Hunters" described how Praescient Analytics, a defense contractor, used data analytics developed by Palantir Technologies and funded by the CIA to disrupt sex trafficking during the Super Bowl. Dan Potocki, who was involved with the operation and part of the Initiatives Group at Praescient had this to say: "Sex trafficking is a really hard-to-see problem. That's where our experience working with other hard-to-see

FIGURE 3. Image from "Super Bowl Prostitution Tracked by Defense Software," Bloomberg video during the lead-up to the 2014 Super Bowl, http://www.bloomberg.com/news/videos/b /a8b60ab8–5902–4cc8–871a-aae450ff9290. Used with permission of Bloomberg L.P. Copyright © 2015. All rights reserved.

problems like terrorism can help."[39] For Potocki and others involved with it, including Cindy McCain and Dominique Roe-Sepowitz, a researcher affiliated with Arizona State University, using technology developed for the military to address underage sex trafficking is a win–win tactic. "I'm thrilled that the technology is used by our military, but I'm equally thrilled that it's going to be used for this. We want to help defend these girls, but also get them help," McCain is quoted as saying.[40]

In another case, John Ryan, formerly with NCMEC, described how technology helped his organization initiate the rescue of a girl that started with just a phone call to a hotline and photo of her. "Starting with a snapshot of the girl," the article notes, "a hotline analyst was able to use Google software and databases to find more than 50 online images advertising her for sex. The ads led the analyst to a phone number that matched other posts from the same pimp and connected him to nine different victims in five states. Then Palantir's software helped map the pimp's movements and location. The hotline operator contacted police, who were able to link the pimp to other crimes and victims."[41] Ryan's quote implicitly suggests that making these kinds of data connections would not have been possible without the availability of technologies in question.[42]

And though some technologically mediated antitrafficking rescues have gotten some press, other, lesser-known interventions have emerged as well. PL4M's "T," who was introduced in chapter 2, told me, for instance, that he had communicated with a third-party company about integrating a big data, business analytic tool into its outreach efforts.[43]

While these efforts vary, what technologically mediated antitrafficking interventions seem to have in common is that they are all broadly geared to (1) gathering data about prospective trafficked persons and the suspected perpetrators and criminal networks assumed to facilitate their exploitation, (2) strengthening communication and/or information-sharing practices between state and nonstate actors, including corporate actors, (3) augmenting state and law-enforcement responses through collaboration, and (4) supplementing state and nonstate actors "offline" antitrafficking activities with sociotechnical tools in the form of algorithms, predictive analytics, big data, and deep-web innovations.

THIRD PARTY COOPERATION AND ALGORITHMIC AND MACHINE-LEARNING INNOVATIONS

In Chapter 2, I examined how law enforcement seeks to leverage technology to build cases against traffickers and identify victims of sex trafficking. Some of this can be attributed to heightened attention to technology in antitrafficking discussions.[44] Yet the sociolegal context in which nonstate actors have sought to disrupt sex trafficking through sociotechnical and technologically mediated interventions also emerges alongside broader neoliberal policing trends where shrinking federal and state budgets have prompted law-enforcement agencies to look to for-profit data-handling organizations to supplement certain aspects of police work.[45] Widely held sentiments that police and law-enforcement agencies don't have sufficient resources, access, or adequate training in how to use technology obscure the fact that there is a growing market for innovators and researchers interested in supplementing law enforcement's work in this area.

What dwindling law-enforcement budgets and the growth of data markets mean is that law-enforcement agencies in the United States may increasingly interface with third-party vendors who collect and store data (e.g., social media and telecommunications companies) as well as other third-party, "data-handling" technology experts[46] who can assist law enforcement obtain and analyze the data. What third-party vendors have to offer law enforcement is a package of "predictive analytics, a catch-all phrase for a broad array of statistical analyses, machine learning, and myriad other algorithmic techniques" to enhance law-enforcement agencies' "predictive policing" capacities.[47]

Predictive analytics comprise but one part of a growing toolkit of innovative technologies that may be employed to assist law enforcement in identifying incidents of trafficking, as well as other crimes. Other sociotechnical solutions in development include face recognition, data mining, mapping, computational linguistics,[48] and the utilization of "big data"[49] and "big compute" to respond to the issue. We are, in fact, in the throes of a big data moment in the United States, a time when more law-enforcement agencies are "turning to predictive policing models of Big Data in the hopes that they will shine investigative light on unsolved cases or help prevent future crimes." For Kate Crawford and Jason Schultz, "big data" is a "generalized and imprecise term that refers to the use of large data sets in data science and predictive analytics." The technology combines "computational power and algorithmic accuracy," and uses different tools to "clean and compare data." The aura of objectivity that surrounds it, coupled with assumptions that it generates more accurate data, has set in motion hopes that big data has the "power to solve problems in numerous disciplines and business arenas,"[50] human trafficking among them.

Other projects that use machine learning and predictive analytic techniques to identity prospective victims have been undertaken by researchers with academic affiliations.[51] Few of the tech innovators I've met divulged specific details about their work. I initially assumed this trepidation to be linked to the proprietary and competitive terrain[52] in which sociotechnical innovation in the antitrafficking space takes place, though I think a broader concern is that sharing specific details about such work could alter suspected trafficker-pimps' future activities, which might, in turn, stymie law-enforcement investigations.

Yet I have been able to piece together details of some technologies in development and the paradigms from which they draw inspiration, including the technology of collaboration. Alex, for example, noted that her organization partnered with a company who has worked with the Department of Defense in developing predictive linguistic analysis of suspected terrorists' e-mail. Upon learning about their work and more about predictive linguistic analysis, her organization reached out to the company. Of the algorithm they developed, Alex is clear "it isn't meant to replace law-enforcement efforts. It's designed to help them do their job better."

Alex's discussion about applying predictive linguistic analysis to identify minors among a population of ad posters comprised of youth and adults alike raises a few questions. What happens when empirically understudied investigative tactics are outsourced from the state to third-party technological innovators and then automated? Recall that Mark, the police officer I introduced in chapter 2, found the investigative technique of combing online classified ads and then trying to distinguish youth from adults unreliable. Through this process, he didn't encounter youth but adult sex workers. How this algorithm or others like it distinguish between voluntary adult sex workers and coerced trafficked victims whose ads appear on the same sites is unclear. What is also unknown is what kinds of data, intelligence, and decision-making went into building the algorithm and how it computationally learns to become more efficient? Here expectations about efficiency and accuracy belie that in function, algorithms operate through probability. While algorithms may predict certain behaviors, they do not traffic in exactitudes. Another resounding challenge is that algorithms developed by nonstate entities are proprietary and not subject to public oversight, provided they do not violate any laws. While an algorithm may not break any laws, it may focus the prioritization of leads on particular individuals and communities already vulnerable to law-enforcement attention, including youth and adult sex workers and communities of color, who are disproportionately subject to criminal justice intervention. And what happens to youth and adults who come into contact with law enforcement after they have been identified by this automated process?

The presumption is that the victims among them will be offered protection. However, as I pointed out in chapter 1 and will also discuss in chapter 4, it is not implausible that some youth may still be arrested, charged, and/or put in detention before receiving state services and protection, assuming services are offered at all. And whether voluntarily engaged in sex work or in an exploitative sex trafficking situation, adults may face a similarly punitive fate, since criminalization is the de facto law-enforcement strategy of first response. While the tool may enhance law enforcement's ability to connect with prospective victims of trafficking, it stands to reason that it will also be used to identify adults voluntarily involved in commercial sex and could therefore contribute to carceral interventions that include some form of punishment.

Developments on the predictive analytic and big data front suggest that third-party actors and networks are poised to play an increasingly important role in shaping the terms, conceptual frames, and algorithmic boundaries through which law enforcement evaluates, assesses, and acts on risk. This applies to assessments based on profiling individuals seen as at risk of perpetrating a crime, such as sex or labor trafficking, or on evaluating an individual's risk of exploitation. Third-party actors like law enforcement are also compelled to weigh the potential gains that these technologies offer against the legal risks they invariably provoke. Algorithmic approaches are new, and they introduce a potential for false positives as well as possible privacy and civil liberties infringements. While it may be useful to look to technology to detect statistical anomalies and to make sense of patterns in the data that could potentially help identify trafficked persons or the individuals who exploit them, pattern identification remains complicated, and algorithms are far from impartial, since their shape and design are constrained by the "procedural logics" and assumptions of the actors who create them.[53]

Furthermore, as Crawford and Shultz's work on the legal ramifications of big data suggests, big data in the form of predictive policing doesn't just authorize the government and its third-party partners to "collect massive amounts of information about individuals."[54] The deployment of predictive analytics may additionally "generate data that reveals private aspects of identity," data that is "subject to abuse,"[55] particularly if aspects of it take shape without government or public oversight. It is already difficult to obtain accurate data about trafficking, which some actors working on data–focused anti-trafficking initiatives also point out.[56] Yet data amassed and produced in the service of anti-trafficking interventions may itself cause harm.[57] Expecting an antitrafficking predictive technology to "mine the data for patterns or expect a clever algorithm to sort things out" may not only be untenable, as one antitrafficking technology innovator suggested, but the tool itself may generate personally sensitive information and data linking particular people to particular crimes, whether as prospective victims or alleged perpetrators, which could contribute to a form of what Crawford and Schultz describe as "predictive privacy harms."[58]

There is also the issue of context, or rather of its absence. Context in antitrafficking work matters. It is the difference between a third-party actor knowing the difference between a voluntary sex worker and a victim of sex trafficking, or distinguishing between people who act as market facilitators,[59] decoys, and bodyguards, on the one hand, and trafficker-pimps who use coercive means to exploit people, on the other. Not only do these issues underscore why it is important not to fetishize sociotechnical solutions or to assume they are singularly capable of addressing the problem, they further highlight how the introduction of new techniques may potentially contribute to harms, which are arguably exacerbated and harder to ameliorate when executed by a constellation of state and nonstate actors.

MEMEX

Not only have algorithms become part of the antitrafficking toolkit, the Department of Defense has also funded research to change the terms under which we search for information online and has done so under the auspices of counter-human-trafficking efforts. In May 2014, the Executive Office of the President released a report titled "Big Data: Seizing Opportunities, Preserving Values." The report identified big data as a "powerful tool for law enforcement" and referenced a counter-trafficking initiative advanced by the Defense Advanced Research Project Agency (DARPA), the Defense Department's go-to research arm using big data. As the report describes:

> Recently advanced web tools developed by DARPA's Memex program have helped federal law enforcement make substantial progress in identifying human trafficking networks in the United States. These tools comb the "surface web" we all know, as well as "deep web" pages that are also public but

not indexed by commonly used search engines. By allowing searches across a wide range of websites, the tools uncover a wealth of information that might otherwise be difficult or time intensive to obtain. Possible trafficking rings can be identified and cross-referenced with existing law enforcement databases, helping police officers map connections between sex trafficking and other illegal activity. Already, the tools have helped detect trafficking networks originating in Asia and spreading to several U.S. cities. It's a powerful example of how big data can help protect some of the most vulnerable people in the world.[60]

DARPA describes the Memex program as seeking a "user-defined, domain-specific search of public information" and says that it "plans to use its groundbreaking research to fight human trafficking."[61] On the Defense Department's motivations, commentator Meghan Neal suggests that the program will provide military, law-enforcement, and intelligence agencies with a new tool in the form of an innovative "search paradigm" to search the hidden depths of the Internet.[62] Memex derives its name from a hypothetical device engineer and inventor Vannevar Bush (1890–1974), director of the Office of Scientific Research and Development during World War II, described in an article in the *Atlantic* in July 1945 titled "As We May Think."[63] Bush's "memex" concept subsequently influenced countless thinkers and served as the inspiration for numerous advancements in computing.[64]

A revived Memex and the technologies that derive from it, have, as research groups IST Research suggested, countertrafficking possibilities. In a blog post in 2014, IST Research's founder and CEO Ryan Paterson quoted DARPA's Memex solicitation as saying:

> Technologies developed under Memex will be applied to example domains, including counter human trafficking. Human trafficking is a line of business with significant web presence to attract customers and is relevant to many types of military, law enforcement, and intelligence investigations. The use of forums, chats, advertisements, job postings, hidden services, etc., continues to enable a growing industry of modern slavery. An index curated for the counter trafficking domain (which includes labor and sex trafficking), along with configurable interfaces for search and analysis will enable a new opportunity to defeat trafficking enterprises.[65]

He then cited two proposals under consideration, naming the academic research institutions involved. DARPA's deep dive jaunt into the hidden activities of the deep web as a way to fight human trafficking suggests that countertrafficking has the potential to inform future military, law enforcement, and security activities. And based on a press release about Memex's accomplishments, it appears to have already helped support trafficking investigations.

For instance, in February 2015, following a *60 Minutes* episode about the program, the New York County District Attorney's Office issued a press release headed: "Memex Has Contributed to 20 Trafficking Investigations and 8 Open Indictments."[66] The press release went on to say that "Memex is used in every human trafficking case brought by the District Attorney's Office" in New York County, noting that it is essential "in building evidence-based prosecutions" and does away with reliance on "traumatized victims alone to testify in these complex cases."[67] District Attorney Cyrus R. Vance, Jr.'s observation about Memex substituting for reliance solely on traumatized trafficked victims' testimony relates to a point I made in chapter 2, namely, that digital evidence appears to have already become a kind of posthuman witness stand-in for victims deemed "at risk." Yet Memex's efforts also put a new spin on what Elizabeth Bernstein has described as antitrafficking's "militarized humanitarian" features.[68] Arguably, DARPA's twenty-first-century resuscitation of and research investment in Memex[69] is not only suggestive of antitrafficking's multifaceted carceral, militarized humanitarian, and networked dimensions,[70] but also reflects a new kind of "data-driven justice,"[71] a vision of assistance and aid for trafficked persons (or any group deemed vulnerable) that utilizes data and innovative tools like search engines with the capacity to plumb the heretofore untapped reaches of the "deep web."

CONCLUSION

This chapter begins by focusing on how U.S. efforts to thwart terror have provided a conceptual blueprint for other exceptional problems like trafficking.[72] Fascinatingly, the links between trafficking and terror paradigms aren't merely discursive. Rather, there is evidence to suggest that efforts to disrupt suspected traffickers' activities have taken a direct cue from intelligence gathered to fight terrorism, insights that may never have come to light. Consider this: during a February 14, 2014, Intelligence Squared debate in which invited speakers were asked to argue for or against a motion to the effect that Edward Snowden was justified in disclosing classified documents, the former director of the Central Intelligence Agency, R. James Woolsey, argued against the motion and cited human trafficking, among other reasons, as to why his disclosures compromised the government's efforts. He elaborated:

In the defense department, working together with the intelligence community, it has come to be possible to utilize cell phones, and their operation, with some very clever software in such a way that you can help an individual member of the military or an individual CIA operations officer know whether he or she is being followed or not.

A very clever system, one that saves people's lives. That also is no longer with us because Snowden betrayed it, and it's now known to our adversaries.

In Latin America, we have come to find how to penetrate the communication networks of some of the worst organizations and groups that are selling women, principally women, into sexual slavery. We had a very good handle on how that was being done, working with other Latin American countries in dealing with it. And that trafficking, that human trafficking network and our knowledge of their capabilities is, of course, now gone, with Snowden having released that to those who are enslaving women in that part of the world [emphasis added].[73]

Woolsey's discussion about intelligence ostensibly obtained for national security purposes that was used to disrupt human trafficking networks adds weight to the idea that sociotechnical responses to trafficking have drawn from initiatives supported by the Defense Department or intelligence community to thwart terrorism. Not only is this suggestive of a "scope" and "mission creeping"[74] overlap between intelligence obtained for national security intelligence efforts and that used to disrupt trafficking networks, it raises questions as to whether the U.S. (or "Latin American") public would have known that disruptive antitrafficking activities were taking shape alongside or as a result of activities forged in the name of national security. Press releases and short blog posts provide little insight as to the design and impact of these interventions. In the absence of more in-depth discussions about the scale, scope, and technical dimensions of investigations like those Woolsey referred to, it is extremely difficult to gauge the ultimate impact of these tools, especially on the groups they're intended to assist. Suffice it to say that technologically mediated antitrafficking efforts raise more questions than answers and this is an area where more research is needed.

I welcome Mahdavi's critique and call for reform in her 2014 book *From Trafficking to Terror,* which offers a compelling comparative examination of the discourses and moral panics that shape the wars on terror and trafficking. Her observation that the conflation of these phenomena has led to "increased policing, criminalization, tightening of borders, and keeping particular populations 'in' and others 'out'" is astute.[75] Her book's concluding note that technology can be leveraged to facilitate positive change also seems promising. Yet what are we to make of technologies aimed at disrupting trafficking but that are explicitly designed with law-enforcement and intelligence goals in mind? Technologies create opportunities for innovation and empowerment just as they can be leveraged to consolidate techniques for heightened social control. The question is whether technical innovations rolled out to disrupt trafficking help the people they purport to assist.

Though there are more questions than answers, what is somewhat clear is that once trafficking is understood to be an exceptional problem,[76] like terrorism,[77] exceptional interventions are authorized and expanded in new directions, for instance, through research and technical innovation. Selected technical tools in development and the collaborative partnerships that enable their development and deployment further suggest that the state can do things that may previously have been impossible. Searching the deep web, infiltrating traffickers' communication networks, using predictive analytics to identify escort ads assumed to be written by victimized youth, and "cross-referencing" data, intelligence, and databases to identify "possible trafficking rings" and help police map "connections between sex trafficking and other illegal activity"[78] are all part of a data-driven model of justice where innovative tools and law-enforcement goals are put in the service of trafficked persons' identification and protection. But if the point of certain tools is to bring the state in general and law enforcement in particular one step closer to finding individuals at risk of being trafficked for sex, it is important to consider what, if any, mechanisms exist to ensure that such interventions minimize potential harms to them? I think this is a basic but still important question to ask, given that state interventions can sometimes produce less-than-protective results, a subject explored in the next chapter.

4

The Switch Up

Justice is a seventeen-year-old black teenager whose first self-reported experiences with prostitution began when she was around fourteen.[1] At the time of our meeting in June 2013, she had been at Dreams & Destiny—a private residential shelter designed for youth who have been in sex trafficking situations—for eight months. She was the oldest teen I met with.

Justice's path to the shelter was paved by numerous encounters with police, probation officers, and counselors, some of which stemmed from her involvement with prostitution, and other contacts that revolved around separate criminal matters, at least at first glance. Like some other youth I interviewed, Justice did not uniformly characterize her interactions with law enforcement as wholly punitive or protective. Instead, she described a process in which law enforcement "switched up" treating her like a victim and an offender. Her first encounter with police took place in the seventh grade after she got into a fight with a girl at school. The school called the police and upon arrival, they threatened to take her to jail if the fighting continued. Despite the fact that she was threated with jail, her take on that first encounter with police was more or less positive. The second time Justice encountered the police, when she was fourteen, she came away with a decidedly more negative view. She had been forced into prostitution at the time, and she had just been raped. The man responsible dropped her off in some random neighborhood, and she had no idea where she was. She knocked on someone's door, and they then called the police. When the responding officer showed up, some of the first words out of his mouth were, "Stop fucking crying. You're pretending. You're acting like you're a victim, and you're out here prostituting." Justice's shame and humiliation at the way she was treated was poignant three years after the encounter. "He [the police officer] didn't know anything about me," she recalled. "He was just like, 'You're fucking on the streets. You're doing this, doing that,' and just like automatically just like judged me." She lamented that he didn't bother to ask why she was there in the first place. "I didn't even know where I was, and I was crying, like, I was just shocked. I was frightened. I was scared, and he came up to me and he said that I was trying to play a victim and I was out here prostituting and they seen me and this and that, which they never seen me." Justice's disorienting encounter with law enforcement didn't end there. "How old are you?" the cop asked after taking her to a police station. "Like twenty-three, twenty-four?" On discovering that she was a minor, however, he started treating her like a victim: " he switched it up. He switched his whole personality up," she said.

Two years later, at sixteen, Justice underwent the first of two stints in juvenile hall on a gun charge and experienced another switch up of sorts. She was given a survey that seemed to focus on diagnosing her exploitation and getting her to view herself more like a victim. "I took his charge and they like did a survey on me," she said. The survey asked her questions like, "Is your pimp abusive?" to which she answered that he did abuse her but wasn't as abusive as she had originally thought. After being charged, Justice learned more details about her pimp's violent history and criminal record. Presumably some authority figure in the hall who authorized the survey wanted Justice to think about the violence her pimp inflicted on her and consider how it might escalate if she returned to him upon release. Justice acknowledged that her pimp hit her, though the survey had the effect of compelling her to think about her experiences with him from a different perspective. "Like he would hit me or he would like slap me or like punch me one time. But like he never like went to the point where—like it just, it kind of escalated. It went from him like calling me baby to calling me bitch to slapping to me to one punch."

After two months in juvenile hall, the gun charge against her was dropped and Justice was subsequently released. Though she spoke of being brainwashed by her pimp, she went back to him after she got out of jail. When she returned to juvenile hall the second time, her mom made her stay to face the consequences of her actions. Eventually, however she was given a few options about where to go next: Option #1: Stay in jail and participate in a local program where they would help her get her GED, find housing, and look for a job. Option #2: Go into a residency program located in another state, which was, by her account, really far away. Option #3: Go into an unlocked shelter specifically designed for girls who have been in situations like hers. In consultation with her mom and the counselor she was assigned to in jail, she chose the third option. When she arrived at the shelter, she was on probation for about eight months. A few days before we met there, she was informed that she was officially off probation due to good behavior.

Justice meets the U.S. federal government's definition of a sex-trafficked domestic minor. When I met her in 2013, her home state had passed a law defining people in situations like hers as victims in need of assistance. Yet by the coarsest of tallies, Justice's journey to the unlocked facility where I met her and her varied encounters with law enforcement at school, on the street, and through arrest, detention, and eight months of probation supervision hardly reads like the typical trajectory of a person legally defined as a victim of a crime entitled to protection and services. On the contrary, her experiences with the criminal and juvenile justice systems, including encounters with carceral actors who had a hand in overseeing her "official" punishment, as well as those who sought to intervene in other ways (e.g., through the survey she was given in juvenile hall) suggest that "protection" for some girls in similar situations may follow a detention-to-protection pathway.[2] Insights from scholars Beth Richie, Kimberlé Crenshaw and other feminist scholars are instructive here and help explain why punitive protection is not color-blind, but rather exacerbated for girls and women of color, who are disproportionately vulnerable to overcriminalization.[3]

Not all sex-trade involved youth now viewed as victims of domestic sex trafficking are arrested, charged, or detained like Justice. Throughout the United States, states have moved to adopt safe harbor laws,[4] generally aimed treating youth involved in the sex trade as victims, rather than offenders, and typically offering services in lieu of criminal sanctions. Moves to decriminalize underage prostitution and shifts in viewing sex-trade involved youth as victims have further authorized collaborative, multi-agency arrangements that are framed as alternatives to criminalization.[5] Yet despite the introduction of state safe harbor laws and other policies aimed at diverting youth to social-service programs instead of subjecting them to traditional forms of punishment—

what legal researcher Brendan Conner describes as an "arrest-referral" approach[6]—my interviews with Justice and other youth reveal that irrespective of whether they are ever formally arrested, charged, or detained as an outcome of their experiences with prostitution or on other charges, the lines between what counts as a punitive intervention or a protective encounter are less than clear. What youth had in common was that their path to the Dreams & Destiny shelter was marked by a series of "switch-ups" where although they were called victims, they were subjected to a variety of carceral encounters consistent with the treatment of juvenile offenders.

This chapter follows the trajectories of youth leading up to their arrival at Dreams & Destiny. In addition to providing insight as to what youths' encounters with carceral actors consist of, it examines what youth take away from interacting with some of the frontline actors—police, federal agents, and public defenders among them—who played some role in finding them or offering assistance. Chapters 1 and 2 highlighted the role some nonstate actors play in helping law enforcement fight trafficking. This chapter argues that bringing youth into closer contact with carceral systems is not the best way to protect them.

MAKING IT COUNT

The range of carceral encounters sex-trade involved youth may experience—including everything from being stopped, questioned, and handcuffed, or having their cell phones searched by law enforcement—are not officially counted by law-enforcement agencies, much less recognized as a form of punishment. Meda Chesney-Lind and Randall Shelden observe that the number of "contacts" youth have with police surpasses the actual number arrested.[7] This is a noteworthy observation when applied to child sex trafficking in the United States: it highlights the fact that whether or not youth and especially girls at risk of being sex trafficked in the United States are ever arrested, charged, or placed in camp or juvenile detention on prostitution or other charges, some may nonetheless interface with police and other law-enforcement personnel who wield the power[8] to "switch up" whether they are to be treated as victims, offenders, or some combination of the two.

Just as arrest data on prostitution are an unreliable metric in documenting the actual number of youth and teens engaged in prostitution (and by extension how many are 'trafficked'), it is misleading to read the relatively low number of youth arrested for prostitution—791 in total in 2009[9]—as an indicator that police, law-enforcement agencies, judges, and other personnel concerned with juvenile justice routinely treat victimized youth in a manner that corresponds with their legally defined status as victims. Put somewhat differently, just because the punitive encounters that youth experience with carceral actors aren't counted, doesn't mean that they are not happening or cause for concern. And just because arrest data for underage prostitution remain low does not mean that minors are consistently treated as victims. There have been some changes. For example, some states have followed New York's lead by adopting safe harbor laws and creating human trafficking intervention courts that purport to treat those referred to it as "victims *rather than* offenders."[10] However, some youth may still be treated like criminals, albeit offenders whose rehabilitation from "victim to survivor" hinges on interacting with state and nonstate agents with a stake in carcerally oriented modes of protection. Rather than being juvenile offenders in the classic delinquency sense of the term, or typical victims who necessarily want or look to the state for help, some trafficked youth and teens fall instead into a hybrid category that researchers have variously described as prostituted youth's and migrant sex workers' "victim–offender" and "victim–criminal" status, respectively. This hybrid discursive category has been observed in different national contexts and used to describe migrant and domestic populations alike.[11] In the case of children and teens deemed to be at risk of sex trafficking in the United States, some occupy a nebulous zone of classification that defies neat categorization as either "victims" or "offenders."

This pattern is not altogether new and corresponds with broader antitrafficking trends. Following the passage of the Trafficking Victims Protection Act in 2000, individuals assumed to be potential victims of trafficking—historically migrant laborers and sex workers—have similarly been treated as both victims and criminals. For instance, migrant sex workers in the United States have been targets of law-enforcement "rescue raids" and sundry forms of punishment that include arrest, detention, and interrogation.[12] The treatment of underage U.S. citizens thus follows trends where migrants and adult sex workers have born the punitive brunt of antitrafficking legislation,[13] and where antitrafficking activities have repurposed carceral procedures pitched as protective but in actuality may include some form of punishment.[14]

But when U.S.-born youth are newly imagined as "trafficked" rather than as victims of commercial sexual exploitation of children (CSEC)[15] and when pimps are reclassified as "traffickers," youth and adults involved in various sex trades may encounter a U.S.-styled version of punitive protection. This is a blend of intervention informed by racialized punishment,[16] criminalized poverty,[17] and broader assumptions that girls and women who trade sex for money, housing, and other forms of survival are best protected when the state and its allies cooperate in carceral interventions to help them.[18]

At first glance, trafficked youths' protection by the carceral state and its partners may seem more gender-sensitized, rehabilitative, and "empowering" than the tools used to punish typical juvenile offenders. This model may indeed assist some victims and may be a better option than more typical forms of juvenile justice. Yet it is still crucial to understand how and why carceral forms of protection function. Doing so helps us to identify areas where youth's needs have yet to be met and why some youth have a great deal in common with the swelling ranks of "typical" women and girl offenders in the United States who have experienced some form of carceral or semicarceral oversight.[19] Understanding the dimensions of trafficked youths' carceral protection thus invites consideration of the broader legacy of punishment in the United States. These trends also necessitate understanding how and why *softened* (read gendered) forms of punitive protection have emerged just when strapped budgets and cost-cutting measures have prompted the carceral state—along with various nonstate and for-profit partners—to invest in forms of rehabilitation, and to do so in the name of assisting victims who may nonetheless be treated like juvenile offenders.

THE SHELTER: DREAMS & DESTINY

In June 2013, I visited Dreams & Destiny. Though it took a few days to interview nine residents placed there, the process of setting up interviews with youth identified as victims of domestic minor sex trafficking was several years in the making. I had tried (and subsequently failed) to conduct interviews at a different shelter, Sunny Dawn. It was only through a shared connection and a vetting period with Janice, the founder of Dreams & Destiny, that interviews with youth there were possible. I came to learn that Dreams & Destiny differs for several reasons from other shelters where trafficked youth may be placed. First, the shelter is a secure but unlocked facility.[20] There are no physical restraints placed on youth at the shelter that would prevent them from walking out if they wanted to. Unlike shelters located in rural and far-off areas that attempt to make it physically difficult for trafficked youth to run away, Dreams & Destiny is in a residential area and within walking distance of public transportation. Contrast this with a shelter located in a rural area that a federal prosecutor told me about. Girls brought to that shelter are required to remove their shoes upon arrival and must always have an adult accompany them whenever they walk outside. These efforts are aimed at preventing them from running away, while at the same time keeping pimps at bay. Even the physical environment is designed as a deterrent to flight and reunion with pimps. As the prosecutor explained, that shelter was built with private money and is located in a place that "includes special accommodations to help the girls out in an area where they don't feel like walking out the backdoor in the middle of the night, because frankly, there's snakes and other harmful animals nearby. The pimp doesn't want to come to that shelter because he has to drive up a long, winding road with trees on both sides with a surveillance camera, and he's just not going to show up."

At Dreams & Destiny, youth do not have to contend with snakes or "other harmful animals" and can essentially walk out the door, shoes and all, if they want to. Though the shelter is outfitted with security cameras and requires all guests to sign in, Janice makes it clear that residents' presence there is voluntary and that they alone ultimately decide whether to stay or leave. What is additionally distinctive about the shelter is that while it maintains relationships with law enforcement, it does not owe its organizational existence or sustainability to it. Janice said she is not opposed to working with law enforcement. She has long-standing relationships with police officers and federal agents throughout the United States. However, even though the shelter welcomes law-enforcement referrals, from what I could discern, the private facility does not rely on them to fill beds and has no observable institutional stake in whether youth there decide to cooperate with law enforcement or not. Instead, Janice fills the beds in her facility through a combination of referrals from law enforcement, parents, and other concerned adults. She also aims to connect directly with youth themselves through different outreach strategies.

Janice spoke at length about the police relationships she has cultivated over the years and all that she is been able to accomplish as a result. Yet she was unwavering in what she sees as her main role: to create a shelter where kids get to act like kids, where they have access to the best educational opportunities, medical care, mental health, and social services her budget allows, and where residents are encouraged to focus on their educations and future dreams. In fact, at Dreams & Destiny, residents learn to speak in the language of dreams and Janice and fellow staffers encourage youth to rehearse the practical contours of their future goals and destinies in fine-grained detail.

PROSTITUTION AS SYMPTOM?

Janice helped coordinate all of the requisite informed-consent procedures and allowed me to ask residents any question related to their experiences with law enforcement or at the shelter itself. However, she placed two conditions on my interviews: a shelter employee was to be present during all interviews with residents, and I was not to ask youth any direct questions about their family histories or any other potentially retraumatizing topics. According to Janice, prostitution was not the main factor that led to placement at Dreams & Destiny; rather, prostitution was a "symptom" of things they had experienced before they ever became involved in prostitution. Given my interest in accounting for what happens to youth now viewed as victims of sex trafficking, I accepted Janice's conditions.

However, despite my asking residents questions focused on their experiences with law enforcement, as well as questions about technology and how they came to be placed at the shelter, they relayed extensive and oftentimes harrowing details about their individual and family histories, experiences related to sex-trade involvement, and the circumstances that preceded their arrival at the shelter. Youth I met represent a small sliver and a selective, biased sample of an otherwise diverse and heterogeneous population who trade sex for money or survival, whether by choice or through coercion, in the United States. Recognition that youth placed at Dreams & Destiny have complicated family backgrounds, and that most were exposed to violence while involved in situations we now call "trafficking" does not mean that their experiences stand in for the whole population of adults and children involved in the sex trade, or that people who have been in sex trafficking situations, no matter their age, are best served when "rescued" by carcerally–oriented antitrafficking responses.[21]

However, I think we can look to the intersecting forms of violence youth I met endured—both at the hands of individual actors and from the state itself—as precisely why criminal justice–centered models of intervention that center solely on prosecutorial outcomes[22] are the wrong systems to help them.[23] If we agree with Janice that youths' experiences with prostitution, now referred to as sex trafficking, is not necessarily the sole source of the problems faced by youth and teens placed at Dreams & Destiny, then we may also begin to understand that the remedies best equipped to assist them are not longer or more intimate contacts with carceral systems but, instead, reimagined safety nets that do not include punishment.

DREAMS & DESTINY RESIDENTS' BACKGROUNDS

Youth placed at Dreams & Destiny came from all over the United States and some had lived in multiple states. Che, whom I introduced in chapter 1, had been at the shelter for less than two weeks. Other residents, like Kyla, had been there longer. Residents' ages varied, as did the circumstances that had led up to their becoming sex-trade involved (table 2).

Four out of nine residents at Dreams & Destiny were on probation when they arrived at the shelter, and all explicitly talked about or implied that they had histories of running away from home, which is consistent with the findings of scholars who have suggested that running away precedes some youths' entrance into prostitution, and that running away or being "thrown away" itself may set the stage for some girls' subsequent involvement with the juvenile justice system.[24] The presence of residents at Dreams & Destiny was voluntary, and none were physically confined. However, since Justice, Lelani, Crystal, and Shayna were on probation when they arrived at the shelter, if they decided to leave, they risked future justice involvement.

Family Disruptions

My aim was not to uncover what contributed to youths' sex-trade involvement, but rather to learn what happened to them after they were officially identified or unofficially labeled a victim of sex trafficking. Even so, youth shared extensive details about their families and interpersonal struggles with adults in their lives, particularly their mothers.[25] Such data lend support to studies that have pointed to a range of factors that shape adolescents' entry into prostitution. Sociologist Sharon Oselin, for instance, has found that "substance-addicted parents, absent parents, or exposure to sexually, physically, or emotionally abusive adults" are among the factors that shape street-level prostitutes' entrance into prostitution as adolescents.[26] Other familial disruptions that youth reported included adoption, housing instability, financial problems, and the incarceration of parents.

TABLE 2   INFORMATION ABOUT YOUTH

Name	Race/ethnicity	Age	Self-reported age when involved in prostitution	Amount of time at shelter (days)
JJ	Black	16	14	14
Shayna	Black	16	13	14
Che	Latina	14	12	10
Vivi	White	15	15	150
Kyla	Black	16	15	365
Araceli	Latina	13	12	14
Crystal	Biracial	17	14	14
Lelani	Black	16	16	14
Justice	Black	17	14	240
Average		15.6	13.9	93.8

Note: n = 9

Youths' reflections on the kinds of familial disruptions they experienced are important to broader scholarly considerations as to what factors shape youth and teens' entry into trading sex, whether on their own or facilitated by other people. Yet their reflections also indicate how they feel about law enforcement, since disruptions within families are what sometimes led to their first encounters with law enforcement. For instance, when I asked Vivi, a fifteen-year-old white teenage girl to describe her first encounter with police, she asked whether I meant a situation that had directly involved her or situations that had involved her family. It turned out that she had had several encounters with police before she was identified as a victim of sex trafficking and prior to her first arrest and subsequent one-night stay in "juvie" at the age of eleven for shoplifting. Before all that happened, police had been called to her house on several occasions, often because of violence that was taking place between her mom and stepfather, which sometimes involved her too. Of her first phone call to 911, she explained, "The police came. They just pushed me aside." Vivi's encounters with unresponsive police officers weren't unique. Kyla, a sixteen-year-old black teenager, expressed similar discontent that calls to police when she was younger had failed to protect her and her sister. "I do not like police officers," she told me. "I just feel like they don't understand where you're coming from when you're trying to tell them something. And then most of the time, they take your parent's side."

Vivi and Kyla had a lot in common. Both of their biological moms have struggled with addiction, both have histories of engaging in prostitution (Kyla's biological mom) and "survival sex"[27] for housing (Vivi's mom) and both have been incarcerated. But what Vivi and Kyla additionally share in common is that during early childhood moments of personal duress and witnessing violence in their homes, both came to view law enforcement as unresponsive actors who did little to improve their situations or offer them protection. All the youth I interviewed at Dreams & Destiny described having a pimp or a person who functioned as what Marcus, Riggs, et al. have referred to as third-party "market facilitators."[28] None of them referred to those who facilitated their engagement in the street-sex economy as "traffickers." They did, however, talk about pimps, boyfriends, and people with whom they were in relationships, whom they described with varying degrees of fear and affection, contempt and indifference. Whereas Crystal, Kyla, Vivi, and Justice described how pimps controlled and coerced them through physical acts of violence, others like Lelani, JJ, and Shayna described their connection to boyfriends and pimps in more nuanced terms.

I heard law enforcement talk about pimps in one of two ways. Some speak of "Romeo" pimps who groom youth through affection and by brainwashing them to believe that they are in love with and in a relationship with them. And then there are law enforcement who refer to pimps as animals, or "gorilla" pimps, who use acts of physical, sexual, and psychological violence to exert control over victims.[29] Yet listening to youth talk about pimps and boyfriends revealed that few described them in ways that fell into either category. To be sure, law-enforcement expectations that pimps-turned-sex traffickers are masters at manipulating youth belie the more complicated relationships some youth develop with them. Marcus, Horning, and Curtis, for instance, find that the term "pimp" is inadequate in capturing the complex relationships that develop between youth and the people who play some role in facilitating their involvement in the sex trade.[30]

Even among youth who talked about their pimps or boyfriends' otherwise exploitative and controlling tactics (table 3), some described ways in which they actively challenged and resisted it.[31] Che and Shayna, for example, described clever ways in which they manipulated their pimps. Che spoke of "cuffing" money from the second pimp she worked with, saying, "Me and the girl, we started cuffing money and then he found out. He's like, 'Why the fuck you cuffing my money?' We're like, 'It's not your money.'" Shayna's pimp controlled her use of her cell phone. "This how they do it," she explained. "Like if we have a phone, the only number that physically in there is his, nobody else. And he has

TABLE 3   DREAMS & DESTINY RESIDENTS' EXPERIENCES IN THEIR OWN WORDS

Name	Person(s) who played a role in facilitating sex-trade involvement	Description of facilitator(s)	Language youth used to describe interactions with pimps, boyfriends, and third parties
JJ	Friend	Boyfriend	"I mean I had a boyfriend and stuff. . . . And remember, I told you I was on the track and stuff? Well, I guess you could say he was mine."
Shayna	Unclear	Pimp	"I've been with him for three years, some girls just go to another one [pimp] because they've been with him for a while. But I've been with him and same thing; like he only had me. He don't have no other girls. Other pimps got like four or five. He only had me."
Che	Man from neighborhood	Pimp, part of a team	"I ran away from rehab, and that's when I met my pimp. I lived on the streets for five days until I met him. . . . I was an amateur. . . . He taught me everything I know practically."
Vivi	Girl from group home	Pimp	"I was with this girl and she sold me."
Kyla	Unclear	Pimp	"I was forced into prostitution by a man who threatened to take my life."
Araceli	Friend	Relationship	"I kinda had a relationship with him but he made me work. . . . One day he put hands on me. He left the house and I was just crying and I called my friend."
Crystal	Friend	Pimp	"Basically, I got forced into the game. I nearly died. Like I got choked up to the point I couldn't breathe. And I almost died that day. I thought I was going to die. I had a gun pointed to my head. I got pistol-whipped and everything."

(Continued)

TABLE 3 *(continued)*

Name	Person(s) who played a role in facilitating sex-trade involvement	Description of facilitator(s)	Language youth used to describe interactions with pimps, boyfriends, and third parties
Lelani	Guys she met on the street	Boyfriend	"He was like a boyfriend, like usual. Like he presents himself as a boyfriend. There's a couple times when I was out on my own and everything or I run away again and he just shows up. . . . I had no reason to be scared of him 'cause we just had that type of relationship where I understood what he was there for, he understood what I was there for."
Justice	Unclear	Pimp	"The person that's controlling you that's behind everything is the pimp. . . . He expects you to do this and expects you to do that. And if you don't do it, then it's like you feel like it sort of ties to him. You feel bad or whatever."

to have your information on his phone. So if I end up leaving him and he knows I have my phone, he can cut it off because he have the information. So that happened before." But Shayna referred to herself "a sneaky person" and explained that though her pimp thought she only had one phone, the phone he alone controlled, she saved enough money to buy her own, a fact she relished.

Lelani described her relationship with her boyfriend as a kind of mutually beneficial arrangement, not unlike some of the online, meet-a-millionaire web sites she sometimes used to set up dates. Lelani had run away from home and started trading sex for food and shelter. After a period of living on her own on the street, she started to "notice things," as she put it. "You start to notice everything especially if you're running away all of the time . . . after a while, I started picking up on stuff like that and kind of like taught myself to flow with everything." I asked her if anyone helped her to flow with everything, to which she replied:

If anything, I just felt I needed to survive. I needed to get things on my own 'cause it's just . . . in my mentality, I feel that if you want something, you go get it yourself. You don't make nobody else do it. So I mean I can say he kind of introduced me to what I can do. But everything's just in a form of "Oh, I have to get it myself. I have to go out there and find a way. If there's a will there's a way."

Lelani described the man who helped her flow in the game as "just some regular dude," not really the forceful type. She knew of a few cases where people were forced into prostitution. But as she saw it, girls who stayed "in the game" for a while were there because they wanted to be. In her own case, she contrasted the lack of coercion she felt entering prostitution to a situation where she was forced to do drugs. "There's this guy who actually forced me to do drugs. He was like, 'Okay, you're going to smoke this and I'm going to take you out.'" Lelani's experience of prostitution was not free of violence, but it was not from the "regular dude" with whom she had an arrangement; rather, based on what she described, some of the dangers she faced seem consistent with vulnerabilities faced by people who engage in sex work outdoors[32] where the threat of arrest looms large and where the criminalized status of prostitution also limits the ability to practice safe sex and screen clients.[33]

"NOT THE WORST THING THAT'S HAPPENED TO ME": JOHNS AND BAD DATES

Justice and Lelani volunteered information about bad dates and violence they had experienced from the men who bought and exploited them. Justice spoke of once going on a date with a black man. Her pimp explicitly forbade that, she said, but she went anyway because it gave her the chance to make the money her pimp demanded of her. She described a horrible experience on the date but added, "that's not the worst situation that I've been in, though." Lelani had had some bad dates too. But unlike Justice, who described a pimp as the controlling force behind her decision-making, Lelani explained her history of bad dates as owing to her lack of experience "in the game." She said that with time and experience, she was able to better gauge whose car she felt safe getting into and which johns she would allow into rooms where they had agreed to meet. Yet she had been robbed by a few guys in the past and had problems with a few regulars who got mad at her because of not getting "what they wanted." One time, a regular with whom she had had previous dates, picked her up in his car. Everything seemed fine at first. But he did not have the amount of money they had agreed upon. When Lelani told him he had to go back and get more money, he responded by using a low-voltage Taser on her. This "really didn't bug me much," she said, but the violence escalated.

> It just turned into a fight going on while he was driving, and he had someone else in the backseat. Like he popped out of nowhere 'cause I know I checked the backseat before I hopped in the car. Nobody was there. So he probably just came from the trunk. So his friend was trying to choke me out. . . . And then eventually, I just told him, I was like, my uncle is an officer. "I know your license plate," and everything. Eventually he was just like, "Okay, we're fixin' to pull over and drop her off, like just throw her out."

The men stole Lelani's shoes and left her stranded on the highway, forcing her to run barefoot back to the area where she was staying. I was familiar with the area where Lelani was dropped off and shocked to learn how far she had to travel on foot. I took the opportunity to ask her if that experience had changed her feelings about prostitution or if it altered how she tried to stay safe afterwards. "If anything," she said, "I wasn't thinking of it as, 'Oh, well, this is the worst thing that's ever happened to me.' If anything, I was just like, 'I'm gonna stick it out because I sure as hell ain't going home. I don't want to be anywhere else.' Like I was just so comfortable in how I was living, I didn't want to go nowhere else. So I was just like, 'Okay, well, I'm not gonna do that no more. I'm gonna have to be a little bit more sly about how I go about doing my thing.'"

Both Justice and Lelani were attacked by adult men and their lives put at risk because of violence inflicted upon them. Yet both were adamant that the violent encounters they experienced were not the worst things that had happened to them, and neither mentioned calling the police or going home as options. "Wrapped into him" is how Justice described her feelings for her pimp, an attachment that made her want to do anything for him. But her pimp's control over her also meshed with her own history and bad experiences with police. "You're brainwashed to think, when you're in that lifestyle, it's like everybody, police is the enemy," she explained. What she said next also helps to illustrate why youth and adults involved in the sex trade may not see police as protectors from violence but rather as prospective buyers: "It's police officers that take girls that are prostituting that are underage, and they have sex with them," Justice said. "When you see the police and they do stuff like that, like what they did to me when I was fourteen, you know what I'm saying? So it's hard to think that they're not the enemy."

None of the youth I interviewed spoke of being raped by police or coerced into having sex with them in to avoid arrest. Yet a former adult sex worker and current antitrafficking outreach worker I interviewed said that in her experience of trading sex for money and drugs, it was not uncommon for police to "have their favorites" and sometimes solicit prostitutes. Her observation is consistent with a report by the Young Women's Empowerment Project that found that police forced some respondents to "trade sex to avoid arrest and then arrested us anyway,"[34] which further underscores why some youth like adults would avoid calling the police.

After the terrible experience she had gone through, the last thing Lelani wanted to do was go home. Already identified as a juvenile offender, she also had good reason to fear calling the police for help. When she was arrested for prostitution at sixteen, she, like Justice had experienced a "switch-up" when an arresting officer treated her in turn as a victim and an offender. When I asked her whether she was treated like a victim or offender, she was clear: an offender. And in her case too, the arresting officer "kind of switched it up. It was like, 'Oh, you're a victim.' But then at the same time, we're going to charge you with this.'"

The officer who charged her with prostitution "twisted the whole story." Lelani learned this after her public defender let her read the report he filed against her. In it, the officer claimed Lelani offered him a sexual favor, a fact she discounted. "I'm not dumb. Like I've been doing this for a while. But he flipped the whole story . . . and I ended up getting charged with it."[35] Lelani's public defender did not offer much in the way of legal advice, according to her, and since there wasn't any evidence to support her version of the story, she thought it best to accept the charges against her rather than prolonging the matter. The rub is that before coming to Dreams & Destiny, she appeared before a specialized court, framed as an alternative to traditional courts designed for typical offenders. Yet with a record of running away from an abusive home, Lelani was charged with trading sex for survival, put in a detention-like shelter, and then later referred to Dreams & Destiny.

Some commentators cite violent encounters women and girls experience from pimps and johns, or the preferred terms among antitrafficking actors—exploiters or buyers[36]—to draw the more generalized conclusion that all prostitution is violent and that heightened criminal justice interventions are needed to respond.[37] Yet such arguments are fraught for the reasons that Justice and Lelani offered: Even if law enforcement acknowledge youth (or adults') victimization in name, they still have the power and leverage of the criminal justice system to "switch it up" and treat them like offenders. I think we can look to youths' exposure to interpersonal and structural violence[38] and the carceral follow-up it provoked not as reason to bolster carcerally–focused interventions, but as the reason why antitrafficking efforts grounded in systems designed to punish can instead inflict harm on the people they aim to assist.[39]

A CLOSER LOOK AT YOUTH CARCERAL ENCOUNTERS

The "switch-ups" Lelani and Justice experienced might seem regrettable but understandable. After all, both were formally arrested, charged, and detained for offenses other than (at least at first glance) prostitution. Cautious readers may further suggest that even if Justice's gun possession or Lelani's history of running away were the result of coercive interpersonal circumstances and family dynamics, respectively, it nonetheless stands to reason that law enforcement first treated them like offenders since both were suspected of being involved in illegal activities. Lelani and Justice were not the only youth formally arrested, charged, and detained; Crystal and Shayna were also picked up by law enforcement for nonprostitution offenses. Crystal's list of offenses is long. She told me that by the age of thirteen, she had been arrested for "lots of reasons," including robbery, possession of marijuana, attempted murder, assault with a deadly weapon, and grand theft. Crystal did not directly state but implied that charges against her stemmed from her involvement with her pimp. Even so, observers may argue that youth who are suspected of committing an offense as serious as attempted murder ought to be processed by the juvenile justice system and treated like other offenders.

To skeptics I offer this rejoinder: Even among youth who were never formally arrested, charged, or detained for prostitution or other offenses, most still reported a range of carceral encounters where they were more or less treated like offenders. These encounters included everything from being stopped and questioned, handcuffed, placed in a juvenile detention facility without any charges against them, having cell phones searched, and feeling used, disrespected, and manipulated by law enforcement. In all but one case, youth who interacted with law enforcement but were not formally arrested reported an encounter that was punitive in nature (table 4).

TABLE 4   CARCERAL ENCOUNTERS RELATED TO PROSTITUTION WITH ARREST AND
FORMAL CHARGES

Name	Arrested for prostitution or other offense(s) committed alone or facilitated by pimp(s)?	Other details related to arrest or probation violation	Placement in juvenile hall or shelter detention with formal charge?
Shayna	Yes	Gave police false information	Juvenile hall
Crystal	Yes	Violated probation. PO went through Facebook account and saw she was engaged in prostitution	Juvenile hall
Lelani	Yes	Charged with running away, drugs, and prostitution	Detention home
Justice	Yes	Gun charge	Juvenile hall (twice)

The police were called to JJ's school when a teacher searched the contents of her cell phone and found out she was using it to set up dates. JJ explained:

> I had run away from home. I went to school the next day 'cause I was over at a guy's house living there and stuff for a couple of weeks. I had sex with him so I could have a roof over my head. So I went to school the next day, and I was trying to figure out where I'm going to stay at, lay my head at. So I went back on Live Links. And my teacher, she was like, "Why are you on the phone? Like you're talking to different people?"

The school called the police. When they showed up, they put JJ in handcuffs and drove her back to the house she had run away from.[40]

In Araceli's case, she was stopped, questioned, and taken to a police station, where her cell phone was also searched and she was threatened with detention, as described in greater detail in chapter 2. Neither JJ nor Araceli was arrested or charged. Yet neither do their experiences conjure up an aura of protection or curiosity on the part of police about the underlying circumstances that led to their involvement in prostitution. Che was identified as a victim through an FBI raid. Yet Che was unequivocal in describing her experiences with law enforcement as manipulative.

TABLE 5   CARCERAL ENCOUNTERS RELATED TO PROSTITUTION WITHOUT ARREST OR CHARGES

Name	Questioned by LE at school for prostitution	Stopped or questioned by LE for prostitution or a related matter without arrest or social-service referral	Handcuffed or physically restrained by LE for prostitution without arrest	LE search of cellphone for prostitution without arrest	LE threat to send youth to juvenile hall for prostitution without formal arrest	Placement in detention facility without formal arrest or charge	Self-reported feelings of disrespect or manipulation by LE
JJ	X		X	X			
Che		X	X			X	X
Vivi							
Kyla							X
Araceli		X			X	X	

Kyla and Vivi were the only teens who voluntarily reached out to law enforcement for assistance. Kyla's experience was negative and Vivi's positive, a point to which I shall return later. Of note here is that law enforcement's unsolicited outreach to JJ, Che, and Araceli translated into a greater frequency of punitive encounters than Kyla and Vivi experienced.

Taken together, these data, though limited, point to three main insights. First, youth who are not formally arrested or charged may nonetheless experience punitive encounters with law enforcement. Second, youth who do not seek out law enforcement's assistance but interact with police through routine patrol activities, street sweeps, raids, online stings, and as a result of the police's presence at schools experience *more* rather than fewer punitive encounters than youth who voluntarily seek law enforcement's help. Third, punitive encounters with police involving youth did not necessarily lead to an immediate social-service follow-up, a finding that tempers assumptions that identifying youth through carceral encounters will necessarily secure appropriate social, medical, and mental health services, or that once identified as victims, youth won't also be subject to additional carceral oversight.

THE COMPLICATIONS OF COOPERATING WITH LAW ENFORCEMENT

Youths' interactions with law enforcement may feel punitive whether they are officially arrested or not. Yet we can further inquire as to what happens to youth tentatively recognized as domestic victims of sex trafficking and encouraged to interface with law enforcement in criminal investigations against the people suspected of exploiting them.

"Like a Piece of Evidence"

Kyla met with police after she went missing and following an independent search for her by her mother and a private investigator. Her meeting with police was voluntary, in the sense that she was not arrested for her involvement in prostitution. Yet encounters with them left her feeling cold, not like a victim whom the police wanted to help but more "like a piece of evidence" they could use to learn about her pimp. "After I got back home and I talked to the police," she said, "they weren't really focused on how I was doing or what they were going to do to help me out. They most wanted to know 'Oh, where's your pimp? Where's he at? Do you know what he looks like? What's his name? Who's his friends?' And I'm like 'Okay, that's nice.' But what about me?"

Kyla had information that the police could use about her pimp; for instance, she could have told them where they could find him. But she opted not to do so, prioritizing her and her family's safety: "I just didn't feel safe enough." Kyla's fears are understandable. She described specific situations that left her and her family members feeling insecure as a result of her pimp's actions and in the face of police inaction. Soon after she was back at home, her mom starting receiving threatening phone calls from Kyla's pimp demanding to know where she was. Meanwhile, she said, on a few different occasions, her sister noticed people following her on her way to work. Kyla described the whole situation as "crazy." All this prompted her mom to search for an out-of-state shelter in which to relocate her.

The challenges Kyla faced after leaving her pimp and in grappling with whether to cooperate with the authorities is not unique to domestic sex trafficking in the United States. Indeed, it is a situation that confronts other forced laborers and victims of crimes where the successful investigation and filing of cases with state and federal prosecutors hinge on the cooperation and testimony of witnesses. Previous scholarly work has documented the constraints migrant victims of forced labor face in cooperating with law enforcement and in deciding whether to testify against the people who facilitated their exploitation. Here researchers have pointed out that the protection of trafficked persons is often problematically tied to their cooperation with law enforcement.[41] Described as antithetical to the goals of a "victim" or "survivor-centered" approach, requiring victims to cooperate with law enforcement has additionally been critiqued on the grounds that it ties protection to the prosecution of traffickers and for migrants, immigration relief.[42] Yet in an antitrafficking environment primarily organized vis-à-vis the criminal-justice system,[43] and where antitrafficking "successes" are measured in terms of arrests, the number of trafficker-pimps prosecuted, and the length of time each convicted trafficker-pimp spends behind bars,[44] youth who are not "formally" processed like typical juvenile offenders may be treated like "pieces of evidence" used to support law-enforcement investigations. Linda Williams rightly calls this "indefensible."[45]

Some antitrafficking actors suggest that victims' testimony against traffickers provides an opportunity for them to tell their stories and feel "empowered."[46] However, victims may fear for their own and their family's safety, as Kyla undoubtedly did.[47] Fears that her pimp would retaliate also likely factored into her decision.[48] She said he had threated her life on multiple occasions. And although not all youth described their pimps in the same violent terms as Kyla, among those who had to decide whether or not to cooperate with law enforcement or testify against their pimps, most said that they did not want to.

Trading Silence for Safety

For Justice and Shayna—girls who had spent considerable time in juvenile hall—remaining silent and refusing to testify against their pimps was strategic: It offered the promise of freedom from fear. For Shayna, refusing to testify against her pimp was a rational calculation. After all, she was in lockup at the time and testifying against him could have made her vulnerable to retaliation. "They asked me to testify but I refused," she said. "Because I don't want to be in jail with the person that if I testify, he's going to jail. So I couldn't testify and they couldn't charge him unless I testified. So I denied it. So he's just out there doing what he doing, and I'm here doing the right thing." Though I met Shayna after she was released from juvenile hall and ostensibly safe from any retaliatory action her pimp might have ordered while she was detained, her ability to "do the right thing" at the shelter by going to school and focusing on her future goals was more firmly secured as a result of, not in spite of, her silence. Justice's own silence and refusal to testify against her pimp was likewise a hedge against a future lived in fear. In the following dialogue, she explains why her silence provided her with an insurance policy of sorts, one that could secure a safe future that the police were incapable of providing for her.

> *Justice*: Nobody wants to testify. I didn't testify against him [her pimp]. It's understandable because people just want to move on. You know what I'm saying?
>
> *Jennifer*: Do you think that's why some people don't testify against their pimps?
>
> *Justice*: It is hard, and then they know because it's scary. My pimp's friend, we used to be really cool together, and he used to call me. And my best friend . . . that I had out there. I guess she had got caught, and then he knew that she snitched on him. So it's easy for them to know, you know what I'm saying?
>
> *Jennifer*: They found out from other people?
>
> *Justice*: Right. It's like they [law enforcement] say, "Oh, you're going to be safe. You'll have confidentiality," but then they don't have the money to move you out of that area. So it's like when they get out, what happens? These are men that live ruthless lifestyles. They don't care about anything.
>
> *Jennifer*: Do you think about that after you leave the shelter here, about how you're going to try to keep yourself safe?
>
> *Justice*: I don't think about that because I didn't say anything, you know what I'm saying? I'm safe.
>
> *Jennifer*: And that [not testifying] helps to keep you safe in some way?
>
> *Justice*: Yeah, it does. And it's sad to say that, but it does. . . . It's like the police, they don't protect you. Where I'm from they don't protect you.

Justice did her best to secure a safe future for herself by refusing to cooperate with a system that is ill equipped to adequately protect her. She paid for her safety with silence, and her arrest, detention, and probation record reveal that she, more than anyone else, has born the punitive costs of her trafficking situation.

WHEN YOUTH COOPERATE

Shayna, Justice, and Kyla were able to secure some modicum of safety for themselves and their families by refusing to cooperate with police. Of the other youth I interviewed, where law enforcement sought to pursue criminal cases against the people accused of exploiting them, three cooperated. However, the terms of their cooperation varied considerably.[49]

For Che, concerns about her safety were not what made interactions with law enforcement difficult. Rather, she was compelled, through an

FBI raid, post-identification questioning, and a grand jury subpoena to give up information about a pimp who had been the closest thing to family she had ever known. The case was closed when I met her. However, she was visibly still grieving the loss of the life she had once had. She was additionally concerned that information she had supplied to federal agents and prosecutors played a role in securing convictions in the government's cases against her pimp and two adult women.

Che's encounters with law enforcement following the FBI raid were marked by a general lack of trust. That the raid that identified her as a victim of trafficking was followed by a two-day placement at a juvenile facility did not seem to help convey a sense that she had much choice in whether or not to cooperate. Once her mother arrived at the facility to take her home, Che was treated like an offender again. "They handcuffed me and they took me to the airport. They handcuffed me till I got on the plane. I mean my mom was there." While Che's description of the handcuffs and placement at a juvenile facility was conveyed in a more matter-of-fact tone, her reflection on how the federal agents questioned her roused more intense emotions.

> I'm a minor. I lied to these people [accused of pimping/trafficking her]. I told them that I was an adult. So I was mad. I didn't want these people [federal agents] to be around me. I was handcuffed. Yeah, I was handcuffed. . . . And then they manipulate. Like they make you answer questions, and then you don't know that everything you say is going to put your pimp in jail. Like you don't know . . . one state line is already a charge, and then another state line is another charge, and then another. And they're asking me, "So, how many states have you guys been in?" . . . I told them everything because I didn't know that I was going to put him in jail. So just stuff like that. . . . I don't really trust law enforcement.

Che thought they treated her disrespectfully and summed up the situation this way: "It was very sketchy, but they said it was a sting operation." Yet her ability remain silent was blunted a few months later when she received what she described as a "letter" but was actually a subpoena to testify before a federal grand jury in the case against her pimp. "They said that I had to testify in grand jury. That I have no real choice. Which I think it was a lie . . . and I never heard anything else after that. I just got the letters of how many years he got, and then that's it . . . and then he has to register as a sex offender wherever he lives."

What Che's reflection of the FBI sting reveals is that participating as a witness did not give her a sense of justice. Rather, she was wracked with guilt about her pimp's sentence and felt manipulated by the process. The impact his lifelong status as a sex offender will invariably have on his relationship with his daughter also causes her emotional turmoil. "At night it hits me. . . . He has a daughter. That's what hurt the most. That he had a daughter. . . . And he was crazy about his daughter. I mean he loved her. She can't be around her dad. She can't be around him now. He's a sex offender."[50]

Federal and some state laws against underage sex trafficking deem Che too young to consent to what happened to her. Some antitrafficking advocates may further read her feelings of remorse at her pimp's punitive fate as evidence that she was too traumatized or unfamiliar with real love to know any better. Yet Che is not too young to know that her pimp's love of his daughter is real. The impact that his federal prison sentence and sex offender status will have on him, his daughter, and even Che puts into sharp focus research that has traced the "collateral" damage and unintended consequences of mass incarceration on convicted offenders, their families,[51] and victims. Criminologists have diagnosed the problems and collateral consequences of mass incarceration and highlighted the logics that have given rise to it, what Natasha Frost and Todd Clear call the "punishment imperative."[52] Arguing that tough-on-crime policies propagate racial disparities, consolidate social inequalities, and have damaging effects on individuals, families, and entire communities, Frost and Clear further suggest that efforts to "incarcerate our way out of crime"[53] have been buttressed by a corresponding social movement to recognize the rights of victims of crime.[54] Taking victims' opinions into account in sentencing, and in subsequent decisions about convicted offenders' probation terms and release from prison, reflects the sentiment that protecting victims and imposing stiffer criminal penalties on offenders go hand and hand, and it has been useful to proponents of carceral systems.[55]

Foregrounding the rights of victims and their families as reason to agitate for stiffer sentences for defendants might make sense if harsher penalties resulted in better overall outcomes for victims of crimes. Unfortunately, as Frost and Clear point out, this is rarely the case, "with many victims leaving the justice process feeling used by the system to 'get' the defendant."[56] Arguably, youth treated both as victims and offenders may feel the detrimental effects of the system more acutely, since they may not just be used by the system but may actually be subjected to punishment themselves, even if framed as a form of protection.

"We're Here to Protect You"

Vivi's situation was distinct in that she identified a girl named Lisa, who had been placed at the same group home, as her pimp. Her situation was also unique among youth I met in that Vivi sought out the police's help, volunteered to cooperate in their investigation against Lisa, and overall reported a positive experience with law enforcement. At the group home, Lisa had told Vivi that she could make Vivi's life better if they ran away together. Lisa borrowed the cell phone of another girl at the group home and called someone she knew to pick them up. A car filled with other people arrived, including a man with a gun and another girl in the back. After they had driven for some time, Vivi said, a man in the front seat of the car asked her, "Can you suck dick, honey?" Her first thoughts? "Oh no, what did I get myself into?"

What Vivi described next included a confusing scene with various people. But even after some time she had no idea what was happening and asked, "Am I like getting a job or something?" It was not that Vivi was unfamiliar with the idea that people trade sex for things. Her mom engaged in a form of survival sex, for instance,[57] so that she and Vivi and could have a roof over their heads. But she had no point of reference for the situation Lisa introduced her to, and neither could she grasp a reality where adults paid money to have sex with girls. "Prior to this I knew nothing about people selling little girls," she told me. "I'm fifteen years old for Christ's sake." Vivi offered few other details about what happened before she encountered police. But after multiple attempts at trying to run away from Lisa, she eventually broke away and ran to a nearby business. Once she got there, she was not sure what to say to the people inside but mustered: "I was with this girl and she sold me last night." They believed her and called the police, who showed up soon afterwards. Vivi explains what happened next: "About four men came, then two of them left. Then it was this older white man, and then this younger Hispanic man. . . . They're like okay, let's go outside. I was like 'No, I can't go outside because she's going to find me. She's going to find me. My pimp.' And they were very, very nice to me. And they were like 'It's okay. We're here to protect you.' And I felt very comforted."

The police also took her to the hospital where Vivi underwent a medical examination. Of the woman who performed it, Vivi said, "She was very nice." Like the attending medical examiner, Vivi unambiguously asserted that the police were really nice to her throughout the whole ordeal, an experience that sharply contrasted with her first experience in juvenile hall.

> In the past when I went to juvenile hall, the police were very mean. . . . And it was just not a pleasant experience. But the last time I had interactions, they were very nice, and they did as much as they could. . . . They were going to take me to the hospital. You know, check me out. And so I got like a full examination . . . there was no handcuffs. No nothing. They just put me in the back of the car, you know, and they made sure I had my seat belt buckled, and they let me fall asleep.

Vivi's experiences differentiate her from other youth in a few ways. First, her involvement with prostitution, while undoubtedly terrifying to her, took place within a relatively short time frame: seventy-two hours, she noted. Second, the responding officers she interacted with did not handcuff, arrest, disrespect, or manipulate Vivi. Instead, they treated her like a scared teen who had just been through an awful situation she didn't want to be in. Vivi thought that being a "ward of the court kid" differentiated her from other girls as well and helped to explain why she didn't get handcuffed or arrested. Yet further distinguishing Vivi's situation is that she actively sought to cooperate with police. Though the police never found Lisa or the other people, she was eager to assist them.

Beyond the details that Vivi shared with me, a few other factors appear to have shaped her experiences. When Vivi ran away from Lisa, she was in a jurisdiction where cases involving missing and kidnapped persons or involving sex trafficking are routed to a unit with detectives specifically trained to handle these crimes. The agency has made human trafficking—specifically domestic sex trafficking—a priority, and everyone from patrol officers to the police chief is trained and well–versed in the topic, insights that partially explain why Vivi's interactions with police were so different from those of other youth. Yet arguably the most salient element that factored into Vivi's experience is race. Vivi is white, and her experiences followed historical white slavery scripts. Scholars have explored how antitrafficking initiatives have resuscitated myths that circulated about white slavery in the late nineteenth and early twentieth centuries.[58] Ronald Weitzer, for instance, has described how legacies of the white slavery panic and the symbolic and haunting mythos that accompanied it have shaped contemporary antitrafficking campaigns. Vivi's situation aligns with historical renderings of white slavery, where victims are imagined as "innocent, young girls dragged off against their will to distant lands to satisfy the insatiable sexual cravings of wanton men."[59] Vivi was not taken to another country. But she was driven to neighboring city, where a group of black men and a young woman coerced her into a situation she said she did not want to be in. I take Vivi's explanation of what happened to her at face value, and I do not discount that the situation she was in was daunting and horrible for her. Yet the legibility of her story aligns with white slavery tropes where innocent, "good" (white) girl victims are victimized by men, and in this case, a girl of color.

Race also likely contributed to her treatment as a victim rather than an offender. Meda Chesney-Lind and Randall Sheldon describe the "new double standard of juvenile justice" that exists for girls in general and for girls of color in particular.[60] In addition to describing how girls of color are differently "processed by the juvenile justice system,"[61] the authors cite a study by Jody Miller, who found that "Caucasian girls were significantly more likely to be recommended for a treatment rather than a detention-oriented placement than either African American or Latina girls."[62] In Vivi's case, the responding officers' treated her like a victim, took her to get a medical examination, and told her in no uncertain terms that they were there to protect her. Ideally, Vivi's experience would be the rule rather than the exception among youth I met at Dreams & Destiny. Unfortunately, as interviews with youth and broader juvenile justice system trends reveal, rather than being offered nonpunitive, rehabilitative options, girls of color are far likelier to be routed to punitive juvenile justice settings.[63]

"Juvenile Hall Is No Place for Somebody to Be"

The switch-ups most youth experienced before arriving at Dreams & Destiny indicate the precarious dimensions of their legal status and the challenges that come with dealing with carceral agents and interfacing with the justice system. I have heard some antitrafficking actors suggest that youth themselves view arrest and detention as a way to assist them. I was skeptical about such sentiments until Justice relayed that she thinks the first step in assisting youth is to arrest them. For her part, Crystal thought she might still be involved with "all that stuff," by which she meant the sex trafficking situation she was in, if her probation officer had not searched her Facebook account and put her in juvenile hall for a probation violation. Yet while Justice and Crystal offered what appear to be tentative endorsements of carceral protectionist interventions, both drew a clear line when it came to detention. An eager practitioner of yoga, Justice liked that the juvenile detention facility where she was placed offered yoga instruction. In a moment of humorous reprieve, she told me that no matter how many yoga classes she could take in the hall, she preferred the unlocked and supportive setting at Dreams & Destiny over detention, saying, "Juvenile hall is no place for somebody to be."

Other youth questioned the logic of punitive forms of protection. Shayna, for instance, offered her own take on prison abolitionism in questioning why pimps go to jail in the first place. Counter to public campaigns that have used the image and symbolic likeness of girls who have been involved in exploitative sex trafficking situations as the reason why trafficker-pimps ought to face stiffer sentences, harsher penalties and mandatory minimums, Shayna countered, "I don't believe in people going to jail even though they're wrong for it. Murder, okay. If you murder someone, I'll testify against it, because that's murder, right? But something stupid like pimping? Come on now." Proponents of prison abolition highlight how "tough law-and-order" efforts to address various types of gendered violence have helped fuel mass incarceration, what some scholars refer to as the prison industrial complex.[64] Prison abolitionists and scholars critical of the prison industrial complex have sought to resist carceral expansion and drawn attention to the short-sidedness of looking to punitive systems of control to undo intersecting systems and structures of domination.[65] Shayna does not deny that her pimp controlled her and had done things that observers may view as unambiguously coercive and exploitative. Yet Shayna's conviction that pimps should not go to jail even if they are "wrong for it" suggests that she and perhaps others involved in the sex trade and who are connected to pimps (or boyfriends, decoys, bodyguards, or market facilitators) are not simply brainwashed. Rather, she perhaps understands that punitive criminal justice tools are ineffective deterrents to preventing interpersonal violence and may not be capable of protecting youth who face both coercive situations and intersecting systems of domination, including racism and poverty.[66]

CONCLUSION

Switching up youth's treatment as victims and offenders and subjecting them to punitive modes of protection in order to fulfill broader antitrafficking goals is not just a side effect or unintended consequence of mass incarceration. Rather these are the results one would expect when a system expressly designed to punish is realigned in the service of a "victim–offender's" protection. Yet if not through arrest or handcuffs, juvenile hall, detention homes, or other carceral encounters, what should happen to youth who are in exploitative situations?

In the dominant antitrafficking discourse, it is not uncommon for commentators to focus on the age at which youth enter prostitution in order to argue for more rigorous carceral interventions. But Araceli challenged youth's seeming lack of agency and offered an alternative story of self-advocacy. Araceli was in a relationship with the gang-affiliated man who facilitated all of her dates with clients. While still in a sex trafficking situation, she was picked up by the police, who did not ask her questions about having a pimp but did threaten her with detention. Sometime after this, she went into rehab for drug addiction. While she was there, a staff member befriended her and told her to call her if she ever needed anything. Araceli went back to her pimp after rehab, but the first time he "laid hands on her," Araceli called her friend from her pimp's house. Her friend promptly came and picked her up, essentially helping Araceli "rescue" herself. With the help of moms, friends, and supportive adults, some youth who were not formally arrested, charged, or identified in an antitrafficking raid advocated on their own behalves through referrals to Dreams & Destiny. These referrals took place without the assistance of law enforcement and outside of carcerally orchestrated antitrafficking raids.[67] Yet based on what youth shared with me, most of these voluntary referrals took place only after they had experienced carceral switch-ups.

Not all youth may feel safe enough to leave a violent situation the way Araceli did. But the fact that she found a way to extricate herself from a daunting situation and asked her friend for help supports research on survival strategies of sex–trade involved youth and teens.[68] It is also consistent with the findings of a report focused on migrant sex workers in the United States where interviewees sought out supportive services on their own and without the help of law enforcement. The net effect of their noncarceral strategy of self-advocacy wielded more positive outcomes than in the case of sex workers who were forcibly removed from situations through more coercive law-enforcement tactics.[69] Unfortunately, these types of harm reduction–oriented interventions now appear to be in short supply, arguably as a result of heightened attention to domestic minor sex trafficking and the carceral and collaborative partnerships engendered, though this is an area where more research is needed.[70] Ideally, all those who find themselves in a violent or coercive situation they do not want to be in would have the chance to interact with law-enforcement personnel who listen to their stories, dedicate time and resources to understanding their backgrounds and current situations, and offer assistance that improves their lives. Training law enforcement to treat youth as victims, and with respect and dignity, rather than like juvenile offenders, is an important step in a more supportive direction.[71] Yet expectations that training alone will prompt law enforcement to treat people as victims rather than offenders reflects the same enforcement-centered logic that gives rise to carceral protectionism in the first place. It also fuels expectations that carceral solutions can be leveraged to ameliorate the very problems these systems produce. Yet as the next chapter suggests, more rather than fewer expert-oriented legal cures are ultimately needed to resolve these problems once people endure switch-ups and interface with carceral systems, even those framed as protective.

Curative Harms and the "Revolving Door" of the Criminal Justice System

In July 2012 I traveled to Washington, DC, to take part in a workshop on trafficking and technology. The workshop was attended by a broad range of actors, including government officials, tech-industry leaders, nongovernmental actors, law-enforcement agents, researchers and a trafficking victim turned survivor-advocate-leader. The meeting was informative on multiple counts, yet it was in an informal exchange that occurred after the workshop ended and during a more casual lunch conversation that my education on trafficking and technology really occurred. It was then that I came more fully to appreciate the longitudinal effects of the criminal-justice system on people who have been in domestic sex trafficking situations, even among the select few who manage to "make it" by transitioning from trafficking victims to survivors, leaders, and area experts.[1]

My teachable moment went down like this: a small group of us decided to grab lunch together after the workshop ended. Chairs crammed together in a cubbyhole corner of a bustling DC bistro, I happened to sit next to Kiara, a poised and articulate twenty-four-year-old black woman, who was working as an advocate for victims of domestic sex trafficking at a nonprofit organization at the time we met. She was also the only self-identified survivor of trafficking in attendance at the workshop. Kiara's experiences illustrate the more visible role that a select group of labor and sex trafficking survivors have come to play in shaping the scope, direction, and agenda of governmental and nongovernmental antitrafficking efforts in a U.S. environment where emphasis has been placed on survivors taking a lead in antitrafficking.[2]

Yet despite all of the ways in which Kiara has established herself as an authority on the topic and proven to be an antitrafficking survivor-leader invited to sit at the anti-trafficking table, the act of physically getting into the meeting and literally sitting down at the table proved extraordinarily difficult, a process she described as "hell on earth." That is because, in order to get into the room where conversations about technology and trafficking were taking place, she needed a government-issued ID to enter the building. At the time, I had naively failed to consider that handing over our IDs would make it possible for the building's security team to run background checks on us, a blind spot born out of the privilege of never having been arrested or charged with a crime.[3] For Kiara, however, this posed a major problem. In recalling the experience, she noted that she didn't pose a threat to anyone in the building or at the meeting. But her criminal record purportedly conveyed a different story.[4] She told me that thanks to the herculean efforts of two people who went to great lengths to help her, she was eventually able to get inside the building and to attend the workshop. But the experience was daunting for her and set the stage for our informal conversation that day, a follow-up interview later, and my subsequent examination about how an arrest or criminal conviction impacts a person days, months, and years after the fact.

During the time Kiara was forcibly involved in prostitution, which was at different times facilitated by a pimp, a madam, and then online classified-ad sites, she had numerous interactions with law enforcement. In addition to the six misdemeanor charges filed against her, she was referred to a prostitution-diversion program and placed on probation for a year. Kiara noted that she was never offered mental health services or referrals outside of the criminal-justice system, though she was arrested for prostitution multiple times on the same track, and sometimes by the same officers. Instead, she was booked, charged, and pled no contest to the charges filed against her. Not only did the lack of mental health services pose a lot of challenges, but her lack of options and inability to access what she called "restorative services" influenced her decision to go back to the track, back to "the life," and back to what Tory, a public defender I interviewed, described as the "revolving door" of the criminal-justice system.

Kiara was eventually sent to a shelter beyond the limits of the city of her last arrest, a change she described as integral to helping her transition out of the life of prostitution for good. Yet despite all of the professional accomplishments she has achieved since leaving the shelter and despite transforming herself from a trafficking victim into a survivor and leader-advocate, Kiara is still dealing with the consequences of having been in a sex trafficking situation, and the carceral interventions that followed, a fact made plain every time she applies for a job, tries to get an apartment, and even when trying to enter a workshop focused on finding technological solutions to assisting people who have been in trafficking situations.

Kiara's story draws our attention to a few sobering realities. First, before a person is ever recognized as a victim of domestic sex trafficking in the United States, they may encounter law enforcement through arrest, detention, or some form of carceral control, commonly equated with the treatment of "typical" juvenile offenders or criminal suspects. As detailed in chapter 4, even though they are legally defined as sex trafficking victims, some youth may still end up getting stopped on the street or arrested, charged, or detained.[5] Others may have their cell phones searched or have their activities watched on online classified-ad sites, all in an effort to protect them. Yet Kiara's case illustrates another important insight; namely, that the punitive encounters she experienced years ago have been temporally suspended and the length of her punishment indefinitely extended due to the digital trail and incriminating data left from the arrest records and misdemeanor charges filed against her. When asked, Kiara is unambiguous in describing her experiences of prostitution: it was forced, involuntary, and a form of sex trafficking. And yet she is unwavering in her assertion that "no girl under eighteen should be arrested on prostitution charges."

This chapter explores the legal consequences and long-term effects of carceral interventions on individuals who have been arrested, charged, and convicted of an offense, yet who are broadly assumed to be victims. I argue that once processed by carceral systems, even those designed with their well-being in mind, people like Kiara are held personally responsible for undoing the harms imposed on them.[6] Previous scholarly analyses have suggested that the carceral "cure" of punitive incarceration—even "new penology" variants that adopt gendered techniques of control[7]—can produce worse results than the supposed "disease" of criminal deviance that gives rise to punitive regimes.[8] This chapter builds on such findings and suggests that just as more typical forms of punishment can produce "cures" with collateral consequences for offenders, their families, and society at large,[9] carceral protectionist interventions can produce iatrogenic cures,[10] exacerbating the hardships of those caught up in a criminal justice net that aims to assist but may include various forms of punishment. One way to think about this is that once people are identified or processed through carceral systems, additional legal and advocacy follow-up is needed to undo these "fixes" and achieve curative relief. What's more, the burden of seeking out these legal remedies falls squarely on at risk victims subject to carceral protectionist interventions.

In addition to drawing attention to the time, resources, and legal burdens that befall Kiara and others who must individually labor to undo the marks left by carceral protectionist interventions, this chapter aims to caution policy makers and antitrafficking stakeholders who suggest that a persons' exposure to the criminal justice system, even programs framed as "alternatives" to more typical criminal and juvenile justice programs, carry minimal risks. Whether we're talking about *softened* (i.e., gender-sensitized) "victim-centered" policing strategies or specialized court initiatives, exposure to these systems can create particular challenges that are not always easy to undo.

TWO YEARS AND THREE MONTHS LATER

More than two years had passed since I first met Kiara at the workshop, and I wanted to learn how she was doing, so I reached out to her to find out. When we reconnected by phone in October 2014, she told me that she had since left her job as an advocate for underage victims of sex trafficking and had just moved to a new city to start her own consulting firm. Though she had strong leads and solid professional contacts to get her antitrafficking consulting business off the ground, she had encountered a range of challenges that directly arose from having a criminal record. Housing and employment were at the top of the list, as was getting the last of the criminal charges against her expunged.

Housing and Employment

Getting an apartment was "the hardest thing in the world" for her, Kiara said, because landlords increasingly run private, third-party background checks to learn about prospective tenants' criminal histories and to weed out those with records, even people whose past justice involvement belies experiences of victimization. As I have sought to make clear throughout this book, not everyone arrested for prostitution is a victim of sex trafficking, and neither is every victim of sex trafficking subject to arrest, charge, or detention. However, as chapter 4 suggests, when people—and here I focus on girls—are involved in the sex trade and presumed victims of sex trafficking, they may be exposed to carceral interventions that "switch up" their treatment as victims and as offenders. Moreover, irrespective of whether someone is involuntarily involved in prostitution or not, an arrest or charge produces a record that subjects voluntary sex workers and victims of sex trafficking alike to heightened surveillance; this occurs through databases,[11] as well as through other forms of control, including background checks initiated by nonstate actors such as employers or landlords. In fact, if there is a link between voluntary sex workers' experiences and those of people who have been in coercive sex trafficking situations, it is that once one has been arrested or charged with an offense—even a low-level state misdemeanor charge like prostitution—a record is produced that can be seen by law enforcement, prospective employers, landlords, or anyone with an interest in running a background check for the purposes of demarcating those deemed "fit" for employment, housing, or professional licensure[12] from those who are not.

According to legal scholar Michelle Alexander, around sixty-five million Americans have criminal records, including "tens of millions of Americans who have been arrested but never convicted of any offense, or convicted only of minor misdemeanors."[13] A criminal record may include documentation about a person's arrest, parole, or probation history, as well as information about "convictions, issuance of warrants by police departments, and court proceedings."[14] Though Kiara has been recognized by different law-enforcement agencies as a victim of sex trafficking, she still falls within the outsized ranks of millions of American citizens whose past arrests, charges, or convictions have marked them with a record, which in turn, create barriers in accessing basic needs and opportunities, such as the ability to secure housing and employment. Kiara's housing challenges aren't solely the result of having a prior arrest and criminal record. That alone would be daunting enough. What has additionally exacerbated the difficulties she's encountered is that each time a landlord runs a background check on her, they can also learn about her past prostitution charges, information that's been used by prospective landlords to coerce her into having sex with them. The same thing has happened to her in seeking employment. Not only has Kiara been turned down for different temp jobs, internships, and educational opportunities in the social-service field (where she was told she lacked the mental fitness to perform such work), she also described a situation where she applied for a job and the employer, upon learning about her past involvement in prostitution, told her she'd have to sleep with him in order to get it. Kiara needed the job and considered his offer, but ultimately decided not to. This kind of extortionist threat would be unacceptable in any circumstance. But it is a situation made worse due to the fact that Kiara is recognized (lauded in fact) as a survivor of trafficking yet she has been treated like a criminal. That the criminal-justice system has played a direct role in magnifying her post-trafficking vulnerability may be unsurprising to some. Yet the ubiquitous use of background checks to sort people for employment and housing purposes puts into sharp focus the protracted control that the carceral state can wield days, months and even years after individuals are arrested, detained, charged, diverted, or rehabilitatively supervised by specialized trafficking courts.[15]

Expungement

Different terms exist to describe the remedies available to those who seek to strike, vacate "seal, purge, or erase" their criminal convictions. Legal researcher Logan Wayne uses the catchall term "expungement" to describe different postconviction legal remedies that exist in different states,[16] which may enable people to seal or retroactively dismiss some or all of their criminal records, assuming such dismissal or expungement is technically possible.[17]

The term *vacatur* (Latin for "it is vacated") is sometimes used by groups who advocate on behalf of both trafficked persons and sex workers in the United States.[18] In a legal memorandum on the topic, the Sex Workers Project advises that *vacatur* is a preferable legal remedy to expungement because "it offers the most complete 'erasure' of a criminal conviction, including the potential impact of a conviction on a person's immigration status."[19] In recognition of these legal burdens, more nongovernmental, policy, and legal reports have surfaced that describe the harmful effects of the criminal-justice system and identify the types of legal remedies that might best assist them.

In 2013, for instance, with the support of law firm Latham & Watkins, the antitrafficking organization Polaris put out a report titled "Vacating the Convictions of Sex Trafficking Victims," which states that

> trafficking victims often are compelled to engage in prostitution and other criminal activity, but are not always identified as victims when they are arrested, detained, prosecuted, convicted, and/or plead guilty to these crimes.

The resulting criminal records inhibit the ability of these victims to move forward with their lives because they can no longer obtain certain jobs or loans, or go to school as a result of the stigma that is attached to having to report a conviction for prostitution.[20]

A year later, in 2014, the International Women's Human Rights Clinic (IWHRC) at the City University of New York School of Law released a report compiled by Suzannah Phillips and Carrie Coates titled "Clearing the Slate: Seeking Effective Remedies for Criminalized Trafficking Victims," which documents the ways in which having a criminal conviction can stigmatize survivors of trafficking. Phillips and Coates discuss a range of practical barriers that face survivors who have criminal records, challenges that include impediments in securing employment, obtaining licenses in certain industries, such as "security, childcare and cosmetology," and barring access to government benefits like welfare and public housing. The report includes testimonies of persons who have been in trafficking situations and, who like Kiara, have been stigmatized and "haunted" by a trafficking past they otherwise seek to "put behind them." The report also includes a number of important recommendations.[21]

Though aimed at different constituencies, these reports broadly draw attention to the fact that antitrafficking law-enforcement interventions may be punitive, and that particular legal remedies are needed to undo them. They also highlight the variability of *vacatur* laws from state to state.[22] For instance, some states impose statutory timelines for sealing and vacating records or may include other impositions.[23] In Kiara's case, she told me she had to wait from five to seven years to start the process of erasing the six misdemeanor charges filed against her. Even then, she had to find a private attorney willing to take on her case gratis or pro-bono. Kiara gave me permission to speak with her attorney— Michael—who also agreed to be interviewed to explain how the process worked in the state in which he sought to vacate some of her records. Michael used a novel legal argument to vacate four of the charges against her. Though an outstanding charge from New Jersey remains on her record, Kiara is "lucky" in that a legal remedy actually exists. That is because New Jersey is one of fifteen states that has adopted *vacatur* laws allowing individuals who have been trafficked to "clear their criminal records."[24] The requisite number of years having passed, Kiara can now begin the process of vacating the last charge against her, but it falls to her to do so herself. That she and others in situations like hers are held personally liable for cleaning up the collateral mess of a broken criminal-justice system adds a "personal responsibility" flourish to the neoliberal ethos that has helped shape the rise of the U.S. carceral state.[25]

Recognizing these challenges, some nongovernmental organizations in the United States, along with various private law firms, have begun to assist formerly trafficked persons to expunge their records. Yet all this assumes that a person self-identifies as a victim in the first place and has access to an organization or skilled legal advocate with expertise in this area. Some people may and others may not. What this means is that for individuals who have been in trafficking situations and who are arrested or charged, but are without access to a knowledgeable public defender, advocate, or antitrafficking organization, they basically have one of three options for undoing the damage:

- Initiate the process yourself
- Hire a private attorney
- Find or get referred to a private attorney, academic clinic, or skilled advocate willing to do the job at low or no cost

All three options additionally require a person or their legal representative(s) to (a) have technical knowledge about vacating and sealing adult or juvenile records in one or more states; (b) have some working familiarity with state and federal antitrafficking laws; and (c) have the time and skill to work on vacating or sealing record(s). In Kiara's case, the first and second options are out of the question for the New Jersey charges. She can't afford to hire an attorney, and like most people who aren't trained in adult criminal, juvenile delinquency, or specialized antitrafficking courts (this researcher included) limited understanding about how different states' sealing and *vacatur* processes work would make it difficult to do this on her own. The third option, while promising, still requires finding or getting a referral to an organization, law firm, or individual advocate competent to do this. Michael told me that a law-enforcement officer had referred Kiara to him. When I asked him to quantify his time spent working on her case, he said expunging domestic cases can take anywhere from fifty to a hundred hours.[26] Michael spent sixty-one hours on Kiara's case. If his firm hadn't agreed to take the case pro bono, it would have cost Kiara around $32,000 to hire Michael and cover related costs to expunge her record. Michael's firm isn't the only one out there willing to take on pro bono cases like this. There are other organizations and advocates willing to help people in situations like Kiara's.[27] Yet for people who don't have the financial means to retain a private attorney or who aren't in touch with agencies or legal advocates with specialized knowledge on antitrafficking legislation, vacatur laws, and recording sealing, escaping the punitive grip of the criminal-justice system may be troublingly out of reach.[28]

PERPETUAL CHALLENGES

Kiara's situation is distinct in that she has become a visible and vocal advocate on behalf of girls and women who have gone through exploitative and coercive experiences. Yet as I came to learn after speaking with public defenders and advocates whose work involves assisting formerly trafficked persons' expunge their records, the challenges she has faced as a result of her record are not wholly unique. Though every person's situation varies, a few general challenges attend the process of sealing or vacating a criminal record.

Providing False Information

People involved in exploitative sex trafficking situations sometimes lie. Some lie to law enforcement about their age or real identity because the person exploiting them has told them to do so, or they may lie to avoid going back to systems they feel to be unsafe. Tory explained the latter motivation:

> Some of our clients were sixteen and seventeen at the time they were arrested and convicted of prostitution. Some of them were even younger than that . . . [and] misrepresented their age. Many young people do that in an effort to avoid being returned to a home environment or child-welfare system that isn't safe. We have a lot of young people who are under the age of sixteen who, when arrested, indicate that they're older than sixteen, seventeen, or eighteen so as to avoid being connected to a lot of these systems and environments that they perceive as harmful . . . [and in New York] there is a criminal charge associated with providing false information to the police.

Not only does Tory's narrative raise questions about the wisdom of returning youth and teens to homes or foster-care systems that are unsafe, it draws our attention to the fact that if people lie about their age or identity to police, even to preserve personal safety, this can complicate efforts to seal or vacate their records, since providing false information is a crime that can result in an a criminal charge. When people lie to conceal their identity and/or are found to have committed a non-prostitution offense, they or their advocate(s) must demonstrate to the court how and why their involvement in an act otherwise defined as a criminal offense was committed under duress and as a result of being in an exploitative situation, which may be difficult to prove without evidence.

A Resource-Intensive Process That Can't Be Streamlined

Tory has extensive experience as a public defender undoing the damage of her clients' interactions with criminal justice and is all too familiar with the harmful of prolonged justice involvement on her clients. Tory works in an adult criminal court system comprised of adults aged 16 and older who are charged with prostitution-related offenses. Some of her clients legally qualify as victims of sex trafficking, even if most don't identify as such. However, the "arrest to assist" model discussed in this book is the default treatment they receive. She contests this approach, holding—I think accurately—that it hasn't changed much even with the rise and expansion of human-trafficking intervention courts.

Tory has thus become well–versed in the myriad challenges that face her clients, including the difficulties some face in vacating their records. As of August 2014, thirty-one of her clients have moved to vacate a total of 253 convictions. To put this number in perspective, Tory told me that in the state of New York, forty-six survivors in all have sought to vacate a total of 467 convictions, which means that she has worked on more than half of the cases in which people have sought to vacate their records in the state. I assumed that a greater number of convictions on someone's record would require more time on a legal advocate's part. Tory made clear, however, that it is not the number of convictions a person has that makes the process of vacating their records difficult. Instead, it is the time that goes into crafting the legal motion itself and the burden of demonstrating that the person petitioning the court to erase the record qualifies as a victim of trafficking, a finding similarly discussed in the CUNY report written by Phillips and Coates.[29] As she described it to me:

> It really doesn't matter whether it was 125 convictions or one conviction, because it's about their experience and you have to capture so much of that. These are resource-intensive motions . . . we've tried to figure out ways to streamline it and make it more accessible . . . but it just can't be, because the

burden is on the person seeking the relief to prove that they were in fact trafficked. . . . So how do you prove you're trafficked, right? I mean, aside from like whipping out the home video that you've stored on your camcorder of you being trafficked, which doesn't exist, or your Rolodex that like marks numbers and phone numbers and dates of birth and important dates in your trafficking experience. It's based on your own narrative, which is usually compiled in an affidavit and the lawyers that work on these motions do a lot of investigative work to try to pull together any corroboration that we can find.

Tory's quip about "whipping out the home video" speaks to the improbability of individuals having ready access to the kind of evidence that would "prove" that they are victims of trafficking. In-depth investigative work is thus needed to corroborate the experiences of those seeking relief, which demands time, skill, and resources.[30] Sometimes the corroborating evidence that helps to undo a record comes from law-enforcement agencies. For instance, Kiara's attorney, Michael, described presenting new material to the court in an attempt to vacate her record, arguing that Kiara had fully cooperated with a local police department and the U.S. Attorney's Office in their criminal investigations against those accused of exploiting her. Michael requested that these law-enforcement agencies submit letters to confirm that Kiara had been a cooperative victim. They did, and in this case, the court was persuaded and moved to vacate all four of the offenses on record in that state.

Becca, an advocate for trafficked youth, isn't an attorney by training but has also learned how to seal and vacate the records of some clients in the organization where she works. She played down the difficulty of expunging records, likening it to learning how to fill out paperwork correctly. Becca further suggested that some nongovernmental organizations were painting expungement processes as more complicated than they are to improve their fund-raising prospects. But as she began to offer specific details about some of her client's situations and the time and effort it took to help them, I couldn't help but think that even the "easy" cases she described—for instance, situations where peoples' arrests or convictions take place in the same state—still seemed labor-intensive even for the most skilled advocate. Becca compared an easy case she had worked on with a more difficult one:

It's a lot of paperwork for me . . . and each case has to be different. Even if it's for the same charge, prostitution, each claim has to be a different petition. . . . I have another kid who . . . got arrested for prostitution twice in the same week. . . . She has two bench warrants [against her] and she's graduating in September, but they won't give her her license because she knows she has these two things. They don't know about it, but she knows, and so now she's trying to work on it. So right now, that's gonna be a legal issue because she's gonna have to appear in court . . . now, she's an adult and she was tried as an adult. She used her real name. She used her real birthday. So that's a good thing. She's still gonna have fines. There's no specialty [remedy] because they were involved in prostitution if there is no actual [trafficking] case. Now, say she was testifying in a case . . . it's easier to get that record maybe thrown out, maybe expunged, maybe sealed, but she doesn't [isn't involved in a case].

In describing a more difficult case, Becca also intimated that some people might have an easier time having their records thrown out if they agreed to testify as witnesses. Michael's corroboration strategy in Kiara's case adds weight to this claim, and is based on the general idea that a record of any sort, including one corroborated by law enforcement or the judiciary, helps to establish a history of victimization. However, as chapter 4 detailed, there are a number of reasons why youth and presumably adults who have been in domestic sex trafficking or other exploitative situations may seek to avoid cooperating with law enforcement or participating in criminal investigations. And, notably, anyone refusing to do so not only risks risk being labeled uncooperative, complicit, or an accessory to sex trafficking but may also make it difficult for someone who has been in such a situation and has an arrest or criminal record as a result of it to provide the kind of corroborating evidence acceptable to courts considering these requests. Becca's somewhat roundabout recognition that all cases—even the easy ones—require a lot of paperwork underscores findings from the CUNY report and Tory's observation that even in "best case" scenarios in which people tell law enforcement their real ages and identities, pay all the requisite court fees, and keep careful track of their legal paperwork, helping people who have been in trafficking situations achieve legal reprieve is still a resource-intensive endeavor where a quick fix isn't guaranteed.[31]

No Quick Fix and Living in Fear

Individuals arrested or charged either with prostitution or other offenses may continue to feel the effects of this months and years after the fact. They may automatically be disqualified from certain jobs, for example, as the CUNY report points out.[32] Tory spoke of hearing many heartbreaking stories from clients still burdened years later by their arrest records. She described one client who had three misdemeanor convictions for prostitution dating from 2006 that she was seeking to erase from her record. Tory explained that whereas other states tend to raise charges to felonies for multiple arrests, prostitution convictions are always misdemeanors in New York State. Notably, Tory's client didn't have any felony charges on her record: she was solely seeking to erase the history of misdemeanors on her record. Since being convicted, Tory's client had made many life changes; she had gone to school, earned her GED, and participated in various job-training programs. Yet when she pursued a security job, a background check eliminated her from consideration. Tory's client continued her job search, but got turned down at every stage of the search process. Shuffling from one retail establishment to the next in the greater New York City metropolitan area, Tory explained "every single one of those places did a background check and excluded her because of her three convictions." She went on.

> She actually had a job offer to be a cashier . . . they did a background check and rescinded her offer. So this is real. This happens to people. Especially in this economic time when jobs are scarce and people are overqualified . . . any exclusionary mechanism is going to be relied on . . . to eliminate people. The difficulty people have had in work environments because of their conviction history [is] heartbreaking. There's an added element when potential employers or human resources departments find out that someone has a prostitution history . . . that leads to harassment, stigma, judgment, inappropriate comments, and all kinds of things that people would rather not experience in their workplace. So even in the event that someone is able to keep a job . . . there's tremendous harm that can result.

Past convictions and outstanding warrants not only limit employment opportunities. They can also disrupt educational plans as Lizzie, a social worker who works with sexually exploited youth, explained. My interview with her and a prior informal exchange with the director of her agency challenged me to appreciate that the arrest-to-assist model I've described in this book no longer applies in her county, where youth picked up by the police are offered services—not arrest or punishment—and those in the program she runs volunteer to be there. Lizzie said there are now systems of support in place to treat youth as sexually exploited victims. She also described her state's many accomplishments in treating youth like victims now. She did recall one situation, the only time this has happened, in which one of her clients had made positive life changes only to have them undone in a moment's notice.

Lizzie's client Alissa had experienced a lot of family disruptions. By the time she was thirteen, she had been in and out of foster care and group homes and had a history of running away from these placements. While at one of the group homes, she was approached by pimps, who recruited her. Lizzie said that Alissa had told her that there were parts of the life she was attracted to. The men, whom Lizzie referred to as traffickers, gave Alissa a fake ID and took her to different states, New York and New Jersey among them. When she was fourteen, police in New York arrested her on prostitution charges, assuming she was nineteen, the age listed on the fake ID she gave them. She was then taken to Rikers Island. Following her release, Lizzie said, she faced abuse from the pimp, ran away again, and had more encounters with police, who would pick her up and bring her back to her home state, only to have her run away again. Eventually, because of her history of running away, Alissa was committed to a locked juvenile justice facility. Six months before her eighteenth birthday, she was released and services were put in place to help her.

It was at that point that Alissa had the opportunity to focus on her education. She excelled at it, which was all the more impressive given the educational disruptions she had experienced. Lizzie said that as a result of supportive services and specialized educational opportunities that were available to her, Alissa had completely turned her life around in a really short period of time. Things were going well for her until one day she got a knock on her door by two local police officers. Apparently, detectives in New York had done a warrant sweep and her name had turned up because she had an outstanding warrant as a result of jumping bail at sixteen and not showing up for her court date. She was taken to the local police station, where she was met by two detectives from New York. They extradited her back to New York and, Lizzie told me, "put her right back in Rikers." Lizzie and the director of her agency made several calls to the prison and tried to explain that Alissa was a victim of trafficking. Lizzie also traveled from her home state to New York to be there for Alissa on her court date. After being locked up for two weeks, Alissa went before a judge in a New York court exclusively dedicated to human trafficking. Apparently, the judge was moved that Lizzie had traveled all the way to New York to show support for Alissa—which the judge said was rare. "I'm letting you go today, and I'm realizing that you were a victim," the judge told Alissa. "You were not an adult when this happened." Alissa is doing okay now, Lizzie said. Yet despite this positive outcome, Alissa, once a role model to other youth served by the agency, was never quite the same again after the arrest, after being locked up, and after her past experiences with the justice system came, as Lizzie put it, "knocking right on her door."

Observers of human trafficking consistently note that reliable data on it are difficult to obtain. As I noted in the Introduction and chapter 4, there is an added "bad data problem" in the case of domestic sex trafficking when carceral encounters like those I described in chapter 4 aren't counted as such. This creates additional challenges since, as Tory highlighted, the criminal justice system is not always understood as harmful, or a system that exacts added penalties on those exposed to it (particularly, though not exclusively, on individuals legally recognized as victims of crimes). It is thus difficult to gauge precisely the extent to which people who meet the legal definition of a "trafficked victim" are barred from employment opportunities, face housing challenges, or have their lives roundly and completely disrupted because of past encounters with the justice system and their records. However, these narratives reveal patterns that are consistent with trends legal scholars and advocates have documented, which include but aren't limited to the following:

- As discussed, having a record makes it difficult to get a job, housing, and public assistance.
- Even if a person is able to secure employment following an arrest or conviction, this does not preclude employment problems at a later date, because more employers at both large and small firms—estimated at 75 percent—now run criminal background checks on prospective employees.[33]
- Employers' demand for criminal background checks has been matched by the growing number of so-called third-party data brokers[34] or background-checking companies (BCCs).[35]

The third point is key, because it reveals the challenges of postconviction work at a time when data increasingly makes the global economy go round, and where big data may be used, not just to disrupt trafficking, but to "keep score" in other areas, including in matters related to employment.[36] Legal scholar Kimani Paul-Emile provides a thorough and compelling analysis of BCCs. She finds that they generate billions of dollars in revenue by running "tens of millions of criminal background checks" and collecting, "all manner of criminal justice information on the more than sixty-five million people [with arrest records] in the

United States."[37] Consider too that the records that show up on a criminal background check aren't limited to an actual charge or conviction, which is to say, someone may be viewed as having a "criminal record" for employment purposes without ever having been found guilty of criminal wrongdoing.[38] Moreover, juvenile records, which are assumed to be "sealed," are sometimes included in the aggregate reports BCCs provide to employers. Paul-Emile observes, too, that data that may be part of the report can include records of "arrest (or notice to appear in lieu of arrest); detention; indictment or other formal criminal charge (and any conviction, acquittal or other disposition arising therefrom); sentencing; correctional supervision; and release of an identifiable individual . . . the offenses catalogued in criminal history reports also vary from juvenile offenses and one-time arrests—where charges are dropped entirely—to extensive, serious, and violent criminal histories."[39]

These broader structural trends give context to and background insight into some of the legal challenges faced by people who have been involved in domestic sex trafficking situations and have records. These trends further demonstrate that a record can hurt people years and decades later. Tory described the experiences of another client, Angel, who had established a successful career following her involvement in prostitution when she was in her early teens. By the most normative assessment, Angel had done everything "right" following her convictions: she left her trafficker, focused on her education and career, and started a family. Yet years later, when leadership at the data-entry company Angel worked at changed hands, her past convictions resurfaced and caused her to lose a job at which she thrived. Tory described Angel's plight:

> She currently has sixteen convictions on her record from when she was fourteen and fifteen years old . . . in accordance with a lot of things...her disinterest in being returned to the child welfare system and [on] the instructions of her older trafficker who was exploiting her in prostitution, she lied to the police when she was arrested and she said she was nineteen or twenty. . . . So she was convicted sixteen times in a six-month period of prostitution offenses. She . . . left her trafficker, went on to pursue education and employment, developed a family, and worked in a brokerage house for about thirteen years doing data entry. But as part of that data entry position, she needed to be bonded in some way. . . . And the outside company that her employer used to do the rebonding did a background check on everyone and came up with these sixteen convictions. She was let go after thirteen years [despite having an exemplary record]. . . . She had been living with the fear that this would somehow impact her and there it was. To say that criminal convictions, in particular criminal convictions for prostitution, can be an

obstacle for people moving forward . . . is a huge understatement. . . .
There's no quick fix in the criminal justice system . . . Postconviction work is
very challenging.

In the timeline Tory provides, Angel was ostensibly arrested before federal or state trafficking laws were on the books. Yet Angel's story and
Tory's description of the challenges that accompany postconviction
work offer an instructive rebuttal to advocates who suggest that an arrest
for something like a low-level misdemeanor carries minimal risk. Complicating matters further still is the expectation that a juvenile record
automatically gets sealed (sometimes they don't) or that expunged or
vacated records ever completely disappear or get erased from the public
record without leaving some trace. Such expectations seem increasingly
untenable in an era when third-party data-brokers and myriad "proprietary" databases keep digitized track of justice encounters.[40] Once a person has a record in either the juvenile or criminal-justice system, guaranteeing that an expunged, vacated, or sealed record won't be accessed by
a background-checking company (BCC) is difficult to prevent.

THE CHALLENGES OF EVER COMPLETELY ERASING, SEALING, OR VACATING A RECORD

There are a few undertheorized dimensions of postconviction work that
has salience for people who have been in domestic sex trafficking situations. First, even records that are technically sealable may be seen by
law enforcement.[41] Second, even if a person is trafficked and processed
by the criminal-justice system, but ultimately prevails in sealing or
expunging their records, guaranteeing that those records won't be seen
by law enforcement or won't be sold to third-party data-brokers may be
challenging. Relatedly, third-party data brokers are able to mine public
records,[42] accumulate data in "proprietary databases,"[43] and sell this
information back to employers, landlords, or any interested person or
party seeking to obtain information about people's arrest and conviction records, even if no formal charges were filed and even if the data
they obtain and sell are no longer accurate.[44]

How does this happen? Each time a person is arrested or charged, it
basically results in a digital strike against them. Records aren't just concrete documents stored in file cabinets in the physical world. They are
pieces of data that get amassed in different law-enforcement and private
databases. The public has limited knowledge of these databases and

BCC reports, much less control of them or the ability to correct inaccurate details.[45] People generally have no way to contest information that turns out to be wrong.[46] For instance, even if Kiara is ultimately successful in vacating the remaining charge on her record, it is not beyond the realm of possibility that this information may nonetheless show up in an employer's background check. Logan Wayne suggests that this is because third-party data-brokers face little regulation and are able to "distribute information from expunged records without any repercussions."[47] And because records previously defined as "public" carry profit-making potential, third-party data brokers have "perverse incentives"[48] to mine and sell them to employers, landlords, and insurers.[49]

CONCLUSION

Talking to Kiara and some of the advocates and attorneys who work with people who have been in comparable situations made me appreciate how little attention has been paid to the adverse side effects of justice involvement in a technologically–mediated world. With respect to domestic sex trafficking, I am not referring to the existence of online classified-ad sites, which are assumed to facilitate it. Rather, here I am concerned with the ways in which a record of past involvement with the criminal-justice system has the potential to flow between different law enforcement and proprietary databases, which may ultimately constrain a person's future life opportunities, an area where more research is needed. Were it not for Kiara's willingness to share her experiences, I too would have had a difficult time "connecting the dots." When trafficked persons' experiences within the criminal and juvenile justice systems don't count as punitive or when well-meaning actors assume that carceral systems have the capacity to protect people without detrimental consequences, this type of analytic "dot connecting" is difficult because it challenges the presumption that any intervention—even a carceral one—is better than nothing.[50] Complicating matters further still is the difficulty of getting any kind of quantitative grasp on the number of people who have been in sex trafficking or other exploitative situations who face these challenges, or in assessing how these challenges are exacerbated or potentially ameliorated through technology. It is not clear.

As BCCs and third-party data brokers expand, and as more employers come to rely on data from them to make decisions about people's employability, the challenges confronting Kiara and others in comparable situations may be harder to control or undo.[51] If the point of antitrafficking efforts is an opportunity to live a life free of control, coercion, and punishment, processing people through systems that makes it difficult to "clear the slate"[52] or that allows them to make a clean break from the carceral state all but guarantees that such efforts miss the mark.

The trouble Kiara had in securing housing and finding regular employment was owing, in part, to a system whose supposed "cures" ended up creating more harms. However, in addition to that, it was the digitized memorialization of her arrest and criminal record that flagged her as criminal and a potential threat, a situation that effectively magnified the punitive terms of the carceral "cure" she's endured. Advances in technology allow different datasets and databases to interact, and automated recordkeeping also makes it easier for information to be shared and/or sold to different agencies.[53] Some technological developments may be welcomed by actors interested in bolstering antitrafficking activities but may arguably magnify the terms in which people who have been in exploitative situations experience the carceral cure of protection, though this is an area where more research is needed.

That such a harrowing situation may impact people who are seen as victims of sex trafficking is troubling. Yet concerns about stigma ought not to be limited to people who are legally defined or legibly viewed by authorities as "good" or "deserving" victims of trafficking.[54] These are challenges that confront countless others whose more "typical" encounters with the justice system and criminal records have been used to deny them employment and housing opportunities. In her book *Marked,* Devah Pager, notes that "prior contacts with the criminal-justice system impose lingering effects on job seekers," diminished opportunities that may be compounded by a prospective applicant's race.[55] In the experimental study she conducted, Pager found that among black and white applicants with equal qualifications, "blacks were less than half as likely to receive callbacks as equally qualified white applicants (14 vs. 34 percent)"[56] underscoring both the centrality of race and past involvement with the justice system as factors that can impede job opportunities. There is also the issue of stigma. Though Logan Wayne focuses her discussion on juvenile offenders, I think her assessment of the problems that come with having a criminal record, victim of trafficking or not, applies to any person stigmatized by having a record, even if a legal remedy is available and achieved. She notes: "Assumptions are made about a person with a criminal record, and once those assumptions are made they cannot be undone. In other words, the social stigmatization of the criminal status is so severe that subsequently learning a conviction was expunged usually does nothing to change the opinions of those people who had previously found out about the crime."[57]

Campaigns to "ban the box" and "remove questions about conviction history from job applications" have sought to address some of these concerns,[58] and more cities, counties, and states have moved to adopt the policy.[59] Yet if we think about a record, conviction, or any piece of data related to a person's involvement with the criminal-justice system in digitized terms, then the legal remedies and postconviction relief needed, demand new models of protection. This is what is at stake: when cures harm and when records can't be completely undone, the system is incapable of providing trafficked persons with the protections and, more important, the rights and justice they deserve.

Conclusion

Fall 2014: Two journalists' e-mails land in my inbox asking questions about recent antiprostitution and antitrafficking developments. Their queries give me a chance to reflect upon the possible future direction of efforts to respond to domestic sex trafficking in the United States. In the first instance, I'm forwarded a story about a group of police, prosecutors, and social-service providers who have come together as part of the CEASE/Cities Empowered Against Sexual Exploitation Network. Funded by an $80,000 grant from the organization Demand Abolition, the Seattle-based group aims to reduce the demand for prostitution in its two-year funding period, an effort that, as one King County federal prosecutor put it, creates "an atmosphere of risk" for anyone looking to purchase sex online. The program "Buyer Beware" additionally flips the criminal justice script of solely targeting girls and women who trade sex, and instead seeks to "get girls and women who are involved in prostitution out of a dark, dangerous life."[1]

In another example, a reporter e-mails me a link to a story from Orange County, California about the District Attorney's Office's creation of an online page featuring the names and mug shots of men convicted of soliciting prostitutes. According to the *Los Angeles Times* story, the Orange County DA makes no distinction between sex trafficking and voluntary sex work. And here adult voluntary sex workers and forced sex-trafficked persons' victimization is acknowledged through convicted buyers' shame, put in sharp focus and permanent display as a result of the DA's decision to "keep the photos online indefinitely," and aided by web-crawling bots whose automated scans will likely turn up on these johns' shots for years to come. The DA's online effort is linked to a broader move to combat sex trafficking, and is illustrative "of a shift among authorities in Orange County and elsewhere in viewing the prostitute as the victim, the pimp as the human trafficker and the customer as the enabler."[2]

Two different cities, two different programs. Both utilize technology and both share a vision to change the culture of law enforcement yet again, this time through end-demand strategies aimed at abolishing prostitution and targeting and shaming buyers who pay to have sex with adults and underage youth. As U.S. media treatment typically goes, end-demand efforts tell a story about a misaligned criminal-justice system. The miscarriage of justice—from the perspective some of its proponents—is that while people who sell sex get arrested, the buyer-exploiters who drive demand typically walk away unscathed. Proponents of end-demand policies—who appear to include everyone from selected law enforcement agents to social workers, carcerally oriented feminists,[3] nongovernmental organizations,[4] and cyber patrol operatives using disruptive techniques to "bring men to the fight"[5]—seek to ameliorate this punitive imbalance by shifting the focus away from people who sell sex, widely presumed to be girls and women, and onto those who purchase sex, typically assumed to be men.[6] Leaving aside the conflation of sex trafficking and sex work, and some of the gender-essentialist, heterosexist assumptions that inform end-demand strategies, research into their efficacy tempers some of the fever-pitched hopes proponents pin on it.

First, proponents of end–demand in the United States typically assume that it is a time-tested policy with evenly beneficial results. Yet researchers have noted that the success of the strategy in the country that put it on the map—Sweden—is less than clear-cut. The Swedish or Nordic model is lauded by some U.S. advocates and commentators for its visionary potential. The implicit goal of the law, implemented in 1999, is to protect those engaged in commercial sex (assumed to be women and victims of violence) by criminalizing those who purchase it. It was seen as a way to reduce "the number of sex buyers or sellers" and curb trafficking.[7] As one Swedish deputy chief prosecutor interviewed about the policy put it, "the beauty of the Swedish system is that we criminalize the strong, the oppressors."[8] However, this attempt to protect the weak (i.e., all those who sell or trade sex) and "criminalize the strong" (i.e., people who purchase sex) has not ended the demand for prostitution. Moreover, even though it is legal to sell sex in Sweden, sex workers are unable to exercise labor rights and prohibited from "taking action to make their work safer or easier."[9] "Assurances that the law will not be of detriment to those selling sex do not ring true, since Sweden's abolitionism, as well as other laws and policies, has harmed sex workers themselves," Jay Levy and Pye Jakobsson note.[10]

Second, supporters of end-demand initiatives assume that these are a departure from criminalizing those involved in prostitution.[11] However, even if the Swedish policy were effective in extending rights and protections to people who sell sexual services, it would not neatly map onto a U.S. sociolegal landscape where people involved in the sex trade are still criminalized.[12] And as is the case with efforts to criminally prosecute trafficker-pimps, going after the facilitators of commercial sex does not foreclose the possibility that youth and adults—now widely viewed as victims—may still be endure carceral encounters that mirror the treatment of criminal offenders. Relatedly, integrating end-demand strategies into law-enforcement activities in the United States will not by itself prevent police from stopping, questioning, misidentifying, or "switching up" the treatment of people involved in the sex trade, whether they are viewed as at-risk victims of sex trafficking or voluntary prostitutes engaged in illegal activity. That is because even if called victims in name, people who are involved in the sex trade may still experience punitive, stigmatizing, and disempowering carceral encounters.

Like the antitrafficking efforts that have preceded them, end-demand efforts sound promising, like a clarion call to end exploitation and demand legal justice and fairness. And if we are talking about individuals under eighteen who trade sex for money, shelter, or survival, few would argue that they can give consent, irrespective of whether they see their experiences as coerced or not. Those who abuse, sexually exploit, or profit from others' forced involvement in various sex trades—whether we are talking about trafficker-pimps or buyers/exploiters—should be held accountable for the harms they impose. There ought to be bright legal lines drawn against sexual abuse, harm, and violence in all of its interpersonal and structural manifestations. Yet laws are unruly and don't always produce their intended effect. If there is a research lesson that can be gleaned from anti-sex-trafficking efforts and the push to "end–demand" in the United States, it is that punitive laws do not necessarily translate into reduced rates of violence. Nor do laws that criminalize perpetrators of violence always translate into reduced punitive oversight of the people they are designed to protect.[13] And just as it is misleading to call a still broadly criminalized population "trafficked" and assume that carceral interventions will produce victim-centered results,[14] so too is it unlikely—as other scholars have also suggested—that more arrests and criminal prosecutions, whether of trafficker-pimps or exploiter-buyers—will stamp out commercial sex altogether or enhance the well-being, safety, and rights of adult voluntary sex workers or adult and underage sex trafficking victims whom such laws aim to protect.[15]

. . .

I wrote this book to reflect on the seemingly contradictory truths I encountered while researching collaborative responses to domestic sex trafficking in the United States, paradoxes I couldn't then or even now can't fully reconcile. For instance, most law-enforcement and nongovernmental actors I met expressed what I thought was sincere care, commitment, and resolve to help sex trafficking victims. Yet some also saw detention, diversion, probation, and protracted involvement of the justice system as the best way to help people in exploitative situations with otherwise limited options. Relatedly, some for-profit, faith-based, and nonprofit actors, and researchers are passionate about addressing the sex trafficking taking place online and in their own corners of the country. Yet few seemed to question that by working to strengthen law-enforcement responses, they may also play a role in getting at-risk victims into systems with the capacity to punish, even as they seek to protect.

Carceral protectionism is a framework I use to help make sense of some of these contradictions. Yet as with all frameworks or working theories, there are exceptions and situations to which it doesn't apply. That is why, throughout the book, I have highlighted instances where people I met challenged my line of thinking, or took issue with my equation of an arrest or detention with a de facto form of punishment. For instance, Lizzie, a social worker, said that youth hadn't been arrested in her county for several years. Some youth I interviewed weren't arrested. Vivi reported a positive experience with police and felt that the responding officers and health-care provider she encountered after running away from a sex trafficking situation did everything they could to help her. Justice, a teen whose situation I discussed in chapter 4, had spent more time in juvenile hall than most other youth I met and described her experiences of prostitution as coercive and the result of getting involved with a pimp who was violent and manipulative. Even so, I was taken aback to find that she viewed her arrest as one of the things that helped her get away from her pimp and out of an exploitative situation. Justice's reflections on the utility of arrests weren't limited to her personal experience, however. Our discussion of the topic prompted her to call for more arrests. For Justice, talk of arrests seemed a way to talk about an unresponsive public that had abandoned her and other girls in situations like hers. "Everybody needs to be arrested," she explained. "You guys, they need to stop letting these girls go." Justice's call aligned with Cara, Becca, and other police and advocates who viewed an arrest as one of the few tools available to keep sex-trafficked victims, especially youth, safe.

Though counterintuitive, I wonder if Justice's and different actors' acknowledgment of the necessity of using a criminal justice tool like arrest or detention speaks to the broader purchase of carceral modes of protection, even as some concede that using punitive methods isn't really the best way to treat youth and adults recognized as victims? Put somewhat differently, could it be that Justice's acceptance of her arrest as a step towards a more stable future reflects a far more disconcerting reality in which the only way she could have accessed services was through the criminal-justice system? My point here is not that the criminal-justice system *should* provide the path to Justice's or other girls' and women's protection, a hallmark of a neoabolitionist, carceral feminist approach to trafficking.[16] Instead, perhaps it speaks to the tangible effects of a trafficking ideology that has placed more emphasis on "saving victims" than on addressing the complex and systemic inequalities that create them.[17] In the United States, such complexities and inequities are varied, and include income inequality, structural racism, and the persistent siphoning off of resources from the welfare state into an expansive carceral state.[18] One major effect of this, Marie Gottschalk points out, is that the carceral state has become one of the main "conduits" through which "the poor and disadvantaged" gain access to social services.[19] However unsettling, Justice's observation suggests that for some youth, the carceral state may be one of the few systems through which a girl in a situation like hers can gain some modicum of state support.[20]

PROTECTIVE IN NAME, PUNITIVE BY DESIGN

Throughout this book, I have aimed to draw attention to something seldom accounted for in mainstream discussions of anti-sex-trafficking strategies, particularly those focused on domestic sex trafficking situations: namely, that carceral interventions directed at women and girls deemed "at risk" of domestic sex trafficking can produce less than protective results.[21] I am certainly not the first person to draw attention to the punitive dimensions of antitrafficking efforts. People who work to secure the rights and safety of sex workers have voiced concerns ever since the issue of sex trafficking was revived in the late 1990s. On the research front, critiques about the "punishing fist"[22] of antitrafficking laws and the "rescue industry"[23] that shape it emerged soon after the passage of the Trafficking Victim's Protection Act and the Palermo Protocol in the early 2000s. However, when I started this project in the late 2000s, few researchers were writing about "domestic" versions of sex trafficking in the United States, and fewer still were exploring collaborative arrangements between state and nonstate actors.

What little research exists on the punitive dimensions of antitrafficking has tended to focus on migrants. For example, migrant sex workers and victims of sex trafficking are sometimes placed in "shelter detentions"[24] and "protective custody.[25] Though such placements may be deemed protective, they cohere with criminalized immigration agendas and carceral and welfarist forms of control.[26] Scholars have also noted that NGOs and intergovernmental actors have a hand in overseeing the "humanitarian deportation" of migrants viewed both as "victims" and as "criminals."[27] What this suggests is that carceral interventions to address sex trafficking aren't limited to the United States, nor are they limited to domestic victims, as research advanced by Elizabeth Bernstein, Sine Plambech, Edith Kinney and others crucially highlights.[28] And if a connective thread exists between migrant and domestic "trafficking" populations in divergent contexts, it is this: when antitrafficking frameworks are shaped by carceral agendas,[29] "caring and controlling,"[30] "helping and policing,"[31] and rehabilitating and disciplining sex workers, migrants,[32] and domestic populations are neither contradictions in terms nor diametrically opposed goals. Rather they're on-the-ground expressions and multisited manifestations of a paradigm of justice that controls to protect.[33]

This book is thus one story within a growing archive of research that accounts for what happens to "at risk" populations subject to state-orchestrated, non-state-assisted efforts to help them. That people deemed "at risk" of domestic sex trafficking in the United States may experience intensified forms of social control when their identification and protection is taken up by different state and nonstate actors and augmented by technology may be surprising, even as it corresponds to the findings of scholars who have followed the evolution of more "typical" forms of gendered punishment.[34] Yet, as different people I got to know over the past few years would sometimes remind me, trafficked persons *aren't* typical victims. Nor are they typical offenders. Instead, as victims sometimes treated more like offenders, they occupy a different subject position altogether. This book has been my attempt to bring these perspectives together and to understand how collaboration can blur the boundaries between state and nonstate authority and result in antitrafficking responses in which control and protection intersect.

IF NOT CARCERAL PROTECTIONISM, THEN WHAT?

Diagnosing the problems that accompany anti-sex-trafficking efforts is relatively straightforward. It is far more difficult to come up with ideas, recommendations, and visionary thinking about where we might go from here. As far as visionary thinking is concerned, it is notable that attention to domestic sex trafficking in the United States invites consideration of the advancement of twin, albeit contrasting visions, of justice to address the problem. The term "abolition" tracks so differently in the antitrafficking and prison-abolition movements, both of which conjure up new imaginaries and visions of justice, yet with decidedly different goals. For some anti-sex-trafficking proponents, neoabolitionist interventions are mounted to reform an unresponsive state oblivious to the exploitation, and specifically the sexual exploitation, taking place in its own backyard. Yet rather than focus on the intersecting racial, economic, and gendered root causes of the problem or the devastating effects of neoliberal economic policies, this brand of neoabolitionism strives to bring the state back by underwriting carceral expansion and expanding the reach of the criminal-justice system. Arguably, the carceral state has gotten back in the business of rehabilitation. However, it is doing so through a softened, gender-sensitized, and collaborative version that still keeps the carceral commitments of the state intact.

Proponents of prison abolition offer a different vision of justice. Highlighting the ways in which criminal-justice-oriented "tough law-and-order" efforts to address violence have helped fuel the growth of the prison-industrial complex,[35] prison abolitionists resist neoliberal carceral expansion and underscore the short-sidedness of utilizing punitive systems of control to undo intersecting systems and structures of domination.[36] This book highlights the limits of a carcerally-focused model of justice for people in situations we now call domestic sex trafficking: one where carcerally protecting to empower is the most legible paradigm for the achievement of justice itself. It is my deepest hope that in the not-so-distant future, anyone who experiences coercion or exploitation and wants help, will be able to access the support they need without interfacing with the state in its most punitive form. And though I'm hesitant to offer "best practice" solutions that run the risk of the minimizing the complexities that surround sex trafficking or worse, suggesting interventions that end up doing more harm than good, there are a few recommendations I can offer.

Decriminalizing Prostitution

A national conversation about decriminalizing prostitution in the United States is overdue.[37] Amnesty International kicked off the topic on a global scale when in August 2015 delegates moved to support the decriminalization of prostitution and called on governments to "repeal most laws that forbid the sale and purchase of sex."[38] Their recommendation comes on the heels of mounting scholarly evidence pointing to the range of documented health risks and violations of human rights that accompany criminalized prostitution "policy regimes," among which the United States is included.[39] One argument against such a change is that decriminalization would serve to protect pimps and promote men's "entitlement to buy sex."[40] My response? Fighting sex trafficking and expanding protections through antiprostitution criminal justice efforts might make sense if they adequately provided protections for youth and adults in coercive situations who want out. Unfortunately, such policies haven't proven to be unilaterally protective.

Criminalization also unnecessarily hurts voluntary sex workers who aren't in exploitive situations and don't see themselves as victimized by prostitution, but who are punished by antitrafficking efforts just the same. Practically speaking, decriminalizing prostitution for adults and youth would mean that law enforcement could no longer arrest, detain, divert, or supervise groups "at risk" of sex trafficking for their own protection or arrest people they view as simply breaking the law. Consequently law enforcement—and especially people on the "front lines of the criminal justice system—"[41]would no longer wield the discretionary power to "switch up" treating people as "victims" and "offenders." They could therefore play a much more direct and potentially positive role in the lives of both adults and youth they encounter in the course of their activities, since fear of arrest would be off the table. This could also potentially make collaborations between law enforcement and social-service providers or other nonstate actors more effective.[42]

This would mean, however, that some people identified as victims of domestic sex trafficking could run away from shelters or refuse to participate in criminal proceedings against people accused of exploiting them. The ability to walk away could also mean that both adults and youth might remain in situations from which nonstate actors and police seek to extricate them, believing this to be for their own safety. Yet youth who are arrested or placed under court supervision already run away. Some people already reject services, even at the risk of legal sanction. Sometimes this is due to the fact that the help, the services, and interventions on offer turn out not to be so helpful and empowering after all. Creating more rehabilitative programs that extend girls' and women's involvement with the criminal-justice system, or that impose stringent requirements on the completion of such programs, would seem counterproductive, though this is another area where more research is needed. What is needed, rather, is a sustainably–funded safety net, replete with educational opportunities, high-quality, expansive primary and mental health care, and social services (not to mention fair living wages) both for people who choose to remain in the sex trade and for those who want to transition out of it, but who face limited options.

Services Not Moored to the Criminal-Justice System

It is astounding that for all of the money that has been dedicated to anti-sex-trafficking efforts in the United States, finding a shelter bed or an appropriate placement for a sex-trafficked girl or woman who actually wants assistance is still so difficult. Long-term housing options are also in short supply. And for all of the housing and social service challenges that confront cisgender girls, the challenges for cisgender boys, women, and transgender youth and adults are even more pronounced, since so few options exist for them to begin with.[43] Then there is the issue of the kinds of services that are available. Providing people with services that are culturally appropriate and grounded in evidence requires more than good intentions. It requires expertise, accountability, and a sustained funding commitment. Important critiques exist that highlight how NGO, nonprofit, and foundation efforts thwart social justice movements and organizing.[44] I share these concerns, particularly as more individuals and groups move into trafficking-victim aftercare work, some of whom appear to have had little if any training or experience in the field or have the kinds of skills to help them. If and where such services are wanted (and choice does matter), they shouldn't be court-mandated. And just as justice for trafficked persons shouldn't be tied to a religious or nonprofit charity,[45] bound to celebrity desires, nor turn on the "redemptive capitalist[46]" sensibilities of corporate philanthropy, so too should people who leave coercive situations have access to services that actually support their needs. Yet services alone do not suffice. People involved in the sex trade who want to transition out of it need access to decent jobs and a living wage. But as long as prostitution is a criminalized activity, alternative employment opportunities for people who identify as victims of sex trafficking, voluntary sex workers, or as people just trying to survive, are that much more difficult to obtain since an arrest and criminal record and the stigma that comes with it can make housing, employment, and educational opportunities troublingly out of reach.

The Right to Be Forgotten?

Law enforcement and antitrafficking advocates increasingly recognize that a connection exists between trafficking and technology.[47] To address it, law enforcement rely on digital evidence in sex trafficking investigations. There has also been heightened focus on shutting down online sites thought to facilitate sex trafficking and a push to identify and disrupt sex trafficking online by developing new tools and techniques. Yet while various technologies give antitrafficking actors new tools and data with which to identify and assist victims, such collaboratively curated data—the kind amassed by different actors, shared between different sectors, and distributed across different state and non-state databases—may pose potential risks to prospective victims, for instance, through heightened carceral interventions that punish. They also create the potential for new types of "networked harm"[48] to occur, harms that are difficult for an individual or even the law to undo, since it isn't just the state or law enforcement that collects and analyzes data, but a distributed network of actors, none of whom has sole control of how and in what context such data are used.[49]

One of the more pressing legal questions right now is whether we have a right to be forgotten, some kind of "delete, undo, and restart" mechanism enabling us to erase digital traces of our history and remedy the "foreverness" of the Internet, which can cause reputational harm, personal shame, and humiliation years after the fact. In May 2014, the European Court of Justice ruled in a case involving Google and decided that EU citizens do indeed have "the right to be forgotten."[50] An important decision in raising questions about what rights and data protection ought to include in an age of surveillance, questions about a person's digital trail and the heighted power of "grey media," of which databases and search are included[51] also puts into sharp focus just how little control any of us have, but especially groups already vulnerable to state and nonstate attention.

Though the 2014 EU ruling may not have immediate salience to people who have been in sex trafficking situations in the United States and seek to erase digital traces of their experiences of exploitation or exposure to the carceral state, it may serve to inspire us to think creatively about what types of legal and technical mechanisms might enable them, and indeed anyone with past involvement with the criminal-justice system, to challenge the "foreverness" of the Internet, even if partially, and gain some control over the way in which data are "scraped, mined, and sold,"[52] for different purposes, including interventions developed in the name of at-risk victims' protection.

WE CAN'T ARREST OUR WAY OUT OF THIS PROBLEM

In considering alternatives to carceral protectionism, I have one final recommendation, which comes from an unlikely source. I first interviewed Pete, a police officer whom I got to know over time, in 2009. I interviewed him on several occasions, accompanied him on a ride-along, and kept in touch with him after he left his post in a unit dually tasked with investigating prostitution and sex trafficking cases. To say that Pete was generous in sharing his time, insights, and perspectives with me would be a gross understatement. In fact, the generosity with which Pete and other police officers shared their insights with me cannot be underestimated. It was clear to me from one of our earliest meetings that Pete saw the writing on the wall and thought that the continued focus on arrests without attention to prevention and structural inequities would do little to actually solve the problem of trafficking. In the years since I first met him, his state has passed a number of new antitrafficking laws, but Pete is aware that more laws and more enforcement-centered antitrafficking activities will ultimately do little to address the precarious conditions and social instability that give rise to exploitation and trafficking in the first place. Pete and I reconnected by phone in August 2014. He e-mailed me soon after with one last thought. I close this book with Pete's e-mail response to me, which shows why even some frontline enforcers of anti-sex-trafficking policies are critical of the laws they have a mandate to enforce. He wrote:

Although there are thousands of penal code sections we enforce, it is up to the public to determine what laws matter most to them. In other words, which laws merit more attention depends on the public's interest.

How much time is the public willing to devote to finding meaningful solutions to the epidemic we now refer to as human trafficking. With human trafficking, there is a public perception that by arresting the trafficker the problem is solved. But it is not that simple. We cannot arrest our way out of this problem.

I was always frustrated that very little attention was devoted to the plight of victims before they came into contact with their traffickers. I was also bothered by society's incongruent values with [regard to] the sex trade.

If the public is serious about combating human trafficking, then we need also [to] look into societal disparities and other complex issues. Please understand that my role as an investigator was simple: enforce human trafficking laws.

Passing more antitrafficking laws and requiring police officers like Pete to serve as the frontline carceral enforcers of social problems we, as a public, are unwilling to solve is futile. What is needed instead is the political will and courage to create systems of protection that aren't tied to punishment. Are we willing to invest in systems of support like schools, mental health services, and safe and affordable housing? Are we willing to take the long view and start addressing the economic, gendered, and racial systems of domination that contribute to exploitation and give rise to different forms of gendered, racialized, and protective punishment? My hope is that we'll rise to the occasion and begin the hard work of imagining a future where protection from sex trafficking, forced labor, or exploitation of any sort doesn't put people at heightened risk from systems that control them.

Appendix

As Timothy Black observes, pivotal moments in qualitative research have the capacity to prompt "new directions of inquiry, new social spaces to comprehend, and definitive departures from the familiar".[1] My own moment of altered insight didn't happen in a familiar or oft-visited location, since this project has taken a more multisited and deterritorialized form of study.[2] Instead, the disruptive moment came by way of watching antitrafficking discourses about domestic sex trafficking and coordinated victim recovery efforts play out, in real time, before my eyes.

The occasion was a 2013 citywide operation that coincided with Human Trafficking Awareness month. As one of the lead officers explained in briefing those assembled to execute it, the main purpose of the operation was to "recover juveniles," which in practice meant that different units would collectively focus their attention on finding sex-trafficked youth on the street. A tactical operation plan was in place and a central post was set up to coordinate the various units gathered to sweep that particular city's streets that night. Representatives from different law-enforcement and social-service agencies gathered at the central location where they would wait in anticipation of the stream of sex-trafficked youth expected to pour in throughout the night. The unit I was with met in another part of the city and by 4 P.M., we rolled out to different streets in search of youth.

Ten or so hours passed, the time broken up by driving past a few streets where prostitution is known to occur. Officers approached and questioned adult women presumed to be involved in prostitution facilitated by pimps. All of these women were arrested, aside from two, who were let go for reasons not entirely clear to me. Towards the tail end of the evening, someone from the main post informed us that a neighboring unit had recovered an underage juvenile, who I believed to be a girl but of whose gender I wasn't sure. The small number of youth identified in the recovery effort that night wasn't lost on one of the officers I was with, who acknowledged that the operation hadn't been particularly successful. He also explained that this kind of work is a numbers game. But the idea that an exercise like this is a numbers game was confusing to me: if the goal of the operation was to recover juveniles, and so few were actually identified, could it be that the number of adult women arrested for prostitution or taken in for probation violations served as the symbolic data marker against which this operation's success was measured? Again, I wasn't sure.

By 2 A.M., the operation was more or less over. As I made my way back to the place where I was staying, I was amped up from a mix of adrenaline and the familiar affective state that has been my steady companion throughout this project: anxiety. I couldn't fall asleep and had trouble staving off feelings of confusion. It wasn't until the next day and in the process of typing up hand-scrawled notes that I experienced a small measure of reflective insight. I wrote:

- The task force was focused on juveniles. But in this unit it was adult women who got arrested and booked.
- Why weren't all of the clients arrested if the purpose is to end demand [for prostitution]? Why were the women rounded up and some brought to jail?
- [Despite all the reference to prostitutes] as victims, I did not see any sizeable difference in how they were treated. This was particularly the case for anyone who was seen as uncooperative.

After rereading my notes, I realized that my confusion stemmed from the fact that though this antitrafficking operation was supposed to focus on youth, its implementation on the ground took the form of policing in which women suspected of being involved in prostitution were questioned, arrested, and treated more or less like criminal offenders. And after I experienced my own pivotal moment of sorts, questions, practical ones emerged: should it have taken a citywide task force and the arrest of women involved in prostitution to get a young person or anyone else in an exploitative situation the assistance they needed, assuming they wanted it? Was this strategy really working?

Researchers have compared trafficking, or rather antitrafficking, to a rescue industry,[3] and a networked one at that.[4] Others have pointed out that moral panics[5] and flawed data[6] undergird contemporary antitrafficking efforts both in the United States and globally. I am familiar with and have in my own small way contributed to these critiques.[7] Yet upon closer inspection and critical reflection of my own role in setting the tone and terms of discussion, I see how rehearsals of seemingly bright line truisms—for instance, that antitrafficking efforts could be made "better" through critique—had shaped my acquiescence and implicit agreement. Though they didn't name it as such, some research participants suggested that the carceral protectionist interventions I have described throughout this book—an arrest, for instance—is a way to help some people in what we now call domestic sex trafficking situations. Even though I never fully accepted this argument, I thought that those who said it had a valid point. I still do. If the carceral state has become a safety net for a host of social problems, poverty, mental illness, and domestic sex trafficking among them,[8] a carceral form of protection may be better than nothing.

It would be disingenuous to suggest that I was completely taken aback by this scene. Perhaps the pivotal moment was instead a way for me to confront and clarify some of the basic assumptions I held onto throughout the research process; namely, that most people, no matter their politics, would likely agree that law enforcement should be trained to assist and sensitively respond to situations where people find themselves in coercive, exploitative, and abusive situations and want help.[9] There *should* be bright legal lines around the sexual exploitation of youth and adults coerced into sex trafficking situations. I reasoned that some elements of antitrafficking could and ought to be made better. I thought that more awareness of the problems of antitrafficking—including recognition of its punitive dimensions for both victims of trafficking and voluntary sex workers alike—would be a first step in fostering a law-enforcement paradigm shift that has elsewhere been discussed.[10]

Suffice it to say that after the operation I was compelled to question my own commitment to antitrafficking as a framework with the capacity for reform and the ability to deliver justice to those who experience its effects most directly. And as counterintuitive as it may seem, coming to this realization made me more fully aware of the daunting and arguably impossible task of requiring actors directly affiliated with the carceral state, including but not limited to local police officers, to step up as protectors of victims of sex trafficking, all the while continuing to enforce laws related to commercial sex. This isn't to suggest that law enforcement does not possess literal life-and-death power over people it polices. Obviously they do, as evidenced by research documenting police harassment of sex workers[11] and police street stops and the racial disparities they produce.[12] These trends underscore the ways in which structural racism and criminalized poverty manifests in everyday policing practices[13] and further point to the pressing need for the American public to focus a spotlight on the ways in which people of color, poor people, gender-nonconforming people, and sex workers have and continue to be targets of carceral control.[14]

However, my point is that law-enforcement agencies now called upon and funded to fight the trafficking problem in their own backyards would face consequences for opting out of policing prostitution or refusing to take domestic sex trafficking seriously, even if superficially. As local enforcers of penal codes and policies that police chiefs, elected officials, and the broader public authorize and expect them to enforce, police have little room to refuse, as heightened public attention to trafficking and the passage of more state laws make clear.[15] It is therefore unsurprising that some are going to use the tools at their disposal when tasked with responding. And as long as the public and different private and nonprofit interest groups demand more investment in law enforcement as the primary system of first response, more arrests or recovery efforts or police training alone will not necessarily produce lasting change.

A NOTE ON METHODS

This book has been many years in the making. It was born out of an attempt to better understand state and non-state efforts to respond to domestic sex trafficking in the United States. Johan Lindquist observes that different modes of analysis are needed to foster "a deeper understanding of the individuals, institutions, and networks that engage with antitrafficking."[16] The interviews, informal conversations, and offline and online observations that have shaped my research and appear in the book have been my attempt to do just that.

In 2011, after completing my dissertation, I decided to recalibrate the project. My dissertation research focused on "multiprofessional" efforts to respond to human trafficking in the Netherlands and the United States.[17] Many of the themes I discuss in this book—*carceral protectionism*—for instance—were ideas and concepts I initially developed while writing my dissertation to make sense of the overlap between law enforcement and NGO/social-service responses to human trafficking in the two countries.[18] I wasn't starting this project from conceptual scratch. However, because of my interest in exploring antitrafficking efforts focused on "domestic" situations in the United States, I realized that though my dissertation research was instructive and a foundation for this project, I needed to conduct a new round of interviews and spend more time learning specifically about domestic antitrafficking efforts, by which I mean activities mostly, though not always exclusively, aimed at U.S. citizens and permanent residents.

Starting in 2011, I drew upon a preestablished network of contacts and personal connections to recruit prospective participants. The recruitment and selection of participants was purposive,[19] which is to say, I was looking to engage with people who could speak to particular elements of anti-trafficking efforts, but which in practice mostly meant efforts that involved "domestic" (e.g., nonmigrant) populations. Between 2011 and 2015, I conducted around forty interviews with anti-trafficking actors, including law-enforcement agents, nongovernmental and legal advocates, social-service providers, and other professionals whose work touches on trafficking in some way.[20]

Also included in this count are youth and adults I interviewed who were identified, deemed to be at risk of, or self-identified as victims of sex trafficking in the United States. My use of approximate language to signal the number of formal interviews has to do with the fact that on a few occasions, people I interviewed invited other colleagues to share their thoughts with me. In other instances, I officially met with law enforcement authorities to discuss my research and they directed me to others in specific units. Denise Brennan has observed that "one time [research] conversations" have limits.[21] I agree with Brennan, and the subpopulation of research participants featured in this book are those with whom I interviewed, observed, or informally interacted with on more than one occasion. There are a few exceptions, including, for instance, youth from Dreams & Destiny whom I interviewed once, though I had occasion to casually interact with Che, Vivi, and Kayla at a later event. In addition to formal interviews, I engaged in approximately twenty-five informal conversations and meetings. Some interviews and meetings were recorded; others were not. In both instances, I took hand-written notes.

To protect respondents' confidentiality and the anonymity of any person or organization mentioned in the context of an interview and observations, I have used pseudonyms in place of all real names and organizations. I have removed details that might be personally identifiable, for instance, the use of particular turns of phrase, nicknames, and, in the case of police officers, rank. I also decided to refrain from referring to participants by their geographical or jurisdictional location. In the case of antitrafficking professionals, I left out racial, ethnic, and other identity details, and in a few instances, I changed professionals' gender identities.

I have also taken steps to avoid compromising the anonymity of underage youth, such as by not identifying their home cities and omitting the names of actual placements, mental health diagnoses, and similar information. I have, however, included youths' ages at the time and their race/ethnicity, since these data are relevant in discussions of domestic sex trafficking. My aim was to provide basic information about these youth, yet with the explicit caveat that youth I met do not represent the entire population of sex trade–involved youth and teens. I also interviewed two adult survivors of sex trafficking. Only "Kiara" appears in the book, however. Though she gave me permission to use her real name, I decided not to so as to reduce any risk to her that may arise. In addition to removing identifiable information, I also added details, for instance, giving an anonymous person referenced in interviews a pseudonymous name. When Lizzie told a story about her client, for example, I gave her a name, "Alissa."

Some formal interviews took place soon after I met with or communicated with research participants, others only after a protracted series of informal interactions. Some people only agreed to be interviewed after receiving a supervisor's approval, or upon learning about my research from someone they knew. The latter point highlights an important aspect of the participants featured in this book—most belong to highly localized networks.[22] In some instances, this provided an opportunity for an introduction to others (i.e., so-called snowball sampling). In other cases, people's connection to other actors made formal interviews untenable.

For example, I interviewed "Mark" on two separate occasions. During the interview, he told me about PL4M, a faith-based organization that had passed tips along to his unit. Based on Mark's reference, I reached out to PL4M and then interviewed "T" to learn about how the organization cooperates with police. T then told me about and connected me with a technology researcher with whom his group was in conversation. I spoke informally with the researcher by phone, but the researcher decided against a formal interview. However, by following up on Mark's initial referral, I had the chance to learn about how stakeholders in different cities and different organizations are connected to one another, connections that would not otherwise have been apparent in the context of a formal interview.

In intermittent phases, I observed different activities ranging from law-enforcement trainings, conferences, workshops, panel discussions, secular and faith-based human-trafficking-awareness bus tours, and task-force meetings focused on domestic sex trafficking. In some cases I participated more actively, such as by presenting on my research at non-academic events, which enabled me to interact with and on a few occasions share a panel with different professionals, advocates, experts, and members of the public interested in the topic. Of the meetings, training sessions, and gatherings I observed, some were open to the public, while others were by invitation only. In both instances, I took field notes and gathered materials that circulated from these gatherings. With respect to closed (i.e., nonpublic) activities, I was invited or asked and received permission to attend by the person with the authority to make such a decision, and I was there in my capacity as a researcher studying human trafficking. I visited courtrooms, holding cells, interview rooms, and suspects' apartments with police officers and was also able to spend an afternoon at the Dreams & Destiny shelter before interviews took place there, a visit I count as one of the highlights of this project.

Having had the opportunity to observe and, in some situations, directly participate in a variety of activities helped me to, as sociologist Nikki Jones has put it, "complement, supplement, test, and at times verify"[23] concepts, insights, and information gathered from interviews and informal conversations. I analyzed data by looking for patterns, recurring themes, and anomalies. Whenever a topic or theme emerged in an interview that I had not heard of or that seemed novel, I took steps verify its accuracy. I did this because I thought it important to determine if what I was hearing about was isolated or part of a broader trend. To offer one example, two police officers I interviewed separately mentioned partnerships they had cultivated with nonstate actors and named the organizations that had accompanied them before and/or after street sweeps and hotel raids. Because some of the nonprofits mentioned by the officers don't advertise this specific type of collaborative partnership with law enforcement, I tried to find other ways to substantiate these claims. Eventually, I interviewed a faith-based advocate who told me that she had accompanied a police unit in her jurisdiction on eleven separate street sweeps. She said she had stopped going on these sweeps because she found them ineffective, which might explain why she was willing to speak with me about the topic. However, though such practices aren't necessarily indicative of a widespread trend, it gave me insight about a type of collaboration between law enforcement and different nonstate actors that isn't isolated.

There are limitations to this study that are important to flag. First, the participants featured in this book do not represent a random sample of antitrafficking actors or people officially identified or who are deemed at risk of domestic sex trafficking. Instead, they are a select group of people geographically located throughout the United States, mostly in cities.[24] Another limitation of this study is that I do not include details of the actual cities and regions where respondents are located. This is purposeful. No matter how "imagined"[25] and expansive the antitrafficking community may be, it is still relatively small, and in my experience, the people in it are pretty well connected. Again, minimizing risks to anyone who formally or informally spoke with me as part of this research has been my number one priority, and one way I sought to do this was to remove personally identifiable information as well as the geographic location in which the activities took place.

The number of formal interviews and informal conversations is limited. What the number does not reveal are the years spent researching human trafficking in the United States for my dissertation and the large pool of antitrafficking actors I have met in the ensuing years. For instance, I have met and/or spoken to different law-enforcement agents, prosecutors, probation officers, nongovernmental advocates, technology stakeholders, judges, a member of a congressman's staff, trafficking survivor-advocates, researchers, and interested members of the public, none of whom I formally interviewed, but whom I met in the course of researching trafficking over the course of many years. I think this detail is important with respect to accounting for how I made sense of what I was seeing, because in my experience, it was sometimes a casual or oft-hand remark in a public context—a postconference discussion, for instance—that would focus my attention on an issue that wouldn't otherwise be apparent in a more formal interview or observational activities.

People's perceptions shape claims about trafficking, ideas that in turn shape antitrafficking interventions. Though it was not possible for me to verify or confirm each person's claims, especially about their experiences, wherever possible, I asked those I spoke with for more information or tried to determine whether what was being described was grounded in reality, even if the data or evidence used to initiate such efforts were based on perceptions. For example, if someone called trafficking a modern-day form of slavery, I didn't question this, despite scholarship that challenges such a conceptual pairing. But if a particular practice or technique was discussed, I tried to learn more about it.

As other scholars have noted, "trafficking" is an ill-fitting term to describe different forms of exploitation. Those now called "trafficked" share "little more than their legal status," Denise Brennan points out.[26] Joel Quirk's elaboration of the trafficking problem additionally highlights some of the methodological challenges it raises. For instance when "trafficking," "forced labor," and "modern-day slavery" are treated as interchangeable or conflated into an aggregate of otherwise disparate sociolegal phenomena, the challenge lies in determining (a) whether the activities lumped together under the "trafficking" or forced-labor rubric are sufficiently similar to warrant empirical comparison, and (b) whether the data folded into this framework adequately capture the complex dimensions of each phenomenon, or if the frame instead obscures important differences among them. The conflation of otherwise distinct phenomena not only makes it extraordinarily difficult to gauge the scope or scale of the global trafficking or forced-labor problem accurately, a challenge Quirk deftly depicts,[27] but risks contributing to misaligned antitrafficking interventions that don't necessarily work or fit the context of the situation.

By way of methodological reflection, in locating particular, specific, and locally circumscribed activities surrounding domestic sex trafficking under the umbrella of "antitrafficking," I have similarly (and perhaps for some, problematically) conflated otherwise distinct countertrafficking activities, for instance, by presuming that efforts to address domestic sex trafficking are one and the same thing as efforts to respond to nonsexual forms of labor exploitation and trafficking involving migrants. This is another limitation of the study and the framework I have used. Yet what I nonetheless find striking is the relative consistency of the discursive and practical effects of antitrafficking as it has shifted from a focus on migrants and is now applied to domestic victims. Migrants and domestic victim populations may not have very much in common except an at-risk status that may lead to both becoming the targets of antitrafficking interventions.

Finally, it is important to stress that my own knowledge of domestic sex trafficking and collaborative antitrafficking efforts in the United

States is partial, "situated,"[28] and shaped by the belief that criminalizing people and limiting their ability to make decisions about their own lives, irrespective of whether they or others see their situations as exploitative, is not the best way to help them. This perspective has undoubtedly trained my attention to particular dimensions of the issue, especially the punitive dimensions. There are of course other sides, facets, and dimensions to the story, and there are details that people I met with, interviewed, and observed talked about that aren't included. I make no claims that this is the "whole" story or the only story. Nor do I seek to draw neat conclusions where my insights and knowledge are limited. This is why, throughout the book, I have used the word "may" a lot. Though this may frustrate some readers, researching and writing this book has helped me to become more comfortable in articulating that which I don't know. I am indebted to anthropologists Anthony Marcus and Edward Snajdr, who observe that though more "self conscious" critical ethnographies on trafficking have begun to emerge, the field is nonetheless marked by its "preliminary and provisional" status, moving "towards" clearer understanding even if full insight has yet to fully arrive.[29]

I don't regard *Control and Protect* as a definitive bookend to the antitrafficking story, but rather as one effort among others to reach a fuller understanding of it.[30] My hope is that this book will spark conversation, debate, and research to more fully account for the multifaceted dimensions of antitrafficking efforts and come up with better ways to promote justice for people who have experienced exploitation.

Notes

PREFACE

1. Maxwell, "Law to Shelter Child Sex Trafficking Victims Could Strain Resources."

2. Ibid.

3. The law was reauthorized in 2008 and 2013. U.S. Congress, *Victims of Trafficking and Violence Protection Act of 2000; William Wilberforce Trafficking Victims Reauthorization Act of 2008; Trafficking Victims Protection Act Reauthorization of 2013*.

4. Hebert, "Sexual Politics," 87.

5. Trafficking Victims Protection Act.

6. The discussion of this in Quirk, "Introduction," is particularly insightful and I return to it in the Appendix.

7. Bernstein, "Carceral Politics as Gender Justice?"; Bernstein, "Introduction."

8. Schilt and Westbrook, "Doing Gender," 461, define "cisgender" as referring to "individuals who have a match between the gender they were assigned at birth, their bodies, and their personal identity." This book focuses primarily on cisgender trafficked girls and women. More research is needed to understand transgender and genderqueer experiences with commercial sex and the respective navigation of antitrafficking policies and systems of response.

9. Discursively conflating human trafficking with slavery is politically expedient, not only for the symbolic weight it carries, but also in its authorization of contemporary antislavery projects whose expansion into new institutional, political, and discursive realms is made possible precisely because of what its seemingly exceptional yet definitionally ambiguous status belies. In this book, I do not delve into comparisons between human trafficking and modern-day slavery, since they have received in-depth treatment elsewhere—see, e.g., Quirk, *Anti-slavery Project;* Bravo, "Exploring the Analogy."

10. Chuang, "Rescuing Trafficking."

11. Vance, "States of Contradiction."

12. Brennan, "Competing Claims of Victimhood?"; Stolz, "Interpreting the U.S. Human Trafficking Debate."

13. Brennan, *Life Interrupted*, 65.

14. Hughes, "Hiding in Plain Sight."

15. Bernstein's research has analyzed Department of Justice data reporting 2,515 human trafficking investigations that took place between 2008 and 2010. Of the "389 confirmed incidents of trafficking," she notes, "85% were sex-trafficking cases, 83% of victims were U.S. citizens, and 62% of confirmed sex-trafficking suspects were African American, while 25% of all suspects were Hispanic/Latino" (Bernstein, "Carceral Politics as Gender Justice?" 253; U.S. Department of Justice, Bureau of Justice Statistics, "Characteristics of Suspected Human Trafficking Incidents").

16. Bernstein, "Carceral Politics as Gender Justice?"; Michelle Alexander, *New Jim Crow;*

17. Michelle Alexander, *New Jim Crow*, 2.

18. Law, "Against Carceral Feminism," Bumiller, *In an Abusive State;* Bernstein, "Carceral Politics as Gender Justice?"

19. Aradau, *Rethinking Trafficking in Women*, 14.

20. For an in-depth examination of how carceral politics shape antitrafficking efforts in the United States, see also Bernstein, "Carceral Politics as Gender Justice?" 253; Bernstein, "Militarized Humanitarianism Meets Carceral Feminism," and Bernstein, "Introduction."

21. Dess, "Walking the Freedom Trail," 172–73.

22. Children's Advocacy Center, "Support to End Exploitation Now."

23. Dess, "Walking the Freedom Trail," 73; Musto, "Domestic Minor Sex Trafficking."

24. See also Bernstein, "Militarized Humanitarianism Meets Carceral Feminism"; Bernstein, "Carceral Politics as Gender Justice?"; Bernstein, "Sexual Politics."

25. Christian, "20+ Arrested in Houston Prostitution Busts."

26. Ibid.

27. Bernstein, "Militarized Humanitarianism Meets Carceral Feminism"; Bernstein, "Carceral Politics as Gender Justice?"

28. U.S. Department of Justice, Office of Justice Programs, "Office for Victims of Crime: Announcements," March 2015 announcement titled "*Funding Opportunity: FY 2015 Enhanced Collaborative Model to Combat Human Trafficking.*"

29. To the last point, I have also tried to heed the critical insight that "no research ought to be done about sex work without input and accountability to sex workers rights' groups." "'Nothing for Us without Us.'"

30. For discussions of moral panics and melodramas in historical and contemporary representations of trafficking, see Weitzer, "Social Construction of Sex Trafficking"; Vance, "States of Contradiction."

31. Aradau, *Rethinking Trafficking in Women*, 14.

32. Vance suggests that "trafficking" operates like a shorthand where victims are assumed to be women and girls and where trafficking for sex is deemed

its most legible and "common form" despite research to the contrary. See Vance, "Innocence and Experiences," 201.

33. A 2015 Urban Institute Report, the first of its kind on "self-reported engagement in survival sex" in New York City, has drawn attention to the fact that transgender and gender-nonconforming youth, queer, lesbian, gay, and bisexual teens, as well as young men who have sex with men (YMSM) and young women who have sex with women (YWSW), engage in survival sex, and thus technically qualify as domestic sex trafficking victims too, even if some do not describe their experiences as such. The report features many important findings including this: "Of the 107 respondents who were asked, less than a quarter reported being profiled by police as trading sex, but all of them reported being *profiled by the police*" (Dank et al., "Surviving the Streets of New York," 32). Perhaps what this suggests is that LGBTQ youth, YMSM, and YWSW who engage in survival sex experience a particular form of gendered punishment without the gloss of protection attached to it (ibid., 2).

34. Elizabeth Bernstein has astutely traced the interconnections between trafficking, neoliberalism, and the carceral state and her research has been path-breaking in shaping the field of critical trafficking studies in general and theorizing neoliberalism and trafficking in particular. See Bernstein, "Carceral Politics as Gender Justice?"; Bernstein, "Introduction."

INTRODUCTION

1. Prokupecz, "NYPD Conducts Pre-Super Bowl Crackdown."

2. United States, Federal Bureau of Investigation, "Sixteen Juveniles Recovered."

3. Wolf, "FBI: 16 Teens Rescued."

4. Vance, "Innocence and Experience."

5. Mogulescu, "The Super Bowl and Sex Trafficking."

6. Mitchell, "Romancing Rescue"; Boff, "Silence on Violence"; Global Alliance against Traffic in Women, "What's the Cost of a Rumour?"

7. Mogulescu, "The Super Bowl and Sex Trafficking."

8. Schneiderman, "To the Editor."

9. Sanctuaries for Families, "Super Bowl Shifts the Spotlight on Sex Trafficking."

10. Schneiderman, "To the Editor."

11. In their edited collection *Theorizing NGOs: States, Feminism, and Neoliberalism,* editors Bernal and Grewal suggest that "The scholarly feminist work on NGOs collected here reveals the fluidity between the supposedly separate domains of state and society." Bernal and Grewal, *Theorizing NGOs,* 6. Earlier versions of my published work have similarly explored the overlap between state and nonstate responses to trafficking. Musto, "The NGO-ification"; Musto, "Institutionalizing Protection." I argued that newfound collaborative partnerships between NGOs and law enforcement agents resulted in NGO's greater dependency on the state. Rather than operating autonomously or independently from the state, I found that NGOs, particularly those antitrafficking NGOs that receive state funding, function as proxy or "satellite" arms

of the state. Musto, "The NGO-ification." I described this process as the "the NGO-ification of the anti-trafficking movement," a theme akin to what Bernal and Grewal call the "NGO-ization" of the state. Musto, "The NGO-ification," 7.

12. In an attempt to reduce the number of prostitutes cycling through the criminal justice systems, prostitution-diversion programs have been introduced throughout the United States. The Midtown Manhattan Community STAR program for instance, was featured in a Center for Court Innovation report. As the report states, several courts in New York have sought to reduce recidivism by creating a court program to divert "prostituted women" to services and support through a court-monitored process—with "comprehensive assessments, court monitoring, and . . . supportive services" to assist women out of a life of prostitution. Schweig, Malangone, and Goodman, *Prostitution Diversion Programs.* http://www.courtinnovation.org/research/prostitution-diversion-programs

13. For a discussion of the links between carceral politics, feminism, and antitrafficking efforts see also Bernstein, "The Sexual Politics"; Bernstein, "Militarized Humanitarianism Meets Carceral Feminism"; Bernstein, "Introduction."

14. I first published ideas about the concept of carceral protectionism in a 2010 article. I developed it further in my dissertation and expand its definition and meaning here. See Musto, "Carceral Protectionism"; Musto, "Institutionalizing Protection."

15. Williams has drawn attention to the "victim–offender dichotomy" among commercially sexually exploited youth (244). In my dissertation, I described how law enforcement viewed potential victims of sex trafficking as both victims and offenders and that they occupy the liminal subject position of "victim–offender" (190). For her part, Sine Plambech has offered accounts of Nigerian migrant sex workers in Denmark, at once viewed by immigration authorities as victims of sex trafficking and treated like criminals subject to detention and deportation. Plambech's ethnographic research of the in-between gray zone that migrant sex workers occupy and how these categories blur further still upon their return to Nigeria offers an illustrative example of how "trafficking" has produced victim–offender and victim–criminal subject positions for migrants and "domestic" groups alike, such as youth in the United States now seen as "at risk" of sex trafficking; Linda M. Williams, "Harm and Resilience among Prostituted Teens," 244; Musto, "Institutionalizing Protection," 190; Plambech, "Between 'Victims' and 'Criminals'"; Chapkis, "Trafficking, Migration, and the Law."

16. To protect the anonymity of Cara and others featured in this book, I have used pseudonyms. I have also changed identifiable details to protect participants' anonymity, including the names of the organizations they represent; e.g., Sunny Dawn is a pseudonym for a faith-based shelter housing sex-trafficked youth.

17. This is not to suggest, however, that there is uniform agreement among service providers who work with domestic victims about how to secure their safety, as Clare Renzetti's research illuminates. Moreover, Renzetti found that social service providers she interviewed described their relationships with law enforcement as fraught. Yet, even as most service providers Renzetti interviewed found the trend "problematic," her finding that "all...noted that most sex trafficking

victims access services through the criminal justice" lends support to my broader argument about the persistence of carceral modes of protection for "at risk" domestic populations. Renzetti, "Service Providers and Their Perceptions of the Service Needs of Sex Trafficking Victims in the United States," 143; 146.

18. National Conference of State Legislatures, "Legislative Intent of 'Safe Harbor' Laws."

19. Geist, "Finding Safe Harbor."

20. Justice for Victims of Trafficking Act.

21. E.g., Sherman, "Justice for Girls." As I was completing the revisions for this book, I became aware of a forthcoming law review article that addresses some of these same topics, including New York's and other states' Safe Harbor and vacatur laws addressing DMST. For a discussion of the laws and punitive treatment of underage persons involved in the sex trade, including the "arrest institutional approach," see Conner, "In Loco Aequitatis."

22. Vance, "Thinking Trafficking, Thinking Sex," 139.

23. The law has subsequently been reauthorized in 2008 and 2013. U.S. Congress, *Victims of Trafficking and Violence Protection Act of 2000*; U.S. Congress, *William Wilberforce Trafficking Victims Reauthorization Act of 2008*; U.S. Congress, *Trafficking Victims Protection Act Reauthorization of 2013*.

24. Antitrafficking laws and activities focused on domestic sex trafficking in the United States follow a pattern that scholars have observed of trafficking instruments focused on migrants—for instance, the 2000 UN Convention Against Transnational Organized Crime: the Palermo Protocol. The link lies in the fact that calling a legal instrument victim centered or human rights focused is discursive, not necessarily prescriptive. As Anderson and Andrijasevic observe, "The Palermo Protocol . . . is not a human rights instrument. It is an instrument designed to facilitate cooperation between states to combat organised crime, rather than to protect or give restitution to the victims of crime. States are to strengthen border controls to prevent trafficking and smuggling. Border controls and police cooperation, not human rights protection, lies at the heart of both the smuggling and trafficking protocols." Bridget Anderson and Andrijasevic, "Sex, Slaves and Citizens," 136.

25. Plambech, "Between 'Victims' and 'Criminals'"; Chapkis, "Trafficking, Migration, and the Law."

26. Chuang, "Rescuing Trafficking."

27. Haynes, "Used, Abused, Arrested and Deported."

28. In her book, *In an Abusive State,* Bumiller draws attention to the ways in which "routine law enforcement blur the distinction between victim and criminal." As Bumiller's discussion of criminal-justice responses to domestic violence and rape further suggests, victims can effectively be transformed into "perpetrators in the eyes of the law." Bumiller's work rightly highlights how the model of criminalization, whether to address rape, domestic violence, or domestic sex trafficking, produces victim and criminal subjects which holds the potential to turn victims into perpetrators. Bumiller, *In an Abusive State,* 14.

29. Dess, for instance has called for mandatory police training at the state level. Dess, "Walking the Freedom Trail."

30. Gottschalk, *Caught,* 1.

31. Young Women's Empowerment Project, *Girls Do What They Have to Do to Survive.*

32. Sharon Oselin refers to police as "discretionary enforcers of law" and refers to this type of police power as a pivot to argue that collaboration between police and prostitute-serving organizations could potentially enhance rather than blunt street-based prostitutes' safety. Oselin, *Leaving Prostitution.* Yet Oselin's argument that collaborations can change perceptions and possibly improve interactions between prostitutes and police implicitly hinges on an ideological contingency. Namely, that in order for PSOs and former sex workers (and I would add victims of sex trafficking) to collaborate with police, they would need to acquiesce to the law-enforcement strategy of criminalizing prostitution, even if criminalization here does not mean arresting or incarcerating prostitutes themselves, but is aimed instead at clients or "buyers." This research complicates the idea that collaboration between different state and nonstate actors always de facto leads to positive outcomes for voluntary sex workers and sex trafficking victims alike even as some self-identified victims of sex trafficking may welcome it along with carceral forms of protection more generally. Self-identified survivors of sex trafficking, like prostitutes who do not view themselves as victims, are not, after all, a homogenous group. Even if collaboration is welcome by some, this does not discount the fact it can still lead to stepped up forms of social control for all women and girls involved in various sex trades, insights this book highlights.

33. Bernstein, "Militarized Humanitarianism Meets Carceral Feminism," 65.

34. Ibid. See also Bernstein, "The Sexual Politics."

35. See also Bumiller for a discussion of responses to sexual assault. Bumiller, *In an Abusive State,* 14.

36. Lacey, "District Attorney Jackie Lacey Unveils New Program."

37. An examination of antitrafficking interventions helps to shed light on how and why voluntary sex workers as well as youth and adults in coercive situations have been targets of heightened policing and criminal justice interventions. It also allows us to better understand how and why antitrafficking efforts have negative consequences not just for victims of sex trafficking, but for sex workers deemed "at risk" and who have similarly been targets of law-enforcement raids. See Ditmore and Project Urban Justice Center, *Sex Workers, Kicking Down the Door.*

38. Vance, "States of Contradiction."

39. Chacón, "Tensions and Trade-Offs."

40. Andrijasevic, *Migration, Agency, and Citizenship.*

41. Bernstein, "Militarized Humanitarianism Meets Carceral Feminism"; Chuang, "Rescuing Trafficking"; Doezema, *Sex Slaves and Discourse Masters;* Weitzer, "The Social Construction of Sex Trafficking"; Chapkis, "Soft Glove, Punishing Fist"; O'Connell Davidson, "Real Sex Slave"; Kempadoo and Doezema, eds., *Global Sex Workers;* Vance, "Innocence and Experience."

42. Koken, "Meaning of the 'Whore,'" 29.

43. Neoabolitionism situates girls and women's participation in commercial sex as intrinsically and transhistorically exploitative. See Outshoorn, "The Political Debates on Prostitution and Trafficking of Women"; Jeffreys, "Prostitution,

Trafficking and Feminism"; Hughes, "The 'Natasha' Trade"; Pateman, *The Sexual Contract;* Barry, *Female Sexual Slavery.* They argue that all forms of prostitution are involuntary and a form of sex trafficking regardless of whether those who participate in the sex trade see their labor as voluntary. Priscilla Alexander, "Prostitution"; Kempadoo and Doezema, eds., *Global Sex Workers.*

44. Farley, *Prostitution and Trafficking in Nevada.*

45. Abolition is further described as something "no woman can ever consent to" in Vance "Innocence and Experience, 202." See also Barry, *The Prostitution of Sexuality;* Hughes, *Trafficking for Sexual Exploitation.*

46. Boris and Salazar Parreñas, eds., *Intimate Labors;* Brents and Hausbeck, "Sex Work Now"; Bernstein, *Temporarily Yours.*

47. Koken, "The Meaning of the 'Whore.'"

48. Ibid., 62; Bernstein, *Temporarily Yours;* Limoncelli, "The Trouble with Trafficking"; Andrijasevic, *Migration, Agency, and Citizenship.*

49. Ditmore, "Trafficking in Lives"; Weitzer, "The Social Construction of Sex Trafficking."

50. Koken, "The Meaning of the 'Whore,'" 44.

51. Chuang, "Rescuing Trafficking." The mainstreaming of neoabolitionist politics is illustrated by Nicholas Kristof's regular *New York Times* features on sex trafficking and the bevy of print and online commentators who now roundly spotlight stories of trafficked victims' exploitation in the sex trade. This mainstreaming has been possible thanks to increased focus on trafficked persons' age. Kristof, "She Has a Pimp's Name Etched on Her."

52. Marcus et al., "Is Child to Adult." Here it is also important to note that youth do not always describe their experiences in terms of force, fraud, or coercion. For instance, in a 2015 report focused on LGBTQ youth, young men who have sex with men, and young women who have sex with women by the Urban Institute and Streetwise and Safe, researchers found that only 15% of youth they interviewed who trade sex in New York City reported exploitative situations even though they meet the federal definition of a victim of sex trafficking. Dank et al., "Surviving the Streets of New York," 68.

53. O'Connell Davidson, *Prostitution, Power, and Freedom,* 28.

54. Agustín, *Sex at the Margins.*

55. Weitzer, "The Social Construction of Sex Trafficking," 459; Musto, "What's in a Name?"

56. Congdon, "Speaking of 'Dead Prostitutes.'"

57. Rights4Girls, "Members of Congress Join Rights4Girls."

58. Dawson, "No Such Thing as a Child Prostitute."

59. Saar, "Stop Calling Kids 'Child Prostitutes.'"

60. Vance draws critical attention to the limits of protectionist interventions, observing: "by definition, [interventions] that aim to rescue the victim, with no consultation about the remedies desired by differentially situated people are patronizing, as well as ineffective." Vance "Innocence and Experience," 211.

61. Kim, "Lost Children"; Vance, "States of Contradiction."

62. Curtis et al., *The Commercial Sexual Exploitation of Children in New York City,* 1.

63. Ibid.

64. Bureau of Justice Statistics, "Arrest Data Analysis Tool." See also Chesney-Lind and Shelden who point out that youth "contacts" with police exceed the number of actual youth arrested. *Girls, Delinquency, and Juvenile Justice,* 19.

65. Federal Bureau of Investigation, "Sixteen Juveniles Recovered."

66. My use of "shadow" here draws inspiration from Jennifer Wolch's description of "shadow states." Just as punitive antitrafficking efforts may be read as the shadow side of victim protection efforts, so too do these efforts emerge within the interstices of a "shadow state" where nongovernmental, non-profit, and corporate actors collaborate to fill in the slack of a welfare state in retreat. See Wolch, "The Shadow State," 201–2.

67. Chapkis, "Soft Glove, Punishing Fist"; Musto, "Domestic Minor Sex Trafficking." As Vance observes, protectionist interventions sometimes mask their punitive effects, just as state antitrafficking masks the role it plays in contributing to the conditions that give rise to sex trafficking. "Vance "Innocence and Experience," 209; 211.

68. See Conner, "In Loco Aequitatis."

69. Global Alliance against Traffic in Women, "Collateral Damage"; Phillips and Coates, "Clearing the Slate."

70. Chuang, "Rescuing Trafficking"; Ditmore and Project Urban Justice Center, *Sex Workers, Kicking Down the Door.*

71. Gallagher, "Human Rights and Human Trafficking."

72. Ibid., 190. Gallagher and Pearson, "The High Cost of Freedom."

73. Agustín, *Sex at the Margins;* Gallagher, "Human Rights and Human Trafficking."

74. Bernstein and Shih, "The Erotics of Authenticity"; Shih, "The Anti-Trafficking Rehabilitation Complex."

75. Plambech, "Between 'Victims' and 'Criminals.'"

76. Lee, "Human Trafficking and Border Control," 135.

77. Conner, "In Loco Aequitatis."

78. Chacón, "Tensions and Trade-Offs," 1640.

79. Sudbury, "Celling Black Bodies," 71.

80. Bernstein, "Militarized Humanitarianism Meets Carceral Feminism"; Bernstein, "Introduction." See also Bernstein, "Carceral Politics as Gender Justice?" for an in-depth theoretical treatment of carceral politics, neoliberalism, and antitrafficking campaigns; Musto, "Domestic Minor Sex Trafficking."

81. Richie, *Arrested Justice,* 2.

82. Obama, *President Obama Speaks at the Clinton Global Initiative.*

83. Luibhéid, "Queering Migration and Citizenship," xxxii; Bernstein, "The Sexual Politics"; Wacquant, "Ordering Insecurity."

84. Bernstein, "Carceral Politics as Gender Justice?"; Bernstein, "Introduction."

85. Bumiller, *In an Abusive State,* 5, 6, 9, 162.

86. Gottschalk, *Caught,* 11.

87. Harvey, *A Brief History of Neoliberalism,* 33, 161–62.

88. Gottschalk, *Caught,* 13.

89. Ibid., 11.

90. Harvey, *A Brief History of Neoliberalism,* 76.

91. Weaver and Lerman, "Political Consequences of the Carceral State."

92. Gottschalk, *Caught*, 1–2.

93. Foucault, *Discipline and Punish*, 297–98

94. Gottschalk, *Caught*, 1.

95. Ibid., 11.

96. Harvey, *A Brief History of Neoliberalism*, 77.

97. Gottschalk, *Caught*, 31–32.

98. Ibid., 32.

99. Ibid., 3–4; Wacquant, "Deadly Symbiosis"; Michelle Alexander, *The New Jim Crow*.

100. Michelle Alexander, *The New Jim Crow*, 1; Gottschalk, *Caught*, 3.

101. Michelle Alexander, *The New Jim Crow*, 1; Gottschalk, *Caught*, 3.

102. Gottschalk, *Caught*, 4–6, 14.

103. See Elizabeth Bernstein for a discussion of the linkages between gender justice, antitrafficking, and carceral politics. Bernstein, "Carceral Politics as Gender Justice?" See also Kristen Bumiller for a discussion of neoliberalism and the ways its criminalized approaches to sexual violence are linked to an "increasingly punitive response of the state." Bumiller, *In an Abusive State*, 162.

104. Harvey, *A Brief History of Neoliberalism*, 76; Haney, *Offending Women*, 15–18.

105. Bernstein, "Militarized Humanitarianism Meets Carceral Feminism"; Bernstein, "Introduction."

106. Marchand and Sisson Runyan, "Introduction," 4.

107. Lind, "Querying Globalization."

108. Marchand and Sisson Runyan, "Introduction."

109. Kantola and Squires, "From State Feminism to Market Feminism?"

110. Harvey, *A Brief History of Neoliberalism*, 77.

111. Ibid., 76.

112. Bernstein, "Militarized Humanitarianism Meets Carceral Feminism," 47.

113. Ibid.; Slavery Footprint—Made in a Free World, "How Many Slaves Work for You?" See also Bumiller for a discussion of how, in the early part of the 21st century, sexual violence was figured as "everybody's problem" and thus invited a broad array of actors, experts, and professionals to detect and respond to it. Bumiller, *In an Abusive State*, 14.

114. See Lynne Haney's and Marie Gottschalk's separate work for a more in-depth discussion about how the carceral state does not, as might be expected, retreat under neoliberalism but rather expands it in diffuse directions. Haney, *Offending Women*, 96; Gottschalk, *Caught*, 13. For her part, Bernstein, argues that against the backdrop of a "devolving state," forms of governance rely on "state and nonstate actors." "Militarized Humanitarianism Meets Carceral Feminism," 67.

115. Gottschalk, *Caught*; Bernstein, "Militarized Humanitarianism Meets Carceral Feminism"; Bernstein, "Introduction."

116. Bernstein, "The Sexual Politics"; Bernstein, "Militarized Humanitarianism Meets Carceral Feminism."

117. Wijers et al., *Trafficking in Women*; Musto, "Institutionalizing Protection."

118. Braidotti, "A Critical Cartography," 5.

119. Scholars who have tracked antiviolence efforts advanced by feminist campaigns and in the service of gender justice—both antitrafficking and against sexual violence—have rightly called attention to the ways in which carceral and criminal-justice-focused efforts divert attention from structural conditions, including neoliberalism. See Bernstein, "Carceral Politics as Gender Justice?"; Bumiller, *In an Abusive State.*

120. Bernstein, "Militarized Humanitarianism Meets Carceral Feminism," 51; Bernstein, "Carceral Politics as Gender Justice?"

121. For a discussion of state surveillance practices unrelated to trafficking, see Ohm, "Fourth Amendment in a World Without Privacy," 1311.

122. The transformation of feminist campaigns to professionalized movement isn't unique to anti-sex-trafficking efforts as Kristen Bumillers's work on sexual violence has compellingly shown. Bumiller, *In an Abusive State,* 61–69.

123. In his book, *The Anti-slavery Project,* Joel Quirk offers a rousing account of the sociopolitical forces at play and the empirical and historiographical questions at stake when a particular phenomenon is analogized as slavery. He finds: "when we designate a problem a species of slavery, we are not only making an empirical claim about the subject at hand, but also invoking a preexisting ethical argument for uncompromising action to correct unconscionable evil." Quirk's insights about the exceptionality afforded to antislavery projects is important to a point I am trying to make here which is that linking domestic sex trafficking to modern-day slavery authorizes exceptional interventions, including varied collaborations between state and nonstate actors. Carceral feminist sensibilities are not necessarily displaced by this exceptional ethos so much as folded into it.

124. Wacquant, "Ordering Insecurity."

125. Ibid., 7.

126. Ibid., 11.

127. Ibid., 14.

128. Wacquant, *Punishing the Poor,* 14.

129. Gallagher, "Human Rights and Human Trafficking," 190; Spivak, "Terror."

130. Bernstein, "The Sexual Politics," 143. See also Bumiller, *In an Abusive State,* for a comparison.

131. Brennan, "Competing Claims of Victimhood?" 54.

132. I received a $5,000.00 unrestricted research grant from Microsoft to examine technology and sex trafficking from the perspective of law enforcement. Microsoft, "Microsoft Names Research Grant Recipients."

133. Flexibility is, as Freeman notes, a key attribute of neoliberalism. Freeman, *Entrepreneurial Selves,* 19.

134. For instance, Haney has critiqued the logic of "penal empowerment" that informs correctional facilities for women and notes that such "doublespeak has been around for centuries." Haney, "Working Through Mass Incarceration, 75–76. See also Haney, *Offending Women.*

135. Haney, *Offending Women,* 15.

136. boyd et al., "Human Trafficking and Technology."

137. A November 2015 conference sponsored by Shared Hope International featured workshop speakers from Albuquerque, New Mexico, who have developed what is described as "an innovative form of risk assessment and an algorithm for services and collaboration of law enforcement officials and clinicians." Shared Hope International, "2015 JuST Conference."
138. Shklovski et al., "The Commodification of Location."
139. Farrell and Fahy, "The Problem of Human Trafficking."
140. Davis, "The Future of Prison?"
141. Tonry, *The Future of Imprisonment*, 12.
142. Ibid., 22.
143. Davis, "The Future of Prison?" 10:57–12:03.
144. Youth records are presumed to be automatically sealed. However, in some situations, these records may be publically available or sold to private companies that gather and sell data, making it difficult to completely excise their criminal justice histories from the public record. Adults with criminal records as a result of their trafficking situations also face steep hurdles to vacate or expunge their records. Doing so requires consultation with experts familiar with the law and skilled in undoing the traces left in government and proprietary databases. I take up this discussion in greater depth in chapter 5. See also Wayne, "Data-Broker Threat."

CHAPTER 1

1. L.M. Williams, "Provide Justice"; Phillips and Coates, "Clearing the Slate." For an important discussion of trafficked persons' placement in "shelter detentions," as well as prisons, jails, and immigration detention centers, see Gallagher and Pearson, "High Cost of Freedom," 76. Gallagher and Pearson find that trafficked persons in countries and regions as far ranging as Bangladesh, Central and Eastern Europe, Thailand, Cambodia, Nigeria, and India, among others, have been "effectively imprisoned in government or private support facilities without being able to leave the shelter grounds beyond the occasional supervised excursion or trip to court" (77). Though the situations of sex trafficked U.S. citizens and legal residents differ from those of migrants, I think there is sufficient research to suggest that the United States is another country where anti-sex-trafficking interventions blur the boundaries between protection and punishment.
2. This research is in conversation with social scientists whose writings form a body of work I would call "critical trafficking studies": Bernstein, "Sexual Politics"; id., *Temporarily Yours;* id., "Militarized Humanitarianism"; id., "Carceral Politics"; id., "Introduction"; Vance, "States of Contradiction"; id., "Innocence and Experience"; Kempadoo and Doezema, eds., *Global Sex Workers;* Kempadoo, Sanghera, and Pattanaik, *Trafficking and Prostitution Reconsidered;* Doezema, *Sex Slaves and Discourse Masters;* Cheng and Kim, "Paradoxes of Neoliberalism"; Parreñas, *Illicit Flirtations;* Andrijasevic, *Migration, Agency, and Citizenship;* Plambech, "Between 'Victims' and 'Criminals'"; Bernstein and Shih, "Erotics of Authenticity"; Marcus et al., "Is Child to Adult." This brand of critical *anti*-antitrafficking research (see Marcus and Snajdr,

"Anti-anti-trafficking?") has its antecedents in scholarly works that emerged in the late 1990s and throughout the 2000s, research that challenged the narrow definition, ill-conceived conceptual framing, and "ideological capture" of anti-trafficking discourses and policies. See, e.g., Chuang, "Rescuing Trafficking"; Agustín, *Sex at the Margins;* Chapkis, "Trafficking, Migration, and the Law"; Kempadoo and Doezema, eds., *Global Sex Workers;* Doezema, "Forced to Choose"; Doezema, *Sex Slaves and Discourse Masters;* Ditmore, "Trafficking in Lives"; O'Connell Davidson, "Real Sex Slave"; Chang and Kim, "Reconceptualizing Approaches"; Weitzer, "Social Construction." Despite their varied conceptual aims, critical-trafficking scholars' projects share a commitment to understanding how antitrafficking policies and efforts promote "the exclusion, condemnation, or acceptance of particular migrants and workers" (Chapkis, "Trafficking, Migration, and the Law," 924), with additional attention to the effects of antitrafficking efforts on individuals who are identified and offered state protection, and the larger swath of irregular migrants, voluntary sex workers, and vulnerable populations who are not, but who are nonetheless subjected to antitrafficking interventions (Plambech, "Between 'Victims' and 'Criminals'"). This research further considers the intended and *unintended* consequences of antitrafficking efforts and eschews facile presumptions that all anti-trafficking efforts are inherently "good" or helpful to the populations that are subjected to them (Lindstrom, "Transnational Responses to Human Trafficking"; Vance, "Innocence and Experience," 200–201; Soderlund, "Running from the Rescuers") In sum, what is "critical" about critical-trafficking studies is the theoretical consideration of that which is elided, concealed, and obfuscated in the dominant scholarly treatment of the issue.

3. There are two bodies of work that inform my discussion here. What we now call domestic-minor sex trafficking has previously been discussed under the rubric of commercial sexual exploitation of children (CSEC). Critiques of the treatment of sex-trade-involved youth as offenders, not victims, have been raised by Sherman, "Justice for Girls," and L. M. Williams, "Harm and Resilience." L. M. Williams, "Provide Justice," 303, advocates a halt to arrests and prosecutions, and calls for broader shifts that include "meaningful partnerships with youth and social services." Yet antitrafficking partnerships between law enforcement and social-service providers may subject youth to additional forms of social control, even if these efforts are framed as a protective and victim-centered. Another body of research that informs my understanding of these topics focuses on interventions for migrants now seen as victims of trafficking who have endured different forms of punitive protection and rehabilitative detention. In India and Southeast Asia, e.g., "rescued" sex trafficking victims have run away from shelters and their rescuers and the "line between rescuers and captors has become increasingly blurry . . . the aftermath of raids often belie the claim that all of the rescued women are sex slaves held captive and against their will in brothels" (Soderlund, "Running from the Rescuers," 65). Ramachandran has also looked at rescue operations in India, drawing attention to the blurred lines between "protection, detention, and reform for sex workers, trafficked women, and individuals 'alleged' to be involved in sex work." On the "rehabilitative" detention of trafficked persons, sex workers, and people

deemed at risk of sexual exploitation in India, Ramachandran cited a shelter in Mumbai which inmates described as "worse than prison," see Ramachandran, "Protection/Detention/Reform," 6. And see also Gallagher and Pearson, "High Cost of Freedom," and Shih, "The Anti-Trafficking Rehabilitative Complex."

4. For a discussion of the arrest and detention of girls involved in commercial sex, see Sherman, "Justice for Girls," and L. M. Williams, "Provide Justice" and "Harm and Resilience." Brennan similarly observes that U.S. citizens and migrant victims of sex trafficking have experienced incarceration, all under the guise of rescuing them. Brennan, *Life Interrupted,* 38. See also Musto, "Domestic Minor Sex Trafficking."

5. In her research on gendered punishment, Haney observes how "government from a distance has created an environment of state hybridity," where public–private partnerships do the work of the state. Importantly, this does not signal the retreat of the state but the diffusion of the state through hybrid public-private partnerships. See Haney, *Offending Women,* 16.

6. Thakor and boyd, "Networked Trafficking," 284.

7. Aradau argues that humanitarian approaches to trafficking have opened up possibilities for knowledge transfer between NGOs and law-enforcement agents. Prompted by NGO advocacy, human-rights or victim-centered approaches to trafficking have been provisionally adopted by state and law-enforcement agents precisely because these allow them to pursue investigations more aggressively; there is "no contradiction between human rights and punitive law enforcement . . . human rights become part of the interventions to deal with trafficking . . . and are mobilized for the purposes of preventing the phenomenon," Aradau, *Rethinking Trafficking in Women,* argues (38). Aradau's analysis is critically important in its theorization of the overlap between state and nonstate responses to trafficking. One notable, albeit slight, distinction between her research and this project, however, is that "human rights" as a language and judicial framework are not what discursively and ideologically link nonprofit and social-service actors with law-enforcement partners in the United States. Rather, it is a protectionist, U.S.-centered discourse that focuses on the vulnerability of sex-trafficked women and girls that links state and nonstate approaches, even if "punitive" interventions like arrest and the prosecution of trafficker-pimps are among law enforcement's overarching goals.

8. Farrell and Fahy, "Problem of Human Trafficking," 624.

9. There is broad agreement that protective efforts are necessary in order to foster trafficked persons' empowerment and right to self-determination (Wijers, "Women, Labor, and Migration"). With acknowledgement of the complicated and highly contested nature of the politics of "rescue" (Agustín, *Sex at the Margins;* Soderlund, "Running from the Rescuers"), NGO advocates and social-service providers are nonetheless presumed to play a crucial role in protecting trafficked persons (Musto, "NGO-ification"; Chuang, "Beyond a Snapshot"; Brennan, "Methodological Challenges"; Aronowitz, "Smuggling and Trafficking in Human Beings"), and protective schemes promote a "victim-centered," "survivor-centered," or even "survivor-driven" approach to human trafficking. Conversely, state or criminal-justice approaches seek to apprehend and prosecute traffickers. Current antitrafficking laws depend upon victim cooperation

with law enforcement to identify and corroborate evidence against traffickers. Without cooperative victims, law-enforcement agents would be markedly hindered in their ability to pursue cases against traffickers. Yet a significant body of feminist and sex-worker-rights literature has emerged, which critically examines the weaknesses of antitrafficking efforts organized through the criminal-justice system, especially where victims are arrested first and offered protection later (Kempadoo, Sanghera, and Pattanaik, *Trafficking and Prostitution Reconsidered,* xix; Ditmore, *Use of Raids to Fight Trafficking*). This research challenges the dominant role that law-enforcement agents have been assigned under international and domestic trafficking policies, and questions law enforcement's centrality, concentrated power, and broad discretion in identifying victims of trafficking and managing their protection. These scholars further contend that historic legacies of police violence, incarceration, and harassment of voluntary sex workers have undermined antitrafficking efforts, and point to the ways in which voluntary and forced prostitutes alike have been harmed by antitrafficking "rescue raids" (Bernstein, *Temporarily Yours;* Ditmore, *Use of Raids to Fight Trafficking;* Soderlund, "Running from the Rescuers").

10. Although I did not see Kirsten Foot's book *Collaborating against Human Trafficking* before its publication in September 2015, I was able to skim the Introduction and parts of chapter 2 following correspondence with the author about two specific questions I had regarding her research. Foot provides an important summary of government initiatives that have advanced collaboration, including a description of Office for Victims of Crime, Bureau of Justice Assistance, and the Enhanced Collaborative Model to Combat Human Trafficking grants (ibid., 4–5).

11. Brennan, *Life Interrupted,* 65. U.S. Attorney's Office, District of Massachusetts, "Massachusetts Task Force to Combat Human Trafficking."

12. Federal Bureau of Investigation, "Innocence Lost."

13. Colorado and Washington State aside, "state funding for coordinating partnerships to counter human trafficking is nonexistent in most of the United States" (Foot, *Collaborating against Human Trafficking,* 35–37). Tracking the amount of money and resources allocated to antitrafficking collaborations is complicated by the fact that they are not orchestrated solely by federal or state authorities. Individuals, nongovernmental, faith-based, private foundations, and businesses contribute to antitrafficking efforts too, and as Foot points out, we really don't have a full picture of antitrafficking funding since "there has been no large-scale analysis to date on the amount of funding given to counter-trafficking efforts from each category of donor" (37).

14. See Haney, *Offending Women,* for an in-depth discussion of how governance strategies function in settings organized around gendered punishment that are not specific to human or sex trafficking.

15. U.S. Department of Justice, Bureau of Justice Assistance, "Anti-human Trafficking Task Force Initiative."

16. U.S. Department of Justice, "Human Trafficking Task Forces."

17. Scholars have consistently pointed out that not all human trafficking is sex trafficking, that sex work is sociolegally distinct from sex trafficking, and a combination of sketchy data (Vance, "States of Contradiction"), and panics

about irregular border crossing (Chacón, "Tensions and Trade-Offs") and women's sexual labor and agency in the commercial sex trade (Andrijasevic, *Migration, Agency, and Citizenship*) have contributed to empirically uninformed expectations that sex trafficking is a more egregious problem than other forms of labor exploitation. See also Bernstein, "Sexual Politics"; id., "Militarized Humanitarianism"; Chuang, "Rescuing Trafficking"; Weitzer, "Social Construction"; Agustín, *Sex at the Margins;* Chapkis, "Soft Glove, Punishing Fist"; Kempadoo and Doezema, eds., *Global Sex Workers;* O'Connell Davidson, "Real Sex Slave"; Chang and Kim, "Reconceptualizing Approaches."

18. MacKinnon, "Trafficking, Prostitution, and Inequality"; Jeffreys, "'Brothels without Walls'"; Farley, *Prostitution, Trafficking, and Traumatic Stress;* id., *Prostitution and Trafficking in Nevada.*

19. Hughes, *Trafficking for Sexual Exploitation;* Farley, *Prostitution, Trafficking, and Traumatic Stress.*

20. Bernstein's discussion of carceral feminism and the neoabolitionist politics that shape it are part of a broader "neoliberal sexual agenda" (Bernstein, "Sexual Politics," 143). Carceral feminist antitrafficking politics follow broader neoliberal shifts, such as the use of the criminal-justice system to address social problems, which "locates social problems in deviant individuals rather than mainstream institutions" (137). See also Bernstein, "Militarized Humanitarianism"; Bernstein, "Carceral Politics." On gender, punishment, and the prison-industrial complex, see also Sudbury, "Celling Black Bodies"; Sudbury, "Unpacking the Crisis"; Gilmore and Marshall, "Girls in Crisis"; Law, "Against Carceral Feminism"; Davis, *Are Prisons Obsolete?* Enforcement regimes such as immigration detention and deportation target migrant women and girls involved in the sex trade (Kempadoo, "Victims and Agents of Crime"). However, people involved in the sex trade in general, and U.S.-born victims in particular, are the most recent groups to find themselves caught up in the antitrafficking protection net and the prison-industrial complex (Sudbury, "Celling Black Bodies," 71). What is missing from mainstream discussions about domestic minor sex trafficking are the ways in which antitrafficking efforts have also contributed to the expansion of the criminal and juvenile-justice systems.

21. Bernal and Grewal, *Theorizing NGOs.*

22. Harvey, *Brief History of Neoliberalism;* Lind, "Querying Globalization," 53; Haney, *Offending Women,* 16.

23. Bernal and Grewal, *Theorizing NGOs,* 10.

24. Bernstein, "Sexual Politics," 137.

25. Gottschalk, *Caught,* 13; Haney, *Offending Women,* 16.

26. Ibid.

27. For an important discussion of sexual violence and its links to neoliberalism and criminalized responses to gender violence, see Bumiller, *In an Abusive State,* 146. Though focused on rape and domestic violence, she also touches on criminalized approaches to trafficking as the most "logical and effective way to solve the problem."

28. U.S. Department of Justice, Bureau of Justice Assistance, "FY 2015 Enhanced Collaborative Model."

29. Lind, "Querying Globalization," 53.

30. Haney, *Offending Women.*

31. Specialized court and diversion programs have emerged to assist sex-trade-involved youth as victims rather than as criminals. Yet even where programs are framed as alternatives to the punitive interventions of the past, they still rely on arrests as a mechanism for referring victims to services. Programs such as the First Step Program in Los Angeles County operate as an "arrest referral" to accessing "counseling, classes, and community services" (Conner, "In Loco Aequitatis," 20; and see also Banks, "First Step Program").

32. Conner, "In Loco Aequitatis," 6; Sherman, "Justice for Girls." Linda M. Williams, "Harm and Resilience among Prostituted Teens," 244. Renzetti, "Service Providers and Their Perceptions of the Service Needs of Sex Trafficking Victims in the United States," 148.

33. Brennan, "Competing Claims of Victimhood?"; L. M. Williams, "Harm and Resilience," 244.

34. I draw this distinction because some self-identified survivors of domestic sex trafficking have begun to tell their stories publicly years after the fact.

35. For an in-depth discussion of Safe Harbor laws in New York and its punitive effects, see Conner, "In Loco Aequitatis."

36. Ibid. House of Representatives, "Stop Exploitation Through Trafficking Act of 2015."

37. Brennan, "Key Issues in the Resettlement."

38. Conner, "In Loco Aequitatis," 6.

39. Fassin and Rechtman, *Empire of Trauma.*

40. Conner, "In Loco Aequitatis," 3.

41. Becca also noted that she disapproves of contract organizations that go into juvenile hall and "cherry-pick." By this, I think she meant occasions where organizations select the victims they want to work with in order to "keep them in juvenile hall so they can testify." Becca's observation highlights another trend, namely that more programs have been brought into carceral spaces where youth reside. The My Life, My Choice (MLMC) program, for instance, has been integrated into "juvenile justice facilities" in order to give "law enforcement and service providers tools to identify victims and vulnerable youth and connect them to services" (My Life, My Choice, "Giving Law Enforcement and Service Providers Tools").

42. See also Bumiller, *In an Abusive State.*

43. The distinction I seek to make here is between gendered forms of punishment leveraged in the service of victims' protection and gendered forms of punishment aimed at women and girls who are seen as more "typical" offenders but subject to rehabilitation, therapy, or empowerment efforts as part of their punishment. With respect to the latter, see further Haney, *Offending Women;* Sered and Norton-Hawk, *Can't Catch a Break.*

44. For brief histories of the juvenile-justice system's treatment of girls involved in prostitution, see Sherman, "Justice for Girls"; Conner, "In Loco Aequitatis."

45. Bumiller discusses "softer forms of power" in the context of neoliberalism and how "more state and quasi state actors become part of a network of responders to sexual violence" (*In an Abusive State,* 8). Her note that some

organizations become "central to the policing function of the state" is notewor-thy (6). Moreover, as the soft rooms and softened carceral processes I learned about from law enforcement demonstrate, the integration of social service prin-ciples, for instance, ideas about trauma and victim centeredness can likewise transform police and law-enforcement activities, even as at-risk victims' reha-bilitation reaffirms the primacy of the carceral state.

46. Notably, only one of the organizations advertises the kind of work it does with law enforcement publicly.

47. For adults seen as potential victims of forced prostitution, the placement options are even slimmer.

48. Haynes, "Used, Abused, Arrested and Deported," 244.

49. Chacón, "Tensions and Trade-Offs," 1626–27.

50. Rieger, "Missing the Mark," 242.

51. Musto, "Posthuman Anti-trafficking Turn."

52. H.E.A.T. Watch, "Alameda County District Attorney's Office."

53. L. M. Williams, "Provide Justice," 300.

54. Ibid.

55. Ibid.

56. In a humorous yet informative exchange, I asked Tory how her cases are "referred" to her. She laughed at my use of benevolent language for such a punitive process. She explained that clients are assigned to her when they get arrested. In a follow-up email about the discussion, she said "referral" is not a term that is used in adult criminal courts. Therein laid my confusion. The TVPA defines any victim of domestic sex trafficking under eighteen as a child, but in New York State, sixteen- and seventeen-year-olds are treated as adults. As Chesney-Lind and Shelden note:"[C]hildren in many parts of the United States are 'referred' to the court rather than be arrested; instead of being held in jail pending court action, they are 'detained' in a 'detention center' or 'adjustment center'; rather than being indicted, children are petitioned to the court; in place of a determination of guilt, there is an 'adjudication,' and those found guilty (i.e., adjudicated) are often 'committed' to a 'training school' or 'reform school' rather than being sentenced to prison" (Chesney-Lind and Shelden, *Girls, Delinquency, and Juvenile Justice,* 194). I had wrongly assumed that since Tory worked with sixteen- and seventeen-year-olds, it was in the context of the juve-nile-justice system. As the exchange clarified, however, depending on the state in which a person is identified as "trafficked," a kid or teen under eighteen involved in prostitution is either "referred" to a juvenile court or arrested and assigned to a public defender in an adult criminal court (Conner, "In Loco Aequitatis," 20, calls this process: "arrest-referral").

57. P. L. Brown, "Court's All-Hands Approach"; Lippman, "Announcement of New York's Human Trafficking Intervention Initiative."

58. See Conner, "In Loco Aequitatis," 21, for a discussion of arrest-referral.

59. On migrants who are treated like victims and criminals, see Plambech, "Between 'Victims' and 'Criminals.'" Linda Williams has similarly argued that "social (and even legal) responses" to youth involved in various sex trades sug-gest that in many states "youth can be arrested and charged in criminal courts" (L. M. Williams, "Harm and Resilience," 244). She identifies "victims, offenders,

and survivors" as three overlapping identities of prostituted teens and argues that a survivor-centered identity "poses a challenge to the victim–offender dichotomy" (244). Anti-sex-trafficking efforts in general and collaborations between state and nonstate actors in particular challenge the resiliency of the survivor-centered approach Williams develops. Moreover, the fact that some police utilize survivor-centered language when describing carcerally focused anti-sex-trafficking efforts suggests that survivor-centered techniques can be folded into carceral strategies.

60. On the linkages between antitrafficking, gender justice, and middle-class attachments to carceral feminist responses, see Bernstein, "Carceral Politics." Middle-class women's engagement with social, nonprofit, and nongovernmental antitrafficking work in the United States also occurs alongside broader transnational trends in which employment in nongovernmental organizations provides "access to national and international networks that expand their opportunities, skill sets, and outlooks" (Bernal and Grewal, *Theorizing NGOs*, 14). On women "rescuers" and "helpers" who attach themselves to antitrafficking rescue efforts in Europe, see also Agustín, *Sex at the Margins*.

61. On criminalization as an antiviolence strategy, see Bumiller, *In an Abusive State*, 162.

62. Haynes, "(Not) Found Chained to a Bed," 345.

63. Bumiller, *In an Abusive State*, 15.

64. A common misconception about state reform "equates state restructuring with state withdrawal" (Haney, *Offending Women*, 96). Rather, the diversification and rerouting of state power in arenas like the U.S. penal system have consolidated state control and power.

65. Thakor and boyd, "Networked Trafficking."

66. Foucault, *Discipline and Punish*, 297–98.

CHAPTER 2

1. In her discussion of the entanglement of carceral politics, neoliberal ideology, and feminist antitrafficking activities, Bernstein describes how a "profamilial strategy" has been leveraged to address sex trafficking. In her formulation, the nuclear family and criminal justice system are imagined as safe spaces that protect "women and children." (Bernstein, "Carceral Politics" 246–47). Bernstein's observations are also instructive in thinking about how carceral feminist commitments shape police perceptions about which victims (perhaps those from "good families?") are determined to be worthy of law enforcement protection.

2. Latonero et al., *Rise of Mobile*, 29.

3. Latonero, *Human Trafficking Online*; Latonero et al., *Rise of Mobile*.

4. California Department of Justice, "State of Human Trafficking."

5. Ibid., 65.

6. boyd et al., "Human Trafficking and Technology."

7. Latonero et al., *Rise of Mobile*, 29.

8. Ohm, "Fourth Amendment," 1311.

9. Bernstein, *Temporarily Yours*.

10. Oselin notes that street-level sex workers are criminalized at prolific proportions. In her study documenting the trajectories of street-based sex workers' movement into and out of prostitution, she found that of the women who "had multiple arrests and extensive criminal records"; fears of future criminalization and "returning to jail and the prospect of serving long-time prison sentences" proved to be a "turning point." (*Leaving Prostitution*, 52). Whether or not the criminalization of street-based sex workers is the ideal way to facilitate such "turning points" out of prostitution, or respond to sex trafficking, is however subject to debate.

11. On domestic sex trafficking and the TVPA, see Chuang, "Rescuing Trafficking," 1704. On how antitrafficking enforcement has contributed to the criminalization of migration, see Chacón, "Tensions and Trade-Offs." Brennan, *Life Interrupted*, 41–43, has also discussed the hostile climate in the United States that confronts migrants, making them vulnerable not only to labor exploitation and sex trafficking but to detention and deportation.

12. Ohm, "Fourth Amendment," 1324.

13. Ibid., 1325.

14. Ibid., 1322.

15. Ibid., 1353.

16. Backpage, Craigslist, and MyRedBook are online sites and platforms that are discussed in anti-trafficking spaces. Craigslist used to have—and Backpage still has—a section dedicated to "adult" services, including escort service. MyRedBook, which closed down in June 2014, functioned as a "social media platform," information source, and resource guide on a range of topics related to sex work. Police interviewed for this study mentioned it as part of their anti-trafficking and antiprostitution investigations. See Kayyali, "Whose RedBook?"

17. Harris, "Google."

18. Latonero, "Online Data and Sex Trafficking," 4, quotes a law-enforcement agent as saying that "child sex trafficking is hidden with prostitution. It's the same online."

19. *Riley v. California*. I am grateful to Edith Kinney for helping me understand the implications of the Riley ruling. See also Savage, "Between the Lines."

20. On the "interface between violence against women, law enforcement intervention, the use of technology, and the boundaries between citizen rights and institutional policies," see Richie, *Arrested Justice*, 101.

21. See http://www.cellebrite.com (accessed December 31, 2015).

22. De La Paz and Fassett, *Law Enforcement Training*.

23. Strandburg, "Home, Home on the Web," 157, notes that law enforcement engaged in undercover activity may "friend" a target of surveillance on Facebook by using either an authentic or a fake identity, or posing as "someone the target knows personally." For instance in a drug-related case, a Drug Enforcement Agency agent used an actual woman's identity to create a fake Facebook page (Hamby, "Government Set Up a Fake Facebook Page"). In a letter to the Drug Enforcement Administration on October 17, 2014, Facebook not only found such activities a violation of its terms of use, but wrote that it "undermines trust in the Facebook community" (Facebook Letter, first cited in Pagliery, "Facebook Tells DEA"). In a separate case, *United States v. Daniel*

Gatson, federal district Judge William Martini ruled that it was legal for law enforcement to create a fake online account, in this instance, an Instagram account, ruling that "no search warrant is required for the consensual sharing of this type of information" (Farivar, "Judge").

24. Facebook, "What Is Tagging and How Does It Work?"

25. Marwick, "Public Domain," 378.

26. Ibid., 379.

27. Marwick and boyd, "I Tweet Honestly," 122.

28. Marwick, "Public Domain," 379–80.

29. Some of these items include photos of victims' tattoos, online classified ads, and data extracted from pimps' and victims' cell phones and computers, including selfies of youth.

30. Another Christian group in California—Safe Passage OC—was featured in a *Los Angeles Times* story in October 2013. The group has also engaged in "rescues" of prostitutes and victims of human trafficking. Greg Reese, a retired Huntington Beach police officer and member of the group explained that "everything is done just like a police operation" and that they look at Backpage and Craigslist, for "potential victims, particularly those who look like minors with emptiness in their faces" (Santa Cruz, "Former Cops Lead O.C. Volunteers in Rescuing Prostitutes"). For an ethnographically rich and theoretically insightful overview of the linkages between faith-based efforts and carceral feminism as they coalesce in antitrafficking efforts, see Bernstein, "Militarized Humanitarianism."

31. Coleman, "Anonymous in Context."

32. Albrechtslund, "Online Social Networking as Participatory Surveillance."

33. Latonero et al., *Rise of Mobile,* 30.

34. Bauman and Lyon, *Liquid Surveillance,* 13.

35. Ibid., 11.

36. Ohm, "Fourth Amendment," 1311.

37. Bauman and Lyon, *Liquid Surveillance;* Leary, "Reasonable Expectations."

38. Oselin, *Leaving Prostitution.*

39. Safe Office, for instance, is a data-management company based in Cyprus that offers a range of services such as encryption and offshore hosting, with a tiered pricing system.

40. Strandburg, "Home, Home on the Web," 674, 672.

41. Solove, *Nothing to Hide.*

42. Ohm, "Fourth Amendment," 1311.

43. Pearson, *Off the Streets;* Wurth et al., "Condoms." See also two articles published in *The Lancet,* "Keeping Sex Workers Safe" and "HIV and Sex Workers."

44. Karen Levy and Marwick, "Privacy and Harm in a Networked Society."

45. Browne, "Project Backpage."

46. Gow, Quinn, and Barlott, "Sexual Exploitation Outreach."

47. Karen Levy and boyd, "Networked Rights and Networked Harms"; Karen Levy and Marwick, "Privacy and Harm."

48. New York State Anti-trafficking Coalition, "Trafficking Victims Protection and Justice Act."

49. End Trafficking Campaign, "Victory at Last."

50. New York State Anti-trafficking Coalition, "Trafficking Victims Protection and Justice Act."

51. As another point of comparison, socioeconomic factors that contribute to both trafficking and domestic violence are often ignored, treating these issues as a matter of "bad guys" who have to be "managed" (Chuang, "Rescuing Trafficking," 1705).

52. Although criminal-justice antitrafficking efforts do not yet amount to a "mandatory arrest regime," it is plausible that responses to DMST will move in that direction in the future, with digital evidence offering a way to prosecute cases without the victims' cooperation. Moreover, "in a mandatory arrest regime, no party to the incident—abuser, officer, or victim—has the ability to preempt the involvement of the criminal system once the officer decides that he has probable cause to make an arrest" (Goodmark, "Autonomy Feminism," 3).

CHAPTER 3

1. Greenwald and MacAskill, "NSA Prism."

2. www.wired.com/2014/01/how-the-us-almost-killed-the-internet (accessed February 17, 2016).

3. For a discussion of tech companies' participation in PRISM and the subsequent transparency deal brokered between the Justice Department and four technology firms—Microsoft, Google, Facebook, and Yahoo—implicated in it, see www.wired.com/2014/01/how-the-us-almost-killed-the-internet; www.theguardian.com/world/2014/feb/03/microsoft-facebook-google-yahoo-fisa-surveillance-requests; www.theguardian.com/world/2014/jan/27/tech-giants-whitehouse-deal-surveillance-customer-data (all accessed February 17, 2016).

4. Katianne Williams, "Untangling the Dark Web."

5. Mahdavi, *From Trafficking to Terror.*

6. Aradau, *Rethinking Trafficking in Women;* Bridget Anderson and Andrijasevic, "Sex, Slaves and Citizens."

7. Mahdavi, *From Trafficking to Terror,* 14.

8. Ibid., 18.

9. Thakor and boyd, "Networked Trafficking."

10. Musto and boyd, "Trafficking–Technology Nexus"; Bernstein and Shih, "Erotics of Authenticity."

11. Alcindor, "Google Helps"; Google, "Human Trafficking Hotline."

12. Google, "Fighting Human Trafficking," para. 1.

13. Mahdavi, *From Trafficking to Terror,* 24. Google Ideas, a "think/do" tank that devises technological solutions to complex social and political issues, organized an event on the topic titled "Illicit Networks: Forces in Opposition," http://www.google.com/ideas/events/info-2012, last updated July 18, 2012; no longer accessible.

14. Discussions about human trafficking as a technological problem invariably assume technical sophistication on the part of traffickers. Yet no empirical

research has shown that individuals accused of trafficking are more technologically sophisticated than the average person. This kind of assumption highlights why more empirical research is needed to track antitrafficking/antislavery efforts and the preconceptions fueling it. See Latonero et al., *Rise of Mobile*.

15. Bauman and Lyon, *Liquid Surveillance*.

16. Bernstein, "Militarized Humanitarianism."

17. Paul Amar's work on "securitized humanism" in Egypt and the "state-serving, semi-privatized, parastatal" enforcement paradigm it engenders provides a different example of how the work of some nonstate entities like NGOs overlap and become enmeshed with military and police agendas. Amar, "Turning the Gendered Politics of Security Inside Out," 306.

18. Rachel Dubrovsky and Megan Wood define "data-valence" as a form of surveillance where people are tracked through data. Dubrofsky and Wood, "Gender, Race, and Authenticity," 94.

19. Quirk, *Anti-slavery Project*.

20. Crawford and Schultz, "Big Data and Due Process."

21. An earlier version of this chapter first appeared in an article coauthored with danah boyd. Musto and boyd, "Trafficking–Technology Nexus." I thank danah boyd for her permission to reproduce parts of our original article.

22. Several ideas in this chapter were first developed and subsequently published in Musto and boyd, "Trafficking–Technology Nexus, " an article in *Social Politics*, and Musto, "Posthuman Anti-trafficking Turn," a chapter in Hoang and Parreñas, *Human Trafficking Reconsidered*. I am grateful to *Social Politics* and Open Society Foundations for permission to reproduce aspects of the article and chapter here. I also want to acknowledge that danah boyd was the first to observe that technology heightens the visibility of sex trafficking, while creating new methods to intervene. However, questions about the relationships between trafficking, technology, and visibility had been raised by other scholars as well. See, e.g., Latonero, "Online Data and Sex Trafficking"; id., *Human Trafficking Online;* Latonero et al., *Rise of Mobile;* boyd et al., "Human Trafficking and Technology."

23. U.S. Department of State, "Trafficking in Persons Report."

24. Thakor and boyd, "Networked Trafficking"; Hinman and Patria, "Girls Sold for Sex Online."

25. National Association of Attorneys General, "Letter to Senator Rockefeller."

26. California Department of Justice, "State of Human Trafficking."

27. National Association of Attorneys General, "Letter to Senator Rockefeller."

28. Block, "Your Digital Trail."

29. Ibid.

30. Ibid.

31. Mark Latonero notes that law enforcement has looked to Backpage and online and digital environments more generally for "instances and evidence of sex trafficking" (Latonero, "Online Data and Sex Trafficking").

32. The Wayback Machine (https://archive.org) functions as a kind of digital preservation and archival tool.

33. On September 3, 2015, the Washington State Supreme Court allowed a case against Backpage brought by three underage victims of sex trafficking, collectively known as "J.S.," to move forward. J.S. alleged inter alia that Backpage not only "provided a forum for illegal content . . . [but] helped develop it" (Washington [State], Supreme Court, "J.S., S.L., and L.C., Respondents, v. Village Voice Media Holdings," 2). As the court further clarified, the case hinges not only on Backpage's third-party, content-hosting status, but also on its role in "helping develop the content of those advertisements" (6). This case is important to observers of CDA Section 230 in that it could remove third-party web sites' immunity from liability for criminal activities that occur on their networks. Groups like the Electronic Frontier Foundation contested the ruling, writing, "online providers do not become content 'developers' merely because plaintiffs claim that it is so" (Cope, "Court Ruling Against Backpage.com"). Yet that is precisely what J.S. suggests, raising important questions about the kinds of remedies some victims of sex trafficking have begun to pursue outside of criminal law.

34. Homeland Security & Government Affairs Permanent Subcommittee Investigations. "Recommendation to Enforce a Subpoena Issued to the CEO of Backpage.com, LLC," 1.

35. Taaffe, "Tech Heavyweights."

36. Musto and boyd, "Trafficking–Technology Nexus"; Latonero et al., *Rise of Mobile,* iv.

37. My use of "Backpage 1.0" and "Backpage 2.0" draws conceptual insight from Scott Peppet's article "Prostitution 3.0," which seeks to introduce a novel approach to the study of prostitution by specifically exploring how law, technology, and market developments converge, and how technologies may condition the sex market in the future, along with legal reforms. Peppet places technology and law at the center of his analysis, an analytic approach that is similarly productive in assessing how technology and law inform antitrafficking interventions.

38. Kayyali, "Whose RedBook?"

39. Riley, "Super Bowl Prostitution Digitally Mapped."

40. Ibid.

41. Taaffe, "Tech Heavyweights."

42. Ibid.

43. Another platform—Orbana—featured on Devpost, a "home for hackers" and site frames its work as "data-driven Social Justice." Orbana also uses scraped data to "visualize, analyze, and respond to human trafficking." On its site, Orbana notes that it uses data in the form of "illegal advertisements" and aims to connect users [of the platform] to officials" (Devpost, "Orbana: Data-Driven Social Justice").

44. Latonero, *Human Trafficking Online;* Latonero et al., *Rise of Mobile.*

45. Ferguson, "Predictive Policing"; Lyon, "Liquid Surveillance," 326.

46. Lyon, "Liquid Surveillance."

47. Bowman, "Predictive Policing"; Ferguson, "Predictive Policing."

48. Latonero, *Human Trafficking Online;* Latonero et al., *Rise of Mobile.*

49. boyd and Crawford, "Critical Questions for Big Data."

50. Crawford and Schultz, "Big Data and Due Process," 103; 96.

51. Young, "Researchers Say."
52. For a broad discussion of how competition and collaboration functions in organized antitrafficking activities, see also Brennan, *Life Interrupted*.
53. Gillespie, "Relevance of Algorithms."
54. Crawford and Schultz, "Big Data and Due Process," 104.
55. Ibid. 104–5.
56. Riley, "Super Bowl Prostitution Digitally Mapped."
57. In "Online Data and Sex Trafficking," Latonero has raised important ideas surrounding big data and harm. For instance, he thinks it is possible that more data could increase at-risk groups' (victims of sex trafficking and people involved in commercial sex) risk of surveillance and enhanced vulnerability. Yet he also suggests that it is plausible that marginalized groups may be further alienated and their needs not sufficiently met without data. His argument about these tensions is valid. So is his point that "data frames," a term he uses to describe "the use of big data to define and frame the perceived reality of social phenomena," could cause risks like perpetuating inequality (6). However, in an environment where sex work is still broadly criminalized, the promise that data—big or small—could be framed in such a way as to reduce rather than enhance vulnerability seems unlikely. However, this is an area where more research is needed.
58. Crawford and Schultz, "Big Data and Due Process," 104.
59. Marcus et al., "Is Child to Adult."
60. Podesta et al., "White House Report. Big Data."
61. Defense Advanced Research Projects Agency, "Memex Aims to Create."
62. Neal, "DARPA's Building a New Search Engine."
63. www.theatlantic.com/magazine/archive/1945/07/as-we-may-think/303881 (accessed December 20, 2015); Gere, *Digital Culture*.
64. Gere, *Digital Culture,* 70.
65. Paterson, "DARPA Memex."
66. New York County District Attorney's Office, "Manhattan District Attorney's Office Applies Innovative Technology."
67. Ibid.
68. Bernstein developed this term to describe the carceral, militarized, and faith-based commitments that shape antitrafficking efforts in the United States and globally in her article "Militarized Humanitarianism."
69. Defense Advanced Research Projects Agency, "DARPA-BAA-14-21."
70. Bernstein, "Militarized Humanitarianism"; id., "Carceral Politics"; Thakor and boyd, "Networked Trafficking"; Latonero, "Online Data and Sex Trafficking."
71. See Devpost. "Orbana: Data-Driven Social Justice" for an example of a platform that describes its work as "data-driven."
72. Quirk, *Anti-slavery Project.*
73. Intelligence Squared U.S., "Snowden Was Justified."
74. Lyon, "Liquid Surveillance," 330.
75. Mahdavi, *From Trafficking to Terror,* 75.
76. Quirk, *Anti-slavery Project.*
77. Agamben, "State of Exception."
78. Podesta et al., "White House Report," 29.

CHAPTER 4

1. The "No Such Thing" movement was launched in 2015 to curb the use of the terms "prostitute" and "child prostitute" to refer to underage youth forced into domestic sex trafficking situations, based on the contention that "prostitute" implies consent, and youth are unable to give this (Dawson, "No Such Thing as a Child Prostitute"). During interviews with youth, I aimed to follow their lead with respect to language. They used a lot of terms to describe their experiences, including "forced into prostitution," "relationship," and "the game." Notably, youth did not refer to their experiences as "sex trafficking," although it seems that other adults they had interacted with used terms like "prostitution" and "sex trafficking" interchangeably. Though mindful of advocates' concerns about the term "child prostitute," in the context and time in which these interviews occurred and based on how youth described their experiences, I use "prostitution," and "sex-trade involved" to allow for a broader range of interpretation of what their experiences meant to them. However, as I have elsewhere noted, I welcome a change in how we talk about youths' experiences with exploitation, no matter its form.

2. Musto, "Domestic Minor Sex Trafficking."

3. Beth Richie's discussion of Sara Kruzan's abuse at the hands of the pimp George Howard is relevant here. In a self-defensive move to get away from him, Kruzan hit her pimp with a pistol, an injury that ultimately led to Howard's death and Sara's subsequent incarceration (Richie, *Arrested Justice,* 28). Kruzan's experiences are salient to my exploration of the racialized dimensions of punitive protection in suggesting that girls of color experience intersecting forms of violence not commonly accounted for in mainstream antitrafficking campaigns, including poverty and structural racism (ibid., 24). See also Crenshaw, "Mapping the Margins."

4. For an in-depth discussion of safe harbor laws and their dangers, see Conner, "In Loco Aequitatis."

5. Oselin, *Leaving Prostitution,* 42.

6. Conner, "In Loco Aequitatis," 21.

7. Chesney-Lind and Shelden, *Girls, Delinquency, and Juvenile Justice,* 19.

8. Ibid., 222.

9. Ibid., 44.

10. P. L. Brown, "Court's All-Hands Approach."

11. Sine Plambech, for instance has followed the trajectories of migrant Nigerian sex workers in Denmark, another group involved in commercial sex who are dually vulnerable to forced labor practices and state sponsored, International Organization of Migration (IOM) facilitated initiatives to remove them from the European Union. Nigerian sex workers in the EU occupy a "victim–criminal" status in that they are deemed in need of state protection but are also the targets of border control schemes designed to remove them from the EU and (forcibly) resettle them back to Nigeria. (Plambech, "Between 'Victims' and 'Criminals'"). L. M. Williams, "Provide Justice," 245, has described prostituted youth's overlapping identities as victims, offenders, and survivors. See also Chapkis, "Trafficking, Migration, and the Law."

12. Ditmore and Project Urban Justice Center, *Sex Workers.*

13. Chapkis, "Trafficking, Migration, and the Law."

14. Ditmore and Project Urban Justice Center, *Sex Workers;* Chuang, "Rescuing Trafficking"; Chacón, "Tensions and Trade-Offs."

15. Trafficking discourse appears to authorize more "exceptional" interventions than efforts of the past focused on protecting youth seen as victims of CSEC, or child prostitution. One possible explanation is that the links now being made between child sex trafficking and modern-day slavery have authorized exceptional antitrafficking solutions, though this is an area where more research is needed. See Quirk, *Anti-slavery Project,* for a discussion of the exceptionality of slavery discourses. See also Musto, "Domestic Minor Sex Trafficking"; Bernstein, "Carceral Politics"; id., "Militarized Humanitarianism." For an intersectional theoretical discussion of how antitrafficking laws have "co-opted feminist resistance that expands criminal enforcement systems that target and endanger women and queers of color," see Spade, "Intersectional Resistance and Law Reform," 1032.

16. Michelle Alexander, *New Jim Crow.*

17. Wacquant, *Punishing the Poor,* 126.

18. Bernstein, "Carceral Politics"; id., "Militarized Humanitarianism."

19. Chesney-Lind and Shelden, *Girls, Delinquency, and Juvenile Justice;* Haney, *Offending Women;* Chesney-Lind, "Jailing 'Bad' Girls."

20. See Renzetti for a discussion about service providers' different perspectives about residential facility security requirements. Renzetti, "Service Providers and Their Perceptions of the Service Needs of Sex Trafficking Victims in the United States," 142–143.

21. For critiques of carceral antitrafficking frameworks, see Bernstein, "Carceral Politics"; id., "Militarized Humanitarianism"; Musto, "Domestic Minor Sex Trafficking."

22. L.A. Smith, Vardaman, and Snow, *National Report on Domestic Minor Sex Trafficking.*

23. See also the Young Women's Empowerment Project 2009 report, *Girls Do What They Have to Do.* Among youth who contributed to the study, many experienced both institutional and interpersonal violence. Like Justice, girls who contributed to the study also reported a combination of "police violence, coercion, and refusal to help." As the report further notes, "Police often accuse girls in the sex trade of lying or don't believe them when they turn to the police for help. Many girls said that police sexual misconduct happens frequently while they are being arrested or questioned." On antiviolence work that is attentive to intersecting forms of interpersonal and state-facilitated violence and its effects on women of color, see further also Crenshaw, "Mapping the Margins"; Andrea Smith, Richie, and Sudbury, *Color of Violence.*

24. Chesney-Lind and Shelden, *Girls, Delinquency, and Juvenile Justice,* 38, 44.

25. L.M. Williams, "Harm and Resilience," 249, notes that when given the chance to reflect on important life events that "shaped them into who they are today, [sex-traded youth] often mentioned experiences with family violence."

26. Oselin, *Leaving Prostitution,* 25.

27. Ibid., 33.

28. Though youth I interviewed discussed interfacing with pimps and boy-friends, this is not to suggest that *all* sex-trade involved youth have pimps and boyfriends. For more on market facilitators, see Marcus, Riggs, et al., "Is Child to Adult."

29. References to pimps as "animals" or "gorillas" draw attention to the ways in which perceptions of pimping and sex trafficking are racially coded and the application of antitrafficking laws is similarly shaped by race. See Bernstein, "Carceral Politics" 253. See also Renzetti whose interviews with service provid-ers revealed that many saw victims they worked with as "brainwashed" by traffickers. Renzetti, "Service Providers and Their Perceptions of the Service Needs of Sex Trafficking Victims in the United States," 148.

30. Marcus, Horning, and Curtis, "Child Sex Trafficking," 46.

31. Discussing the ways in which the teens she studied described "harm, hurt, and survival," L.M. Williams, "Harm and Resilience," 246, observes that they did not "see themselves as damaged or harmed." This highlights the gap that sometimes exists between youths' perceptions and those of the actors that assist them.

32. Oselin, *Leaving Prostitution.*

33. A July 2014 *Lancet* article provides a more in-depth discussion of the power police exercise over sex workers. In a discussion about the vulnerabilities that street-based prostitutes face, the authors observed: "Police repression forces sex workers to move their work off main streets into lesser-known areas," where they risk "being pressured into unprotected sex by clients, violence, and other hazards" (Decker et al., "Human Rights Violations"). A 2012 Human Rights Watch report also documented law enforcement's use of "condoms as evidence" in New York, Los Angeles, Washington DC, and San Francisco. Police profiled sex workers and used condoms found on their person as cause to arrest them. Law enforcement's use of condoms as evidence provokes pressing public health concerns in that it discourages sex workers from carrying con-doms and practicing safe sex. (Human Rights Watch, "Sex Workers at Risk"). Though the criminalized nature of prostitution in most states in the United States makes it difficult for individuals involved in street-based prostitution to screen clients, groups that advocate for the rights of sex workers, such as the Sex Worker Outreach Project (SWOP Denver), have put together bad-date sheets to report violent customers in an effort to reduce the harm and violence others may face. (Sex Workers Outreach Project—Denver Chapter, *Denver Bad Date Sheet*).

34. Young Women's Empowerment Project, *Girls Do What They Have to Do,* 36.

35. The Young Women's Empowerment participatory study also described youth who encountered police who lied about youths' activities or who did not believe their accounts of their experiences. Ibid.

36. The preferred terms among some antitrafficking actors are "exploiters" and "buyers." Farley, *Prostitution, Trafficking, and Traumatic Stress;* L.A. Smith and Vardaman, "Domestic Human Trafficking Series."

37. On this antitrafficking approach and the carceral feminist logic it shores up, see Bernstein, "Sexual Politics"; id., "Militarized Humanitarianism."

38. Mahdavi, *From Trafficking to Terror*.

39. Variations of this argument have been made from different theoretical angles. On the limitations of carceral feminism and carceral systems, see Bernstein, "Carceral Politics"; id., "Militarized Humanitarianism"; Musto, "Domestic Minor Sex Trafficking." For a critical intersectional analysis, see Spade, "Intersectional Resistance and Law Reform."

40. A 2015 report titled "Black Girls Matter" notes that "school-age black girls experience a high incidence of interpersonal violence" in an educational climate of "zero-tolerance policing" that is "particularly problematic for girls" (Crenshaw, Ocen, and Nanda, "Black Girls Matter," 11, 30). JJ's experiences at school are reflected in some of the report's findings. That is why future discussions about creating systems of support, environments of safety, and opportunities for empowering youth who have been in sex trafficking situations must also include "gender and race-conscious prisms" (43).

41. Haynes, "Used, Abused, Arrested and Deported," 244.

42. Chacón, "Tensions and Trade-Offs," 1627; Shigekane, "Rehabilitation and Community Integration," 114.

43. Chuang, "Human Trafficking," 148.

44. Bernstein, "Carceral Politics," 253.

45. L. M. Williams, "Harm and Resilience," 300.

46. Kennedy and Pucci, *Domestic Minor Sex Trafficking,* 53.

47. Rieger, "Missing the Mark," 231.

48. Laczko, "Human Trafficking."

49. From what they shared with me, no youth at the time of interviews appeared to be active participants in cases against people accused of exploiting them.

50. Megan Comfort has examined the impact of "secondary prisonization." Tracing the ways in which women "do time together" with imprisoned male partners with whom they maintain romantic partnership, Comfort's research raises broader questions about how mass incarceration shapes and constrains other intimate relationships, including incarcerated parents' relationships with children (Comfort, *Doing Time Together,* 111).

51. Mauer and Chesney-Lind, *Collateral Consequences;* Clear and Frost, *Punishment Imperative*.

52. Clear and Frost, *Punishment Imperative*.

53. Ibid., 138.

54. Ibid., 128.

55. Ibid., 127.

56. Ibid.

57. Oselin, *Leaving Prostitution,* 33.

58. Weitzer, "Social Construction of Sex Trafficking"; Vance, "Thinking Trafficking, Thinking Sex," 135–43.

59. Weitzer, "Social Construction of Sex Trafficking," 667.

60. Chesney-Lind and Shelden, *Girls, Delinquency, and Juvenile Justice*.

61. Ibid., 235.

62. Miller, "Race, Gender and Juvenile Justice," 235.

63. Sickmund and Wan (1999), as quoted in Chesney-Lind and Shelden, *Girls, Delinquency, and Juvenile Justice,* 236.

64. Sudbury, "Celling Black Bodies," 71.

65. Ibid.; Sudbury, "Unpacking the Crisis"; R. Gilmore, *Golden Gulag;* Davis, *Are Prisons Obsolete?*

66. Crenshaw, "Mapping the Margins."

67. Ditmore and Project Urban Justice Center, *Sex Workers.*

68. L.M. Williams, "Harm and Resilience"; Dank et al., "Surviving the Streets."

69. Ditmore and Project Urban Justice Center, *Sex Workers,* 57.

70. The Young Women's Empowerment Project, a peer-based project organized to support sex-trade-involved youth in Chicago dissolved in 2013 after twelve years of operation. The closure of YWEP and other organizations that do not partner with law enforcement appears to suggest that the rise of carceral antitrafficking interventions has (a) curtailed the role of community and peer-based organizations with expertise working with youth and adults in the street and sex economies, and (b) contributed to challenges, constraints, and threats organizations face if they refuse to acquiesce to carcerally oriented antitrafficking interventions though again, this is an area where more research is needed. Young Women's Empowerment Project, *Please Support Our Staff.*

71. Phillips and Coates, "Clearing the Slate."

CHAPTER 5

1. It has become increasingly common for self-identified survivors of human trafficking to talk about their transition from victim to survivor to leader. During the October 6, 2014, WBUR radio program *Under the Radar,* for instance, two survivors of trafficking, Katie Price and Audrey Morrissey, were interviewed by host Callie Crossly and discussed survivor-led antitrafficking efforts (WGBH News, "Survivor-Led Program Aims to Curb Child Sex Trafficking"). Morrissey is associate director of My Life, My Choice, an organization that has developed survivor-led mentorship programs for young people who have been involved in commercial sex and are now legally defined as victims of domestic sex trafficking.

2. Brennan, "Methodological Challenges"; Musto, "NGO-ification."

3. To the countless lists that have riffed off of McIntosh's original white-privilege checklist, I would add the privilege of never having been arrested, charged, or convicted of a crime. See McIntosh, *White Privilege.*

4. On the disconnect between criminal records as "depersonalized" texts and how some expungement-seekers differentially account for their personal histories, lives, and sense of self, see Myrick, "Facing Your Criminal Record," 97–98.

5. Here I am referring to the ways in which antitrafficking protection efforts impact "domestic" populations who may be subject to carceral and/or carceral protectionist oversight by the juvenile and criminal justice systems. Yet research outside the United States has similarly traced the punitive dimensions of antitrafficking protection efforts. On antitrafficking's overlap with immigration

regimes, see, e.g., Lee, "Gendered Discipline and Protective Custody," Gallagher and Pearson, "High Cost of Freedom," and Plambech, "Between 'Victims' and 'Criminals,'" 398, on the different types of carceral, semicarceral, and intergovernmental oversight and control to which migrants are subjected.

6. In a legal commentary focused on the challenges that confront individuals who have expunged their records but where data about their criminal pasts may still circulate in databases owned by third-party data brokers, Wayne notes that "enforcing postconviction privacy rights is on individuals with expunged records" (Wayne, "Data-Broker Threat," 256). My argument similarly suggests that achieving postconviction legal relief remains the burden and sole responsibility of individuals who have been in coercive sex trafficking situations but who are still criminally punished for their activities.

7. McCorkel, *Breaking Women,* 220; Haney, *Offending Women.*

8. McCorkel, *Breaking Women,* 213; Davis, "Future of Prison?"

9. McCorkel, *Breaking Women,* 213; Myrick, "Facing Your Criminal Record"; Phillips and Coates, "Clearing the Slate."

10. Tonry, *Future of Imprisonment.*

11. Myrick, "Facing Your Criminal Record," 76.

12. Phillips and Coates, "Clearing the Slate."

13. Michelle Alexander, *New Jim Crow,* 147.

14. Myrick, "Facing Your Criminal Record," 79.

15. Bauman and Lyon, *Liquid Surveillance,* 13. The "ubiquitous use of criminal-background checks" in employment, licensing, and housing decisions is addressed in Blumstein and Nakamura, "Paying a Price," which argues that criminal records should have a shelf life, or "expiration date." This is challenging, however, given the growth of the data-broker industry and the circulation of public records in public and privately owned databases. See also Wayne, "Data-Broker Threat."

16. Wayne, "Data-Broker Threat," 253. Two attorneys I interviewed jointly, who have extensive experience working in the juvenile justice system, helped me understand that "expungement" is not a technical legal term in the state in which they work but is used to refer to remedies that allow a person to seek a retroactive dismissal of their record.

17. Each U.S. state's statutory repertoire of postconviction remedies takes the form of a "complex state apparatus taking the form of statutes, courts, records departments, police departments, and myriad individuals working anonymously within them," whose partial and incomplete records may "impede the ability of ex-arrestees to manage or repair their relationship with the state that has punished them" (Myrick, "Facing Your Criminal Record," 73). In the unnamed midwestern state where Myrick did research, "sealing" and "expungement" are both defined as "statutory processes through which a person with a state criminal record can petition a judge to either order its destruction (expungement) or order it to be selectively sealed from public access (sealing)" (ibid., 79).

18. Broudo and Baskin, *Vacating Criminal Convictions;* Phillips and Coates, "Clearing the Slate"; Polaris Project, "Vacating Convictions."

19. Broudo and Baskin, *Vacating Criminal Convictions,* 6.

20. Polaris Project, "Vacating Convictions."

21. Phillips and Coates, "Clearing the Slate," 23.
22. Ibid. Polaris Project, "Vacating Convictions."
23. Phillips and Coates, "Clearing the Slate," 34–35.
24. Ibid., 30.
25. Myrick, "Facing Your Criminal Record," 75; Bernstein, "Introduction"; Bernstein, "Carceral Politics as Gender Justice?"; Gottschalk, *Caught.*.
26. Michael said that human trafficking cases involving migrants are typically more time- and resource-intensive.
27. As Tory explained, however, not all those involved in antitrafficking postconviction work have the expertise to help people like Kiara navigate complex legal situations. Complexity is the norm in such cases, which means that advocates working to vacate or seal records must have the requisite experience and should commit to "do no harm." For discussion of a "trauma-informed model of care" in working with formerly trafficked persons in ways that seek to avoid subjecting them to additional and unnecessary harms, see Fehrenbacher, "First, Do No Harm."
28. Phillips and Coates, "Clearing the Slate," 30.
29. Ibid., 36.
30. Ibid.
31. Ibid.
32. Ibid., 5, 21.
33. Paul-Emile, "Beyond Title VII," 895–96.
34. Wayne, "Data-Broker Threat," 253.
35. Paul-Emile, "Beyond Title VII," 903.
36. Saagar, "Monetizing Data"; Hicken, "Big Data Is Secretly Scoring You"; Lake, "Can 'Big Data' stamp out human trafficking?"
37. Paul-Emile, "Beyond Title VII," 903.
38. Ibid., 907.
39. Ibid., 904.
40. Wayne, "Data-Broker Threat," 259.
41. On the "expansive databases" maintained by the FBI through its National Crime Information Center and the "Interstate Identification Index," see Paul-Emile, "Beyond Title VII," 905–7. Since searches in such databases can be run for "employment purposes" and/or accessed by "certain state and federal governments, and by nongovernmental personnel in specific government-regulated jobs and industries" (ibid., 906), formerly trafficked persons may encounter problems obtaining employment in both the private and public sectors.
42. For more on how BCCs come to obtain data from various criminal justice agencies, see ibid.
43. Wayne, "Data-Broker Threat," 259.
44. Paul-Emile, "Beyond Title VII," 908.
45. Ibid., 909.
46. Myrick, "Facing Your Criminal Record," 73, 90.
47. Wayne, "Data-Broker Threat," 255.
48. Ibid., 263.
49. Ibid., 253.

50. Carole Vance notes that antitrafficking activists and advocates are critical of what they see as abolitionists' overemphasis on police intervention, treating it "as unproblematic, effective, and positive" (Vance, "Innocence and Experience," 202).

51. Here again, I think Levy and boyd's discussion of networked harm is salient because of the ways in which networks challenge older models of privacy premised on individual rights and don't account for the ways networks function. See Karen Levy and boyd, "Networked Rights and Networked Harms."

52. Phillips and Coates, "Clearing the Slate."

53. Paul-Emile, "Beyond Title VII," 906–7.

54. Plambech, "Between 'Victims' and 'Criminals,'" 387.

55. Pager, *Marked*, 71.

56. Ibid., 90.

57. Ibid., 259–60. See also Phillips and Coates, "Clearing the Slate," for an in-depth discussion of the stigma that trafficking survivors face as a result of criminal convictions.

58. Rodriguez, "'Ban the Box.'"

59. Rodriguez and Mehta, "Ban the Box."

CONCLUSION

1. Green, "Tougher Police Tactics Stinging Sex Buyers."

2. Foxhall, "Orange County Prostitution Fight"; Orange County District Attorney's Office, "Sex Purchasers."

3. Bernstein, "Militarized Humanitarianism."

4. Massachusetts-based Demand Abolition seeks to address "the driver of sex trafficking: demand for illegal commercial sex" (Demand Abolition, "Why Demand?").

5. The EPIK Project, for instance, views men as integral to the fight to end demand and aims, as the group notes on its web site, to "end the demand for prostituted kids in America by 2020" (EPIK Project, "Our Mission").

6. See also Elizabeth Nolan Brown, "What the Swedish Model Gets Wrong."

7. Jordan, "Swedish Law to Criminalize Clients," 1.

8. Crouch, "Swedish Prostitution Law Targets Buyers."

9. Jordan, "Swedish Law to Criminalize Clients," 5.

10. Levy and Jakobsson, "Sweden's Abolitionist Discourse and Law," 12. Niina Vuolajarvi and Carole Vance aimed to raise *New York Times* readers' awareness to a similar point. In a March 23, 2015, letter to the editor about the promise of Sweden's law, they offer a cogent overview of academic research on the policy, arguing that, "the law has detrimental effects on the well-being and safety of people selling sexual services, whether they are doing so voluntarily or in a coercive relationship" (Vuolajarvi and Vance, "Letter to the Editor"). See also Jordan, "Swedish Law to Criminalize Clients," 5.

11. Decker et al., "Human Rights Violations."

12. On how and why translating end-demand policies to the United States would cause extensive problems, including criminalizing people who sell sex, see Thrupkaew, "Misguided Moral Crusade."

13. On the ways in which mandatory policies against domestic violence have detrimentally impacted women, especially poor women and racial minorities, and "the criminalization of victims" as a direct outcome of "a sexual violence agenda that has been incorporated into state policy," see Bumiller, *In An Abusive State,* 11–12.

14. Musto, "Domestic Minor Sex Trafficking"; Bernstein, "Carceral Politics"; id., "Militarized Humanitarianism."

15. Elizabeth Bernstein has drawn attention to the limits of end-demand, citing a lack of evidence that this Swedish strategy would likely result in a "decreasing demand for off-street sexual services or improving the lives of women in prostitution" (Bernstein, *Temporarily Yours,* 183).

16. Chuang, "Rescuing Trafficking," 1704; Bernstein, "Militarized Humanitarianism."

17. Chuang, "Rescuing Trafficking," 1705.

18. Gottschalk, *Caught,* 46.

19. Ibid.

20. Ibid

21. See also Phillips and Coates, "Clearing the Slate"; Conner, "In Loco Aequitatis"; Sherman, "Justice for Girls." Linda M. Williams, "Harm and Resilience among Prostituted Teens."

22. Chapkis, "Trafficking, Migration, and the Law," 924.

23. Agustín, *Sex at the Margins.*

24. Ramachandran, "Protection/Detention/Reform"; Gallagher and Pearson, "High Cost of Freedom."

25. In Asia, e.g., "the protective custody of trafficking victims constitutes a key site for examining the hybridity of care and control and their gendered consequences in the global borderlands" Lee, "Gendered Discipline," 218.

26. Lee, "Gendered Discipline"; Ramachandran, "Protection/Detention/Reform"; Plambech, "Between 'Victims' and 'Criminals'"; Kinney, "Raids, Rescues, and Resistance"; Agustín, *Sex at the Margins.*

27. Plambech, "Between 'Victims' and 'Criminals,'" 384.

28. Bernstein, "Carceral Politics"; id., "Militarized Humanitarianism"; Plambech, "Between 'Victims' and 'Criminals'"; Kinney, "Raids, Rescues, and Resistance"; Ramachandran, "Protection/Detention/Reform"; Gallagher and Pearson, "High Cost of Freedom."

29. Bernstein, "Carceral Politics."

30. Lee, "Gendered Discipline," 218.

31. Plambech, "Between 'Victims' and 'Criminals'"; Bernstein, "Introduction."

32. Ramachandran, "Protection/Detention/Reform," 7; Shih, "The Anti-Trafficking Rehabilitative Complex."

33. See also Bernstein, "Carceral Politics."

34. Haney, *Offending Women,* 213.

35. Sudbury, "Celling Black Bodies," 71.

36. Ibid.; Sudbury, "Unpacking the Crisis"; R. Gilmore, *Golden Gulag;* Davis, *Are Prisons Obsolete?*

37. Other scholars and advocates have also called for the decriminalization of prostitution. Decriminalization would also potentially inspire a move away

from an antitrafficking "rescue" framework and the narratives that sustain them, which, as Vance astutely suggests, "tend to ignore a range of proven strategies, including peer organizing, decriminalization, and health education" (Vance "Innocence and Experience, 211").

38. Carvajal, "Amnesty International Votes for Policy."
39. Decker et al., "Human Rights Violations," 2.
40. Moran, "Buying Sex Should Not Be Legal."
41. Gottschalk, *Caught*, 264.
42. Oselin, *Leaving Prostitution*, 166.
43. Dank et al., "Surviving the Streets of New York."
44. INCITE! Women of Color against Violence, *Color of Violence*.
45. Agustín, *Sex at the Margins*.
46. Bernstein, "Introduction."
47. Musto and boyd, "Trafficking–Technology Nexus."
48. Karen Levy and boyd, "Networked Rights and Networked Harms."
49. Thakor and boyd, "Networked Trafficking"; Karen Levy and boyd, "Networked Rights and Networked Harms." I thank Mark Latonero for sharing his thoughts on this topic and helping me clarify my argument.
50. Reuters, "Europe's Top Court."
51. Pettinger, "Judgement Machine," 139.
52. Ibid., 137. See also Karen Levy and boyd, "Networked Rights and Networked Harms."

APPENDIX

1. Black, "From a Study to a Journey," 24.
2. Merry, *Human Rights and Gender Violence*, 29.
3. Agustín, *Sex at the Margins*.
4. Thakor and boyd, "Networked Trafficking."
5. Weitzer, "Social Construction of Sex Trafficking."
6. Vance, "States of Contradiction."
7. See, e.g., Musto, "Domestic Minor Sex Trafficking."
8. Gottschalk, *Caught*; Bumiller, *In an Abusive State*; Bernstein, "Carceral Politics."
9. Legal researcher Melissa Dess has recommended mandatory law-enforcement training at the state level, along with the decriminalization of underage prostitution in the state on which her legal note is based, Massachusetts. I agree with her recommendations. However, it seems that like the decriminalization of underage prostitution, the overall benefits of mandatory training would be limited if not accompanied by a broader push to decriminalize prostitution for adults and youth. See Dess, "Walking the Freedom Trail," 181. For an argument in favor of decriminalizing all aspects of consensual adult sex work, see also Amnesty International, "Global Movement Votes."
10. Buettner, "Prosecutors Focus on Pimps and Clients."
11. Decker et al., "Human Rights Violations"
12. Fagan et al., "Stops and Stares," 9.

13. *New York Times,* "Q&A: What Happened in Ferguson?"; Wacquant, *Punishing the Poor.*

14. Michelle Alexander, *New Jim Crow;* Nat Smith, and Stanley, eds., *Captive Genders.*

15. One example of a state law is Proposition 35. In voting for Proposition 35, the Californians against Sexual Exploitation Act, Californians signed off on a sweeping legislative agenda that included (a) harsher penalties and steeper fines for traffickers, (b) the legal classification and registration of convicted traffickers as "sex offenders," and (c) the requirement that they provide law enforcement with their online identities and information about their other Internet activities. Proponents of the measure viewed it as a key way to strengthen the state's response to human trafficking. Almendrala, "Prop 35 Passes"; California Secretary of State, "Text of Proposed Laws."

16. Lindquist, "Beyond Anti-anti-trafficking," 322.

17. Musto, "Institutionalizing Protection."

18. Musto, "Institutionalizing Protection"; Musto, "Carceral Protectionism."

19. Polkinghorne, "Language and Meaning," 141.

20. My dissertation research and this book are based on engaging with different antitrafficking stakeholders. Other scholars have similarly taken this approach in their research into antitrafficking in the United States and Thailand. See, e.g., Thakor and boyd, "Networked Trafficking"; Kinney, "Raids, Rescues, and Resistance."

21. Brennan, *Life Interrupted,* 26.

22. Thakor and boyd, "Networked Trafficking."

23. Jones, *Between Good and Ghetto,* 16–17.

24. Another limitation of this study is that participants were primarily drawn from urban areas. For a more in-depth discussion of methods and sampling, see Hertz, *Single by Chance,* 225.

25. Benedict Anderson, *Imagined Communities.*

26. Brennan, *Life Interrupted,* 14.

27. Quirk, "Introduction."

28. Haraway, "Situated Knowledges."

29. Marcus and Snajdr, "Anti-anti-trafficking?" 194.

30. Ibid.

Bibliography

Agustín, Laura María. *Sex at the Margins: Migration, Labour Markets and the Rescue Industry*. New York: Zed Books, 2007.

Albrechtslund, Anders. "Online Networking as Participatory Surveillance." *First Monday* 13, 3 (2008). http://journals.uic.edu/ojs/index.php/fm/article/view/2142. Accessed February 10, 2016.

Alcindor, Yamiche. "Google Helps Bring Hotline to Human-Trafficking Battle." *USA Today,* April 9, 2013. https://www.google.com/ideas/projects/human-trafficking-hotline-network. Accessed September 18, 2015.

Alexander, Michelle. *The New Jim Crow: Mass Incarceration in the Age of Colorblindness*. New York: New Press, 2012. https://books.google.com/books?hl=en&lr=&id=_SKbzXqmawoC&oi=fnd&pg=PA1.

Alexander, Priscilla. "Prostitution: A Difficult Issue for Feminists." In *Feminism and Sexuality,* edited by S. Jackson and S. Scott, 342–57. New York: Columbia University Press, 1996.

Almendrala, Anna. "Prop 35 Passes: California Voters Approve Harsher Sentencing for Human Traffickers." *Huffington Post,* November 7, 2012. www.huffingtonpost.com/2012/11/07/prop-35-passes-california_n_2089305.html. Accessed December 29, 2016.

Amar, Paul. "Turning the Gendered Politics of Security Inside Out: Charging the Police with Sexual Harassment in Egypt." *International Feminist Journal of Politics* 13 (2011): 299–328.

Anderson, Benedict. *Imagined Communities: Reflections on the Origin and Spread of Nationalism*. 1983. London: Verso Books, 2006.

Anderson, Bridget, and Rutvica Andrijasevic. "Sex, Slaves and Citizens: The Politics of Anti-trafficking." *Soundings* 40 (2008): 135–45.

Amnesty International. "Global Movement Votes to Adopt Policy to Protect Human Rights of Sex Workers." August, 11 2015. https://www.amnesty.org

/en/latest/news/2015/08/global-movement-votes-to-adopt-policy-to-protect-human-rights-of-sex-workers. Accessed September 28, 2015.

Andrijasevic, Rutvica. *Migration, Agency, and Citizenship in Sex Trafficking.* London: Palgrave, 2010.

Aradau, Claudia. *Rethinking Trafficking in Women: Politics Out of Security.* New York: Palgrave Macmillan, 2008.

Aronowitz, Alexis A. "Smuggling and Trafficking in Human Beings: The Phenomenon, the Markets That Drive It and the Organisations That Promote It." *European Journal on Criminal Policy and Research* 9 (2001): 163–95.

Banks, Sandy. "First Step Program Gives Girls a Chance to Put Street Life Behind Them." *Los Angeles Times,* February 20, 2015. www.latimes.com/local/california/la-me-banks-trafficking-victims-20150221-column.html. Accessed February 10, 2016.

Barry, Kathleen. *Female Sexual Slavery.* Englewood Cliffs, NJ: Prentice-Hall, 1979.

———. *The Prostitution of Sexuality: The Global Exploitation of Women.* New York: New York University Press, 1995.

Bauman, Zygmunt, and David Lyon. *Liquid Surveillance: A Conversation.* Malden, MA: Polity Press, 2013.

Bernal, Victoria, and Inderpal Grewal. *Theorizing NGOs: States, Feminism, and Neoliberalism.* Durham, NC: Duke University Press, 2014.

Bernstein, Elizabeth. "Carceral Politics as Gender Justice? The 'Traffic in Women' and Neoliberal Circuits of Crime, Sex, and Rights." *Theory and Society* 41, no. 3 (2012): 233–59.

———. "Introduction: Sexual Economies and New Regimes of Governance." *Social Politics* 21, no. 3 (2014): 345–54.

———. "Militarized Humanitarianism Meets Carceral Feminism: The Politics of Sex, Rights, and Freedom in Contemporary Antitrafficking Campaigns." *Signs* 36, no. 1 (2010): 45–71.

———. "The Sexual Politics of the 'New Abolitionism.'" *Differences* 18, no. 3 (2007): 128–51.

———. *Temporarily Yours: Intimacy, Authenticity, and the Commerce of Sex.* Chicago: University of Chicago Press, 2007.

Bernstein, Elizabeth, and Elena Shih. "The Erotics of Authenticity: Sex Trafficking and Reality Tourism in Thailand." *Social Politics* 21, no. 3 (2014): 430–60. doi:10.1093/sp/jxu022.

Black, Timothy. "From a Study to a Journey: Holding an Ethnographic Gaze on Urban Poverty for Two Decades." In *Open to Disruption: Time and Craft in the Practice of Slow Sociology,* edited by Anita Ilta Garey, Rosanna Hertz, and Margaret K. Nelson, 23–44. Nashville, TN: Vanderbilt University Press, 2014.

Block, Melissa. "Your Digital Trail: Data Fuels Political and Legal Agendas." National Public Radio, October 3, 2013. www.npr.org/sections/alltechconsidered/2013/10/04/228199021/your-digital-trail-data-fuels-political-and-legal-agendas. Accessed February 10, 2016.

Blumstein, Alfred, and Kiminori Nakamura. "Paying a Price, Long After the Crime." *New York Times,* January 9, 2012. https://www.nytimes.com/2012

/01/10/opinion/paying-a-price-long-after-the-crime.html. Accessed February 1, 2016.

Boff, Andrew. "Silence on Violence: Improving the Safety of Women. The Policing of Off-Street Sex Work and Sex Trafficking in London." 2012. http://glaconservatives.co.uk/wp-content/uploads/downloads/2012/03/Report-on-the-Safety-of-Sex-Workers-Silence-on-Violence.pdf. Accessed February 15, 2014.

Boris, Eileen, and Rhacel Salazar Parreñas, eds. *Intimate Labors: Cultures, Technologies, and the Politics of Care.* Stanford, CA: Stanford Social Sciences, 2010.

Bowman, Courtney. "Predictive Policing: A Window into Future Crimes or Future Privacy Violations" (blog). Palantir Technologies, 2012. www.palantir.com/2012/09/predictive-policing-a-window-into-future-crimes-or-future-privacy-violations. Accessed February 1, 2016.

boyd, danah, Heather Casteel, Mitali Thakor, and Rane Johnson. "Human Trafficking and Technology: A Framework for Understanding the Role of Technology in the Commercial Sexual Exploitation of Children in the U.S." Microsoft Research, 2011. http://research.microsoft.com/en-us/collaboration/focus/education/htframework-2011.pdf. Accessed February 2, 2016.

boyd, danah, and Kate Crawford. "Critical Questions for Big Data." *Information, Communication and Society* 15, no. 5 (2012): 662–79.

Braidotti, Rosi. "A Critical Cartography of Feminist Post-postmodernism." *Australian Feminist Studies* 20 (2005): 169–80.

Brennan, Denise. "Competing Claims of Victimhood? Foreign and Domestic Victims of Trafficking in the United States." *Sexuality Research and Social Policy* 5 (2008): 45–61.

———. "Key Issues in the Resettlement of Formerly Trafficked Persons in the United States." *University of Pennsylvania Law Review* 158 (2010): 1581–608.

———. *Life Interrupted: Trafficking into Forced Labor in the United States.* Durham, NC: Duke University Press, 2014.

———. "Methodological Challenges in Research with Trafficked Persons: Tales from the Field." *International Migration* 43, no. 1–2 (2005): 35–54.

Brents, Barbara G., and Kathryn Hausbeck. "Sex Work Now: What the Blurring of Boundaries around the Sex Industry Means for Sex Work, Research, and Activism." In *Sex Work Matters: Exploring Money, Power, and Intimacy in the Sex Industry,* edited by Melissa Hope Ditmore, A. Levy, and A. Willman, 9–22. London: Zed Books, 2010.

Broudo, Melissa, and Sienna Baskin. *Vacating Criminal Convictions for Trafficked Persons: A Legal Memorandum for Advocates and Legislators.* New York: Sex Workers Project, 2012.

Brown, Elizabeth Nolan. "What the Swedish Model Gets Wrong about Prostitution." *Time,* July 19, 2014. http://time.com/3005687/what-the-swedish-model-gets-wrong-about-prostitution. Accessed February 10, 2016.

Brown, Patricia Leigh. "A Court's All-Hands Approach Aids Girls Most at Risk." *New York Times,* January 28, 2014. www.nytimes.com/2014/01/29/us/a-courts-all-hands-approach-aids-girls-most-at-risk.html. Accessed January 24, 2016

Browne, Rachel. "Project Backpage Uses Text-Messages to Help Women Involved in Prostitution, but Some Sex Workers Label it as 'Harassment.'" *National Post,* March 20, 2014.

Buettner, Russ. "Prosecutors Focus on Pimps and Clients, Instead of Prostitutes." *New York Times.* May 2, 2012. www.nytimes.com/2012/05/03/nyregion/manhattan-prosecutors-focus-on-pimps-instead-of-prostitutes.html?_r=0. Accessed February 10, 2016.

Bumiller, Kristin. *In an Abusive State: How Neoliberalism Appropriated the Feminist Movement against Sexual Violence.* Durham, NC: Duke University Press, 2008.

California. Department of Justice. "The State of Human Trafficking in California Report." 2012. http://oag.ca.gov/human-trafficking. Accessed December 29, 2012.

———. Secretary of State. "Text of Proposed Laws." Sacramento: California Secretary of State. 2012. http://vig.cdn.sos.ca.gov/2012/general/pdf/text-proposed-laws-v2.pdf. Accessed December 29, 2016.

Carroll, Rory. "Microsoft and Google to Sue over U.S. HopsSurveillance Requests." *Guardian,* August 30, 2013. www.theguardian.com/law/2013/aug/31/microsoft-google-sue-us-fisa. Accessed February 10, 2016.

Carvajal, Doreen. "Amnesty International Votes for Policy Calling for Decriminalization of Prostitution." *New York Times.* August 11, 2015. www.nytimes.com/2015/08/12/world/europe/amnesty-international-votes-for-policy-calling-for-decriminalization-of-prostitution.html. Accessed February 12, 2016.

Chacón, Jennifer M. "Tensions and Trade-Offs: Protecting Trafficking Victims in the Era of Immigration Enforcement." *University of Pennsylvania Law Review* 158 (2010): 1609–53.

Chang, Grace, and Kathleen Kim. "Reconceptualizing Approaches to Human Trafficking: New Directions and Perspectives from the Field(s)." *Stanford Journal of Civil Rights and Civil Liberties* 3, no. 2 (2007): 317–44.

Chapkis, Wendy. "Soft Glove, Punishing Fist: The Trafficking Victims Protection Act of 2000." In *Regulating Sex: The Politics of Intimacy and Identity,* edited by Elizabeth Bernstein and Laurie Schaffner, 51–67. New York: Routledge, 2005.

———. "Trafficking, Migration, and the Law: Protecting Innocents, Punishing Immigrants." *Gender and Society* 17, no. 6 (2003): 923–37. doi:10.1177/0891243203257477.

Cheng, Sealing, and Eunjung Kim. "The Paradoxes of Neoliberalism: Migrant Korean Sex Workers in the United States and 'Sex Trafficking.'" *Social Politics: International Studies in Gender, State and Society* 21, no. 3 (2014): 355–81

Chesney-Lind, Meda. "Jailing 'Bad' Girls: Girls' Violence and Trends in Female Incarceration." In *Fighting For Girls: New Perspectives on Gender and Violence,* edited by Meda Chesney-Lind and Nikki Jones, 57–79. Albany: State University of New York Press, 2010.

Chesney-Lind, Meda, and Randall G. Shelden. *Girls, Delinquency, and Juvenile Justice.* New York: John Wiley & Sons, 2014.

Children's Advocacy Center. "Support to End Exploitation Now (SEEN)." 2015. www.suffolkcac.org/programs/seen. Accessed September 28, 2015.

Christian, Carol. "20+ Arrested in Houston Prostitution Busts; HPD Vice Demonstrates Changed Philosophy on Sex Crimes." *Houston Chronicle*, September 24, 2015. www.chron.com/houston/article/20-arrested-in-Houston-prostitution-busts-HPD-6524386.php. Accessed September 28, 2015.

Chuang, Janie. "Beyond a Snapshot: Preventing Human Trafficking in the Global Economy." *Indiana Journal of Global Legal Studies* 13 (2006): 137–63.

———. "Human Trafficking (panel summary)" In *Proceedings of the 99th Meeting of the American Society of International Law,* edited by Lawrence Helfer and Rae Lindsay. Washington, DC: American Society of International Law, 2005.

———. "Rescuing Trafficking from Ideological Capture: Prostitution Reform and Anti-trafficking Law and Policy." *University of Pennsylvania Law Review* 158 (2010): 1655–728.

Clear, Todd R., and Natasha A. Frost. *The Punishment Imperative: The Rise and Failure of Mass Incarceration in America.* New York: New York University Press, 2013.

Coleman, Gabriella. "Anonymous in Context: The Politics and Power Behind the Mask." CIGI Internet Governance Papers. September 23, 2013. www.cigionline.org/publications/2013/9/anonymous-context-politics-and-power-behind-mask. Accessed February 10, 2016.

Comfort, Megan. *Doing Time Together: Love and Family in the Shadow of the Prison.* Chicago: University of Chicago Press, 2008.

Congdon, Jason. "Speaking of 'Dead Prostitutes': How CATW Promotes Survivors to Silence Sex Workers" *OpenDemocracy,* November 26, 2014. https://www.opendemocracy.net/beyondslavery/jason-congdon/speaking-of-%E2%80%9Cdead-prostitutes%E2%80%9D-how-catw-promotes-survivors-to-silence-se. Accessed August 26, 2015.

Conner, Brendan. "In Loco Aequitatis: The Dangers of 'Safe Harbor' Laws for Youth in the Sex Trades." *Stanford Journal of Civil Rights and Civil Liberties* 12, no. 1 (forthcoming).

Cope, Sophia. "Court Ruling against Backpage.com Is a Setback for Online Speech in Washington State." Electronic Frontier Foundation. September 8, 2015. https://www.eff.org/deeplinks/2015/09/court-ruling-against-backpagecom-setback-online-speech-washington-state. Accessed September 18, 2015.

Crawford, Kate, and Jason Schultz. "Big Data and Due Process: Toward a Framework to Redress Predictive Privacy Harms." *Boston College Law Review* 55, no. 1 (2014): article 3.

Crenshaw, Kimberlé. "Mapping the Margins: Intersectionality, Identity Politics, and Violence against Women of Color." *Stanford Law Review* 43 (1991): 1241–99.

Crenshaw, K.W., P. Ocen, and J. Nanda. "Black Girls Matter: Pushed Out, Overpoliced and Underprotected." African American Policy Forum. Columbia Law School Center for Intersectionality and Social Policy Studies, 2015.

www.aapf.org/recent/2014/12/coming-soon-blackgirlsmatter-pushed-out-overpoliced-and-underprotected. Accessed September 20, 2015.

Crouch, David. "Swedish Prostitution Law Targets Buyers, but Some Say It Hurts Sellers." *New York Times,* March 14, 2015. www.nytimes.com /2015/03/15/world/swedish-prostitution-law-targets-buyers-but-some-say-it-hurts-sellers.html. Accessed September 23, 2015.

Curtis, Ric, Karen Terry, Meredith Dank, Kirk Dombrowski, and Bilal Khan. *The Commercial Sexual Exploitation of Children in New York City.* New York: Center for Court Innovation, 2008.

Dank, Meredith, Jennifer Yahner, Kuniko Madden, Isela Banuelos, Lilly Yu, Andrea Ritchie, Mitchyll Mora, and Brendan Conner. "Surviving the Streets of New York: Experiences of LGBTQ Youth, YMSM, and YWSW Engaged in Survival Sex." Urban Institute, 2015. www.urban.org/research/publication /surviving-streets-new-york-experiences-lgbtq-youth-ymsm-and-ywsw-engaged-survival-sex. Accessed September 16, 2015.

Davis, Angela. *Are Prisons Obsolete?* New York: Seven Stories Press, 2003.

———. "The Future of Prison? A Sign of Democracy?" Lecture at the University of California Santa Cruz Center for Cultural Studies, Santa Cruz, CA, September 17, 2007. www.youtube.com/watch?v=Q25-KJ55k_0.

Dawson, Stella. "No Such Thing as a Child Prostitute, Anti-trafficking Groups Say." *Reuters,* January 8, 2015. www.reuters.com/article/2015/01/08/us-trafficking-us-children-idUSKBN0KH26920150108. Accessed August 26, 2015.

Decker, Michele R., Anna-Louise Crago, Sandra K.H. Chu, Susan G. Sherman, Meena S. Seshu, Kholi Buthelezi, Mandeep Dhaliwal, and Chris Beyrer. "Human Rights Violations against Sex Workers: Burden and Effect on HIV." *Lancet* 385, no. 9963 (2015): 186–99. doi:10.1016/S0140-6736(14)60800-X.

Defense Advanced Research Projects Agency. "DARPA-BAA-14-21: Memex." 2014. https://www.fbo.gov/index?s=opportunity&mode=form&id=426485 bc9531aaccba1b01ea6d43 16ee&tab=core&_cview=0. Accessed February 10, 2016.

———. "Memex Aims to Create a New Paradigm for Domain-Specific Search." 2014. www.darpa.mil/news-events/2014–02–09. Accessed February 10, 2016..

De La Paz, Catherine, and Byron Fassett. *Law Enforcement Training: Corroborating the Child Sex Trafficking Investigation.* PowerPoint slides, June 16, 2011.

Demand Abolition. "Why Demand?" https://www.demandabolition.org/why-demand. Accessed December 25, 2015.

Dess, Melissa. "Walking the Freedom Trail: An Analysis of the Massachusetts Human Trafficking Statute." *Boston College Journal of Law and Social Justice* 33 (2013): 147–82.

Devpost. "Orbana: Data-Driven Social Justice vs Human Trafficking." Accessed February 12, 2016.

Ditmore, Melissa Hope. "Trafficking in Lives: How Ideology Shapes Policy." In *Trafficking and Prostitution Reconsidered: New Perspectives on Migration, Sex Work, and Human Rights,* edited by Kamala Kempadoo, Jyoti Sanghera, and Bandana Pattanaik, 107–26. Boulder, CO: Paradigm, 2005.

————. *The Use of Raids to Fight Trafficking in Persons*. New York: Urban Justice Center, 2009.

Ditmore, Melissa Hope, and Project Urban Justice Center. *Sex Workers, Kicking Down the Door: The Use of Raids to Fight Trafficking in Persons*. New York: Sex Workers Project, 2009. www.sexworkersproject.org/publications/KickingDownTheDoor.html. Accessed July 31, 2012.

Doezema, Jo. "Forced to Choose: Beyond the Voluntary v. Forced Prostitution Dichotomy." In *Global Sex Workers: Rights, Resistance and Redefinition*, edited by Kamala Kempadoo and Jo Doezema, 34–50. New York: Routledge, 1998.

————. *Sex Slaves and Discourse Masters: The Construction of Trafficking*. London: Zed Books, 2010.

Dubrofsky, Rachel, and Megan Wood. "Gender, Race, and Authenticity: Celebrity Women Tweeting for the Gaze." In *Feminist Surveillance Studies*, edited by Rachel Dubrofsky and Shoshana Amielle Magnet. Durham, NC: Duke University Press, 2015.

Edison International, "L.A. County DA Lacey Urges Audience to Keep the Dream Alive for Future Generations at SCE's Black History Month Celebration." February 12, 2014. http://newsroom.edison.com/stories/l-a-county-district-attorney-jackie-lacey-urges-audience-to-keep-the-dream-alive-for-future-generations-at-sce-s-black-history-month-celebration. Accessed August 27, 2015.

End Trafficking Campaign. "Victory at Last: NY Finally Passed the TVPJA & I Was There to See It." Unicef United States Fund. April 8, 2015. www.unicefusa.org/stories/victory-last-ny-finally-passes-tvpja-i-was-there-see-it/23566.

EPIK Project. "Our Mission." www.epikproject.org/#/what-we-do/our-mission. Accessed December 25, 2015.

Facebook. "What Is Tagging and How Does It Work?" https://www.facebook.com/help/124970597582337. Accessed September 15, 2015.

Fagan, Jeffrey, Anthony A. Braga, Rod K. Brunson, and April Pattavina. "Stops and Stares: Street Stops, Surveillance and Race in the New Policing." Columbia Public Law Research Paper no. 14–479. 2015. http://papers.ssrn.com/sol3/papers.cfm?abstract_id=2650154. Accessed September 28, 2015.

Farivar, Cyrus. "Judge: It's OK for Cops to Create Fake Instagram Accounts." *ArsTechnica*. December 20, 2014. http://arstechnica.com/tech-policy/2014/12/judge-its-ok-for-cops-to-create-a-fake-instagram-account-friend-you/. Accessed September 8, 2015.

Farley, Melissa. *Prostitution and Trafficking in Nevada: Making the Connections*. San Francisco: Prostitution Research & Education, 2007.

————. *Prostitution, Trafficking, and Traumatic Stress*. New York: Haworth Press, 2003.

Farrell, Amy, and Stephanie Fahy. "The Problem of Human Trafficking in the U.S.: Public Frames and Policy Responses." *Journal of Criminal Justice* 37 (2009): 617–26.

Fassin, Didier, and Richard Rechtman. *The Empire of Trauma*. Translated by R. Gomme. Princeton, NJ: Princeton University Press, 2009.

Fehrenbacher, Annie. "First, Do No Harm." UCLA Center for the Study of Women. 2013. https://escholarship.org/uc/item/8m39h3jq. Accessed February 8, 2016.

Ferguson, Andrew. "Predictive Policing and Reasonable Suspicion." *Emory Law Journal* 62, no. 2 (2013): 259–325.

Foot, Kirsten. *Collaborating against Human Trafficking: Cross Sector Challenges and Practices.* Lanham, MD : Rowman & Littlefield, 2015.

Foucault, Michel. *Discipline and Punish: The Birth of the Prison.* New York: Random House, 1977.

Foxhall, Emily. "Orange County Prostitution Fight Puts New Focus on Shaming of Johns." *Los Angeles Times,* November 20, 2014. www.latimes.com /local/orangecounty/la-me-john-shaming-20141120-story.html#page=1. Accessed February 10, 2016.

Freeman, Carla. *Entrepreneurial Selves.* Durham, NC: Duke University Press, 2014.

Gallagher, Anne. "Human Rights and Human Trafficking: A Reflection on the Influence and Evolution of the U.S. Trafficking in Persons Reports." In *From Human Trafficking to Human Rights: Reframing Contemporary Slavery,* edited by Alison Brysk and Austin Choi-Fitzpatrick, 172–94. Philadelphia: University of Pennsylvania Press, 2011.

Gallagher, Anne, and Elaine Pearson. "The High Cost of Freedom: A Legal and Policy Analysis of Shelter Detention for Victims of Trafficking." *Human Rights Quarterly* 32 (2010): 73–114.

Geist, Darren. "Finding Safe Harbor: Protection, Prosecution, and State Strategies to Address Prostituted Minors." *Legislation & Policy Brief* 4, no. 2 (2012): 67–127. http://digitalcommons.wcl.american.edu/lpb/vol4/iss2/3.

Gere, Charlie. *Digital Culture.* London: Reaktion Books, 2008.

Gillespie, Tarleton. "The Relevance of Algorithms." In *Media Technologies,* edited by Tarleton Gillespie, Pablo Boczkowski, and Kirsten Foot, 167–94. Cambridge, MA: MIT Press, 2014.

Gilmore, Leigh, and Elizabeth Marshall. "Girls in Crisis: Rescue and Transnational Feminist Autobiographical Resistance." *Feminist Studies* 36 (2010): 667–90.

Gilmore, Ruth Wilson. *Golden Gulag: Prisons, Surplus, Crisis, and Opposition in Globalizing California.* Berkeley: University of California Press, 2007.

Global Alliance against Traffic in Women. "Collateral Damage: The Impact of Anti-trafficking Measures on Human Rights Around the World." Bangkok, Thailand, 2007. www.gaatw.org/Collateral%20Damage_Final/singlefile_ CollateralDamagefinal.pdf. Accessed January 10, 2013.

———. "What's the Cost of a Rumour?" 2011. www.gaatw.org/publications /WhatstheCostofaRumour.11.15.2011.pdf. Accessed January 5, 2014.

Goldstein, Dana. "Sex is Not a Service: A Former Prostitute Makes the Case for Busting Johns." Marshall Project, September 18 2015. https://www.themarshallproject.org/2015/09/18/sex-is-not-a-service. Accessed September 24, 2015.

Goodmark, Leigh. "Autonomy Feminism: An Anti-essentialist Critique of Mandatory Interventions in Domestic Violence Cases." *Florida State University*

Law Review 37, no. 1 (2009): 1–35. http://humanizingideas.law.fsu.edu
/journals/lawreview/downloads/371/goodmark.pdf. Accessed July 11, 2014.

Google. "Fighting Human Trafficking." Official Blog, April 9, 2013. http://
googleblog.blogspot.com/2013/04/fighting-human-trafficking.html.
Accessed January 2, 2016.

———. "Human Trafficking Hotline Network." www.google.com/ideas
/projects/human-trafficking-hotline-network. Accessed January 20, 2016.

Gottschalk, Marie. *Caught: The Prison State and the Lockdown of American
Politics.* Princeton, NJ: Princeton University Press, 2015.

Gow, Gordan, Kathleen Quinn, and Timothy Barlott. "Sexual Exploitation
Outreach with Text Messaging: Introducing Project Backpage." 2014. www
.frontlinesms.com/wp-content/uploads/2014/01/frontlinesms_casestudy_
Sexual-Exploitation-Outreach-with-Text-Messaging.pdf. Accessed April 15,
2014.

Green, Sara Jean. "Tougher Police Tactics Stinging Sex Buyers." *Seattle Times,*
October 15, 2014. http://seattletimes.com/html/localnews/2024779850_sex-
buyerprogramxml.html. Accessed December 25, 2015.

Greenwald, Glenn, and Ewen MacAskill. "NSA Prism Program Taps In to User
Data of Apple, Google and Others." *Guardian,* June 6, 2013. www
.theguardian.com/world/2013/jun/06/us-tech-giants-nsa-data. Accessed January 18, 2016.

Hamby, Chris. "Government Set Up a Fake Facebook Page in This Woman's
Name." BuzzFeed, October 6, 2004. www.buzzfeed.com/chrishamby
/government-says-federal-agents-can-impersonate-woman-online#.
fp7qwrmn1. Accessed September 15, 2015.

Haney, Lynne Allison. *Offending Women: Power, Punishment, and the Regulation of Desire.* Berkeley: University of California Press, 2010.

———. "Working through Mass Incarceration: Gender and the Politics of
Prison Labor from East to West. *Signs* 36, 1 (2010): 73–97.

Haraway, Donna. "Situated Knowledges: The Science Question in Feminism
and the Privilege of Partial Perspective." *Feminist Studies* 14, no. 3 (1988):
575–99.

Harris, Derrick. "Google: Our New System for Recognizing Faces is the Best
One Ever." *Fortune,* March 17, 2015. http://fortune.com/2015/03/17
/google-facenet-artificial-intelligence/. Accessed September 15, 2015.

Harvey, David. *A Brief History of Neoliberalism.* Oxford: Oxford University
Press, 2005.

Haynes, Dina Francesca. "(Not) Found Chained to a Bed in a Brothel: Conceptual, Legal, and Procedural Failures to Fulfill the Promise of the Trafficking
Victims Protection Act." *Georgetown Immigration Law Journal* 21 (2006):
337–82.

———. "Used, Abused, Arrested and Deported: Extending Immigration Benefits to Protect the Victims of Trafficking and to Secure the Prosecution of
Traffickers." *Human Rights Quarterly* 26 (2004): 221–72.

H.E.A.T. Watch. "Alameda County District Attorney's Office Unveils H.E.A.T.
Watch." District Attorney's Office, Nancy E. O'Malley, 2010. www.alcoda.
org/about_us/files/heat02212010.pdf. Accessed February 12, 2016.

Hebert, Laura. "The Sexual Politics of U.S. Inter/National Security." In *From Human Trafficking to Human Rights: Reframing Contemporary Slavery,* edited by Alison Brysk and Austin Choi-Fitzpatrick, 86–106. Philadelphia: University of Pennsylvania Press, 2011.

Hertz, Rosanna. *Single by Chance, Mothers by Choice: How Women Are Choosing Parenthood without Marriage and Creating the New American Family.* Oxford: Oxford University Press, 2006.

Hicken, Melanie. "Big Data Is Secretly Scoring You." *CNN Money,* April 2, 2014. http://money.cnn.com/2014/04/02/pf/consumer-scores/index.html?iid =EL. Accessed September 21, 2015.

Hinman, Katie, and Melia Patria. "Girls Sold for Sex Online, Backpage Defends Decision to Keep Ads Up." *ABC News,* April 24, 2012. http://abcnews .go.com/US/girls-sold-sex-online-backpage-defends-decision-ads /story?id=16193220. Accessed December 29, 2015.

"HIV and Sex Workers." www.thelancet.com/series/hiv-and-sex-workers. Accessed September 15, 2015.

Hoang, Kimberly Kay, and Rhacel Salazar Parreñas, eds. *Human Trafficking Reconsidered: Rethinking the Problem, Envisioning New Solutions.* Brussels: International Debate Education Association, 2014.

Homeland Security & Government Affairs Permanent Subcommittee Investigations. "Majority & Minority Report - Recommendation to Enforce a Subpoena Issued to the CEO of Backpage.com LLC." http://www.hsgac.senate .gov/download/?id=687782F1-7AE9-4884-9025-F6F1C07E064C. Accessed March 4, 2016.

Hughes, Donna M. "Hiding in Plain Sight: A Practical Guide to Identifying Victims of Trafficking in the U.S." Women's Studies Program, University of Rhode Island, 2003. www.uri.edu/artsci/wms/hughes/hiding_in_plain_sight. pdf. Accessed November 13, 2014

———. "The 'Natasha' Trade: Transnational Sex Trafficking." *National Institute of Justice Journal,* no. 246 (2000): 1–9.

———. *Trafficking for Sexual Exploitation: The Case of the Russian Federation.* Geneva: International Organization for Migration, 2002.

Human Rights Watch. "Sex Workers at Risk: Condoms as Evidence of Prostitution in Four U.S. Cities." 2012. www.hrw.org/sites/default/files/reports /us0712ForUpload_1.pdf.

INCITE! Women of Color against Violence. *Color of Violence: The INCITE! Anthology.* Cambridge, MA: South End Press, 2006.

Intelligence Squared U.S. "Snowden Was Justified." Transcript by National Capitol Contracting, February 13, 2014. http://intelligencesquaredus.org /images/debates/past/transcripts/021214%20Snowden.pdf. Accessed January 1, 2016.

Jeffreys, Sheila. "'Brothels without Walls': The Escort Sector as a Problem for the Legalization of Prostitution." *Social Politics: International Studies in Gender, State and Society* 17, no. 2 (2010): 210–34.

———. "Prostitution, Trafficking and Feminism: An Update on the Debate." *Women's Studies International Forum* 32 (2009): 316–20.

Jones, Nikki. *Between Good and Ghetto: African American Girls and Inner-City Violence.* New Brunswick, NJ: Rutgers University Press, 2009.

Jordan, Ann. "The Swedish Law to Criminalize Clients: A Failed Experiment in Social Engineering." Center for Human Rights and Humanitarian Law, Washington College of Law, 2012, 5. www.nswp.org/sites/nswp.org/files/Issue-Paper-4%5B1%5D.pdf. Accessed September 23, 2015.

Kantola, Johanna, and Judith Squires. "From State Feminism to Market Feminism?" *International Political Science Review* 33, no. 4 (2012): 382–400.

Kayyali, Nadia. "Whose RedBook? Why Everyone Should Be Concerned by the Seizure of MyRedBook.Com." Electronic Frontier Foundation, 2014. https://www.eff.org/deeplinks/2014/07/whose-redbook-why-everyone-should-be-concerned-seizure-myredbookcom. Accessed February 8, 2016.

"Keeping Sex Workers Safe." *The Lancet* 386, no. 9993 (2015): 504. doi:10.1016/S0140-6736(15)61460-X.

Kempadoo, Kamala. "Victims and Agents of Crime: The New Crusade Against Trafficking." In *Global Lockdown: Race, Gender and the Prison Industrial Complex,* edited by Julia Sudbury, 35–55. New York: Routledge, 2005.

Kempadoo, Kamala, and Jo Doezema, eds. *Global Sex Workers: Rights, Resistance, and Redefinition.* New York: Routledge, 1998.

Kempadoo, Kamala, Jyoti Sanghera, and Bandana Pattanaik. *Trafficking and Prostitution Reconsidered: New Perspectives on Migration, Sex Work, and Human Rights.* Boulder, CO: Paradigm, 2005.

Kennedy, M. Alexis, and Nicole Joey Pucci. *Domestic Minor Sex Trafficking. Las Vegas, Nevada.* Vancouver, WA: Shared Hope International, 2008. http://www.northeastern.edu/humantrafficking/wp-content/uploads/Las_Vegas.pdf.

Kim, Gilbert. "Lost Children: Addressing the Under-identification of Trafficked Alien Minors in Los Angeles County." 2006. http://164.67.121.27/files/Lewis_Center/Publications/studentreports/2006_Kim.pdf. Accessed February 1, 2016.

Kinney, Edith. "Raids, Rescues, and Resistance: Women's Rights and Thailand's Response to Human Trafficking." In *Negotiating Sex Work: Unintended Consequences of Policy and Activism,* edited by Carisa R. Showden and Samantha Majic, 145–70. Minneapolis: University of Minnesota Press, 2014.

Koken, Juline. "The Meaning of the 'Whore': How Feminist Theorists on Prostitution Shape Research on Female Sex Workers." In *Sex Work Matters: Exploring Money, Power, and Intimacy in the Sex Industry,* edited by Melissa Hope Ditmore, A. Levy, and A. Willman, 28–64. London: Zed Books, 2010.

Kristof, Nicholas. "She Has a Pimp's Name Etched on Her." *New York Times,* May 23, 2012. www.nytimes.com/2012/05/24/opinion/kristof-she-has-a-pimps-name-etched-on-her.html?-_r=1. Accessed February 5, 2016.

Lacey, Jackie. "District Attorney Jackie Lacey Unveils New Program Aimed at Helping Young Victims of Sex Trafficking." Press Release. February 12, 2014.

Laczko, Frank. "Human Trafficking: The Need for Better Data." *Migration Information Source* 1 (November 1, 2002).

Lake, Maggie, "Can 'Big Data' stamp out human trafficking?" CNN. August 11, 2015. www.cnn.com/2015/08/10/world/can-big-data-help-stamp-out-human-trafficking. Accessed September 21, 2015.

Latonero, Mark. *Human Trafficking Online: The Role of Social Networking Sites and Online Classifieds.* Los Angeles: USC Annenberg Technology and Human Trafficking, 2011. https://technologyandtrafficking.usc.edu/report/. Accessed December 29, 2012.

———. "Online Data and Sex Trafficking: Exploring Bias among Data Set." Draft Research Note for the NYU Institute for International Law and Justice Conference on Measurement and Data in the Governance of Illicit Activities, 2014.

Latonero, Mark, Jennifer Musto, Zhaleh Boyd, Ev Boyle, Amber Bissel, Kari Gibson, and Joanne Kim. *The Rise of Mobile and the Diffusion of Technology-Facilitated Trafficking.* Los Angeles: USC Annenberg Center on Communication Leadership and Policy, 2012. http://technologyandtrafficking.usc.edu/files/2012/11/HumanTrafficking2012_Nov12.pdf. Accessed December 31, 2015.

Law, Victoria. "Against Carceral Feminism." *Jacobin,* 2014. https://www.jacobinmag.com/2014/10/against-carceral-feminism. Accessed January 3, 2016.

Leary, Mary. "Reasonable Expectations of Privacy for Youth in a Digital Age." *Mississippi Law Journal* 80 (2011): 1035–93.

Lee, Maggy. "Gendered Discipline and Protective Custody of Trafficking Victims in Asia." *Punishment and Society* 16, no. 2 (2014): 206–22.

———. "Human Trafficking and Border Control in the Global South." In *The Borders of Punishment: Migration, Citizenship and Social Exclusion,* edited by Katja Franko Aas and Mary Bosworth, 128–41. Oxford: Oxford University Press, 2013.

Levy, Jay, and Pye Jakobsson. "Sweden's Abolitionist Discourse and Law: Effects on the Dynamics of Swedish Sex Work and on the Lives of Sweden's Sex Workers." *Criminology and Criminal Justice* 14, no. 5 (2014): 593–607. doi:10.1177/1748895814528926.

Levy, Karen, and danah boyd. "Networked Rights and Networked Harms." Paper presented at International Communication Association's Data & Discrimination Preconference, May 14, 2014.

Levy, Karen, and Alice Marwick. "Privacy and Harm in a Networked Society." www.datasociety.net/initiatives/privacy/privacy-and-harm. Accessed September 15, 2015.

Limoncelli, Stephanie. "The Trouble with Trafficking: Conceptualizing Women's Sexual Labor and Economic Human Rights." *Women's Studies International Forum* 32, no. 4 (2009): 261–69.

Lind, Amy. "Querying Globalization: Sexual Subjectivities, Development, and the Governance of Intimacy." In *Gender and Global Restructuring: Sightings, Sites, and Resistances,* edited by Marianne H. Marchand and Anne Sisson Runyan, 48–65. New York: Routledge, 2011.

Lindquist, Johan. "Beyond Anti-anti-trafficking." *Dialectical Anthropology* 37, no. 2 (2013): 319–23.

Lindstrom, Nicole. "Transnational Responses to Human Trafficking: The Politics of Anti-trafficking in the Balkans." In *Human Trafficking, Human Security, and the Balkans,* edited by H. Friman and S. Reich, 61–80. Pittsburgh, PA: University of Pittsburgh Press, 2007.

Lippman, Jonathan. "Announcement of New York's Human Trafficking Intervention Initiative." 2013. www.courtinnovation.org/research /announcement-new-yorks-human-trafficking-intervention-initiative. Accessed September 10, 2015.

Luibhéid, Eithne. "Queering Migration and Citizenship." In *Queer Migrations: Sexuality, U.S. Citizenship and Border Crossings,* edited by Eithne Luibhéid and Lionel Cantú, ix–xxxv. Minneapolis: University of Minnesota Press, 2005.

Lyon, David. "Liquid Surveillance: The Contribution of Zygmunt Bauman to Surveillance Studies." *International Political Sociology* 4, no. 4 (2010): 325–38.

MacKinnon, Catherine A. "Trafficking, Prostitution, and Inequality." *Harvard Civil Rights-Civil Liberties Law Review* 46 (2011): 271–309.

Mahdavi, Pardis. *From Trafficking to Terror: Constructing a Global Social Problem.* New York: Routledge, 2014.

Marchand, Marianne H., and Anne Sisson Runyan. "Introduction. Feminist Sightings of Global Restructuring: Old and New Conceptualizations." In *Gender and Global Restructuring: Sightings, Sites, and Resistances,* edited by Marianne H. Marchand and Anne Sisson Runyan, 1–24. New York: Routledge, 2011.

Marcus, Anthony, Amber Horning, and Ric Curtis. "Child Sex Trafficking: Toward an Agent Centered Approach." In *Human Trafficking Reconsidered: Rethinking the Problem, Envisioning New Solutions,* edited by Rhacel Salazar Parreñas and Kimberly Hoang, 41–49. New York: International Debate Education Association, 2014.

Marcus, Anthony, Robert Riggs, Amber Horning, Sarah Rivera, Ric Curtis, and Efram Thompson. "Is Child to Adult as Victim is to Criminal? Social Policy and Street-Based Sex Work in the USA." *Sexuality Research and Social Policy* 9, no. 2 (2012): 153–66.

Marcus, Anthony, and Edward Snajdr. "Anti-anti-trafficking? Toward Critical Ethnographies of Human Trafficking." *Dialectical Anthropology* 37, no. 2 (2013): 191–94.

Marwick, Alice E. "The Public Domain: Surveillance in Everyday Life." *Surveillance & Society* 9, no. 4 (2012): 378–93.

Marwick, Alice E., and danah boyd. "I Tweet Honestly, I Tweet Passionately: Twitter Users, Context Collapse, and the Imagined Audience." *New Media and Society* 13, no. 1 (2011): 114–33.

Mauer, Marc, and Meda Chesney-Lind. *The Collateral Consequences of Mass Imprisonment.* New York: New Press, 2002.

Maxwell, Robert. "Law to Shelter Child Sex Trafficking Victims Could Strain Resources." KXAN, August 30, 2015. http://kxan.com/investigative-story /law-to-shelter-child-sex-trafficking-victims-could-strain-resources. Accessed September 28, 2015.

McCorkel, J. A. *Breaking Women: Gender, Race, and the New Politics of Imprisonment.* New York: New York University Press, 2013.

McIntosh, Peggy. "White Privilege: Unpacking the Invisible Knapsack." In id., *White Privilege and Male Privilege: A Personal Account of Coming to See Correspondences through Work in Women's Studies,* 31–36. Working Paper 189. Wellesley, MA: Wellesley College Center for Research on Women, 1988. http://ted.coe.wayne.edu/ele3600/mcintosh.html. Accessed January 2, 2016.

Merry, Sally Engle. "How Big Is the Trafficking Problem? The Mysteries of Quantification." *OpenDemocracy,* January 26, 2015. https://www.opendemocracy.net/beyondslavery/sally-engle-merry/how-big-is-trafficking-problem-mysteries-of-quantification. Accessed August 26, 2015.

———. *Human Rights & Gender Violence: Translating International Law into Local Justice.* Chicago: University of Chicago Press, 2006.

Microsoft. "Microsoft Names Research Grant Recipients in Fight against Child Sex Trafficking." June 13, 2012. http://blogs.microsoft.com/on-the-issues /2012/06/13/microsoft-names-research-grant-recipients-in-fight-against-child-sex-trafficking/. Accessed September 17, 2015

Miller, Jody. "Race, Gender and Juvenile Justice: An Examination of Disposition Decision-Making for Delinquent Girls." In *The Intersection of Race, Gender, and Class in Criminology,* edited by M. D. Schwartz and D. Milovanovic, 219–46. New York: Garland Press, 1994.

Mitchell, Gregory. "Romancing Rescue: Lessons for Brazil from London and Cape Town on Global Sporting Events, Sex Trafficking and Moral Panics." Lecture at Cambridge University, May 29, 2014.

Mogulescu, Kate. "The Super Bowl and Sex Trafficking." *New York Times,* January 31, 2014. www.nytimes.com/2014/02/01/opinion/the-super-bowl-of-sex-trafficking.html?_r=0. Accessed January 3, 2016.

Moran, Rachel. "Buying Sex Should Not Be Legal." *New York Times,* August 28, 2015. www.nytimes.com/2015/08/29/opinion/buying-sex-should-not-be-legal.html. Accessed September 23, 2015.

Musto, Jennifer Lynne. "Carceral Protectionism and Multi-professional Anti-trafficking Human Rights Work in the Netherlands." *International Feminist Journal of Politics* 12 (2010): 381–400.

———. "Domestic Minor Sex Trafficking and the Detention-to-Protection Pipeline." *Dialectical Anthropology* 37 (2013): 257–76.

———. "Institutionalizing Protection, Professionalizing Victim Management: Explorations of Multi-professional Anti-trafficking Efforts in the Netherlands and the United States." PhD diss., University of California, Los Angeles, 2011.

———. "The NGO-ification of the Anti-trafficking Movement in the United States: A Case Study of the Coalition to Abolish Slavery and Trafficking." *Wagadu* 5 (2008): 6–20.

———. "The Posthuman Anti-trafficking Turn: Technology, Domestic Minor Sex Trafficking, and Augmented Human–Machine Alliances." In *Human Trafficking Reconsidered: Rethinking the Problem, Envisioning New Solutions,* edited by Kimberly Kay Hoang and Rhacel Salazar Parreñas, 123–38. Brussels: International Debate Education Association, 2014.

———. "What's in a Name? Conflations and Contradictions in Contemporary U.S. Discourses on Human Trafficking." *Women's Studies International Forum* 32 (2009): 281–87.

Musto, Jennifer Lynne, and danah boyd. "The Trafficking–Technology Nexus." *Social Politics* 21, no. 3 (2014): 461–83. doi:10.1093/sp/jxu018.

My Life, My Choice. "About Us." www.fightingexploitation.org/about. Accessed September 10, 2015.

———. "Giving Law Enforcement and Service Providers Tools to Identify Victims and Vulnerable Youth, and Connect Them to Services." www.fighting-exploitation.org/professional-training. Accessed September 10, 2015.

Myrick, Amy. "Facing Your Criminal Record: Expungement, and Wrongfully Represented Self as a Collateral Consequence." *Law and Society Review* 47, no. 1 (2013): 73–104.

National Association of Attorneys General. "Letter to Senator Rockefeller, Senator Thune, Representative Upton, and Representative Waxman." July 23, 2013. https://www.eff.org/sites/default/files/cda-ag-letter.pdf. Accessed January 3, 2016.

National Conference of State Legislatures. "Legislative Intent of 'Safe Harbor' Laws." www.ncsl.org/research/civil-and-criminal-justice/human-trafficking-overview.aspx#Safe%20Harbor. Accessed August 25, 2015.

Neal, Meghan. "DARPA's Building a New Search Engine to Crawl the Deep Web." *Motherboard,* February 10, 2014. http://motherboard.vice.com/blog /darpas-building-a-new-search-engine-to-crawl-the-deep-web. Accessed February 10, 2016.

New York County District Attorney's Office. "Manhattan District Attorney's Office Applies Innovative Technology to Scan the 'Dark Web' in the Fight Against Human Trafficking." February 9, 2015. http://manhattanda.org /press-release/manhattan-district-attorney%E2%80%99s-office-applies-innovative-technology-scan-%E2%80%9Cdark-web%E2%80%9D-fig. Accessed September 18, 2015.

New York State Anti-trafficking Coalition. "The Trafficking Victims Protection and Justice Act." 2010. www.tvpja.com. Accessed July 10, 2014.

"'Nothing for Us without Us': Sex Workers the Decision-Makers in New Fund." 2013. www.theguardian.com/global-development/poverty-matters /2013/jan/03/sex-workers-decision-makers-new-fund. Accessed December 29, 2015.

O'Connell Davidson, Julia. *Prostitution, Power, and Freedom.* Oxford: Polity Press, 1998.

———. "Will the Real Sex Slave Please Stand Up?" *Feminist Review* 83 (2006): 4–22.

Obama, Barack. *President Obama Speaks at the Clinton Global Initiative Annual Meeting* [video]. Washington, DC: The White House, 2012. www .whitehouse.gov/photos-and-video/video/2012/09/25/president-obama-speaks-clinton-global-initiative-annual-meeting.

Ohm, Paul. "Fourth Amendment in a World without Privacy." *Mississippi Law Journal* 81 (2012): 1309–39.

Orange County District Attorney's Office. "Sex Purchasers." http://
orangecountyda.org/media/sexpurchasers.asp. Accessed February 10,
2016.

Oselin, Sharon S. *Leaving Prostitution: Getting Out and Staying Out of Sex
Work.* New York: New York University Press, 2014.

Outshoorn, Joyce. "The Political Debates on Prostitution and Trafficking of
Women." *Social Politics: International Studies in Gender, State and Society*
12 (2005): 141–55.

Pager, Devah. *Marked: Race, Crime, and Finding Work in an Era of Mass
Incarceration.* Chicago: University of Chicago, 2007.

Pagliery, Jose. "Facebook Tells DEA: Stop Impersonating Users." *CNN Money,*
December 29, 2014. http://money.cnn.com/2014/10/20/technology/security
/facebook-dea/?iid=EL. Accessed September 15, 2015.

Parreñas, Rhacel. *Illicit Flirtations: Labor, Migration, and Sex Trafficking in
Tokyo.* Stanford, CA: Stanford University Press, 2011.

Pateman, Carole. *The Sexual Contract.* Stanford, CA: Stanford University
Press, 1988.

Paterson, Ryan. "DARPA Memex and Counter Human Trafficking."
IST Research, February 4, 2014. http://istresearch.com/blog/2014/4/17
/hi4w40kxa9l6z9k7vfvw9a8wv5ijec. Accessed February 12, 2016.

Paul-Emile, Kimani. "Beyond Title VII: Rethinking Race, Ex-Offender Status,
and Employment Discrimination in the Information Age." *Virginia Law
Review* 100 (2014): 893–952.

Pearson, Elaine. *Off the Streets: Arbitrary Detention and Other Abuses against
Sex Workers in Cambodia.* New York: Human Rights Watch, 2010. http://
www.hrw.org/sites/default/files/reports/cambodia0710webwcover_2.pdf

Peppet, Scott R. "Prostitution 3.0: A Comment," *Iowa Law Review* 98 (2013):
131–41.

Pettinger, Lynne. "The Judgement Machine: Markets, Internet Technologies
and Policies in Commercial Sex." *Social Policy and Society* 14, no. 1 (2015):
135–43.

Phillips, Suzannah, and Carrie Coates. "Clearing the Slate: Seeking Effective
Remedies for Criminalized Trafficking Victims." City University of New
York School of Law, 2014. www.law.cuny.edu/academics/clinics/iwhr
/publications/Clearing-the-Slate.pdf.

Plambech, Sine. "Between 'Victims' and 'Criminals': Rescue, Deportation, and
Everyday Violence Among Nigerian Migrants." *Social Politics* 21, no. 3
(2014): 382–402. doi:10.1093/sp/jxu021.

Podesta, John, Penny Pritzker, Ernest J. Moniz, John Holdren, and Jeffrey
Zients. "White House Report. Big Data: Seizing Opportunities, Preserving
Values." www.whitehouse.gov/sites/default/files/docs/big_data_privacy_
report_5.1.14_final_print.pdf. Accessed July 18, 2014.

Polaris Project. "Vacating Convictions for Sex Trafficking Victims." Analysis of
State of Human Trafficking Laws. 2013. https://www.google.com/url?sa=t&
rct=j&q=&esrc=s&source=web&cd=2&ved=0ahUKEwiIpJrL7_fKAhUKV
z4KHUVPAJsQFgglMAE&url=https%3A%2F%2Fpolarisproject
.org%2Fsites%2Fdefault%2Ffiles%2F2013-State-Ratings-Analysis

.pdf&usg=AFQjCNFAqcOfoxuU-4X85_3siPSmOyQ6vQ&bvm=bv.11419
5076,d.cWw. Accessed February 12, 2016.

Polkinghorne, Donald E. "Language and Meaning: Data Collection in Qualitative Research." *Journal of Counseling Psychology* 52, no. 2 (2005): 137–45.

Prokupecz, Shimon. "NYPD Conducts Pre-Super Bowl Crackdown on Sex Trafficking." *CNN,* January 31, 2014. www.cnn.com/2014/01/28/justice /pre-super-bowl-sex-trafficking-busts. Accessed January 3, 2016.

Quirk, Joel. *The Anti-slavery Project: From the Slave Trade to Human Trafficking.* Philadelphia: University of Pennsylvania Press, 2011.

———. "Introduction: Contemporary Slavery as More than Rhetorical Strategy." In *Contemporary Slavery and Human Rights,* edited by Annie Bunting and Joel Quirk, forthcoming. Vancouver: University of British Columbia Press, 2014.

Ramachandran, Vibhuti. "Protection/Detention/Reform: Shelters, Sex Workers, and the Law in India." Paper presented at South Asia by the Bay: Feminist Interventions on Gender and South Asia, 2014.

Renzetti, Claire. "Service Providers and Their Perceptions of the Service Needs of Sex Trafficking Victims in the United States." In *Global Human Trafficking: Critical Issues and Contexts,* edited by Molly Dragiewicz. New York: Routledge, 2015.

Reuters. "Europe's Top Court: People Have the Right to Be Forgotten on Internet." www.reuters.com/article/2014/05/13/eu-google-dataprotection-idUSL6N0NZ23Q20140513. Accessed February 12, 2016.

Richie, Beth. *Arrested Justice: Black Women, Violence, and America's Prison Nation.* New York: New York University Press, 2012.

Rieger, April. "Missing the Mark: Why the Trafficking Victims Protection Act Fails to Protect Sex Trafficking Victims in the United States." *Harvard Journal of Law and Gender* 30 (2007): 231–56.

Rights4Girls. "Members of Congress Join Rights4Girls and the McCain Institute to Combat Child Sex Trafficking." *PRNewswire,* January 8, 2015. www.prnewswire.com/news-releases/members-of-congress-join-rights4girls-and-the-mccain-institute-to-combat-child-sex-trafficking-300017851.html. Accessed August 26, 2015.

Riley, Michael. "Super Bowl Prostitution Digitally Mapped by Data Trackers." *Bloomberg Business,* January 31, 2014. www.bloomberg.com/news/articles /2014-01-31/super-bowl-prostitution-digitally-mapped-by-data-trackers. Accessed January 3, 2016.

Rodriguez, Michelle Natividad. "'Ban the Box' Is a Fair Chance for Workers with Records." National Employment Law Project Fact Sheet, July 1, 2015. www.nelp.org/publication/ban-box-fair-chance-workers-records. Accessed September 21, 2015.

Rodriguez, Michelle Natividad, and Nayantara Mehta. "Ban the Box: U.S. Cities, Counties, and States Adopt Fair Hiring Policies." National Employment Law Project Toolkit, September 1, 2015. www.nelp.org/publication /ban-the-box-fair-chance-hiring-state-and-local-guide. Accessed September 21, 2015.

Saagar, Ksira. "Monetizing Data: Milking the New Cash Cow." *Wired,* February 13, 2013. http://insights.wired.com/profiles/blogs/monetizing-data-milking-the-new-cash-cow. Accessed May 1, 2014.

Saar, Malika Saada "Stop Calling Kids 'Child Prostitutes.'" *Huffington Post,* September 23, 2015. www.huffingtonpost.com/malika-saada-saar/stop-calling-kids-child-p_b_8173342.html. Accessed February 10, 2016.

Safe Office. "Features: Loaded with Features that All Work Together Seamlessly." https://safeoffice.com/pp.php?t=i_Features. Accessed February 10, 2016.

Sanctuaries for Families. "Super Bowl Shifts the Spotlight on Sex Trafficking in New York City." 2014. www.sanctuaryforfamilies.org/index.php?option=content&task=view&id=710. Accessed February 20, 2014. Link no longer active.

Santa Cruz, Nicole. "Former Cops Lead O.C. Volunteers in Rescuing Prostitutes." *Los Angeles Times,* October 2, 2013. www.latimes.com/local/great-reads/la-me-c1-prostitute-squad-20131002-dto-htmlstory.html. Accessed September 15, 2015.

Savage, Charlie. "Between the Lines of the Cellphone Privacy Ruling." *New York Times,* June 25, 2014. www.nytimes.com/interactive/2014/06/25/us/annotated-supreme-court-cellphone-privacy-decision.html. Accessed February 10, 2016.

Schilt, Kristen, and Laurel Westbrook. "Doing Gender, Doing Heteronormativity: 'Gender Normals,' Transgender People, and the Social Maintenance of Heterosexuality." *Gender and Society* 23 (2009): 440–64.

Schneiderman, Eric. "To the Editor." *New York Times.* February 5, 2014. www.nytimes.com/2014/02/06/opinion/the-victims-of-human-trafficking.html?emc=edit_tnt_20140208&tntemailo=y&_r=1. Accessed February 10, 2016.

Schweig, Sarah, Danielle Malangone, and Miriam Goodman. *Prostitution Diversion Programs.* New York: Center for Court Innovations, 2012. www.courtinnovation.org/research/prostitution-diversion-programs.

Sered, Susan, and Maureen Norton-Hawk. *Can't Catch a Break: Gender, Jail, Drugs, and the Limits of Personal Responsibility.* Berkeley: University of California Press, 2014.

Sex Workers Outreach Project—Denver Chapter. *Denver Bad Date Sheet.* https://docs.google.com/document/d/19x7f_Qo4dmrFDSopGiGlZn-mi2CexrhikDeAjchfzmvQ/edit?usp=sharing. Accessed January 1, 2016.

Shared Hope International. "2015 JuST Conference Agenda and Workshop Descriptions." https://sharedhope.org/just2015/2015-conference-workshops. Accessed August 26, 2015.

Sherman, Francine T. "Justice for Girls: Are We Making Progress?" *UCLA Law Review* 59 (2012): 1584–628.

Shigekane, Rachel. "Rehabilitation and Community Integration of Trafficking Survivors in the United States," *Human Rights Quarterly* 29 (2007): 112–36.

Shih, Elena. "The Anti-Trafficking Rehabilitation Complex: Commodity Activism and Slave-Free Goods." https://www.opendemocracy.net/beyond-slavery/elena-shih/antitrafficking-rehabilitation-complex-commodity-activism-and-slavefree-goo. Accessed February 13, 2016.

Shklovski, I., J. Vertesi, E. Troshynski, and P. Dourish. "The Commodification of Location: Dynamics of Power in Location-Based Systems." In *Proceedings of the International Conference on Ubiquitous Computing (Ubicomp 2009), Orlando, Florida.* New York: ACM Press, 2009.

Slavery Footprint—Made in a Free World. "How Many Slaves Work for You?" http://slaveryfootprint.org. Accessed February 10, 2016.

Smith, Linda A., and Samantha Healy Vardaman. "Domestic Human Trafficking Series: A Legislative Framework for Combating Domestic Minor Sex Trafficking," *Regent University Law Review* 23 (2011): 265–96.

Smith, Linda A., Samantha Healy Vardaman, and Melissa A. Snow. *The National Report on Domestic Minor Sex Trafficking: America's Prostituted Children.* Vancouver, WA: Shared Hope International, 2009. http://sharedhope.org/wp-content/uploads/2012/09/SHI_National_Report_on_DMST _2009.pdf.

Smith, Nat, and Eric A. Stanley, eds. *Captive Genders: Trans Embodiment and the Prison Industrial Complex.* Oakland, CA: AK Press, 2011.

Soderlund, Gretchen. "Running from the Rescuers: New U.S. Crusades Against Sex Trafficking and the Rhetoric of Abolition." *NWSA Journal* 17, no. 3 (2005): 64–87.

Solove, Daniel. *Nothing to Hide.* New Haven, CT: Yale University Press, 2011.

Spade, Dean. "Intersectional Resistance and Law Reform." *Signs* 38, no. 4 (2013): 1031–55.

Spivak, Gayatri Chakravorty. "Terror: A Speech after 9/11." *Boundary* 31 (2004): 82–111.

Stolz, Barbara Ann. "Interpreting the U.S. Human Trafficking Debate through the Lens of Symbolic Politics." *Law and Policy* 29 (2007): 311–38.

Strandburg, Katherine J. "Home, Home on the Web and Other Fourth Amendment Implications of Technosocial Change." *Maryland Law Review* 70 (2011): 614–80. http://digitalcommons.law.umaryland.edu/cgi/viewcontent. cgi?article=3460&context=mlr.

Sudbury, Julia. "Celling Black Bodies: Black Women in the Global Prison Industrial Complex." *Feminist Review* 70 (2002): 57–74.

———. "Unpacking the Crisis: Women of Color, Globalization and the Prison-Industrial Complex." In *Interrupted Life: Experiences of Incarcerated Women in the United States,* edited by Rickie Solinger, Paula C. Johnson, Martha L. Raimon, Tina Reynolds, and Ruby C. Tapia, 11–25. Berkeley: University of California Press, 2010.

"Survivor-Led Program Aims to Curb Child Sex Trafficking." WGBH News, October 6, 2014. http://wgbhnews.org/post/survivor-led-program-aims-curb-child-sex-trafficking. Accessed February 10, 2016.

Taaffe, Linda. "Tech Heavyweights Take on Human Trafficking with Big Data." *Upstart,* March 8, 2014. http://upstart.bizjournals.com/companies /innovation/2014/03/08/google-Palantir-human-trafficking.html?page=all. February 10, 2016.

Thakor, Mitali, and danah boyd. "Networked Trafficking: Reflections on Technology and the Anti-trafficking Movement." *Dialectical Anthropology* 37 (2013): 277–90.

Thrupkaew, Noy. "A Misguided Moral Crusade." *New York Times,* September 22, 2012. www.nytimes.com/2012/09/23/opinion/sunday/ending-demand-wont-stop-prostitution.html. Accessed September 24, 2015.

Tonry, Michael. *The Future of Imprisonment.* Oxford: Oxford University Press, 2004.

United States. Attorney's Office, District of Massachusetts. "Massachusetts Task Force to Combat Human Trafficking." www.justice.gov/usao-ma/civil-rights/human-trafficking/massachusetts-task-force. Accessed September 10, 2015.

United States. Congress. Justice for Victims of Trafficking Act, 18 U.S.C. §§201 et seq. (2015), https://www.congress.gov/bill/114th-congress/senate-bill/178. Accessed January 3, 2016.

———. "Stop Exploitation through Trafficking Act of 2015." 2015. https://www.congress.gov/bill/114th-congress/house-bill/159. Accessed September 10, 2015.

———. Trafficking Victims Protection Act, 22 U.S.C. §7101 (2000). 106th Congress, Washington, DC. https://www.gpo.gov/fdsys/pkg/USCODE-2010-title22/html/USCODE-2010-title22-chap78.htm. Accessed January 3, 2016.

———. *Trafficking Victims Protection Act Reauthorization of 2013.* 113th Congress, Washington, DC, 2013.

———. *Victims of Trafficking and Violence Protection Act of 2000.* 106th Congress. Washington, DC, 2000.

———. *William Wilberforce Trafficking Victims Reauthorization Act of 2008.* 110th Congress, Washington, DC, 2008.

United States. Department of Justice. Bureau of Justice Assistance. "Anti-human Trafficking Task Force Initiative." 2015. https://www.bja.gov/ProgramDetails.aspx?Program_ID=51 Accessed February 10, 2016.

———. "FY 2015 Enhanced Collaborative Model to Combat Human Trafficking Competitive Solicitation." OMB No. 1121–0329. 2015.

———. Bureau of Justice Statistics. "Arrest Data Analysis Tool: Definitions and Terms." 2014. www.bjs.gov/index.cfm?ty=datool&surl=/arrests/index.cfm. Accessed February 12, 2014.

———. "Characteristics of Suspected Human Trafficking Incidents, 2008–2010." April 2011. http://bjs.ojp.usdoj.gov/content/pub/pdf/cshtio810.pdf. Accessed September 28, 2015.

———. Department of Justice. "Human Trafficking Task Forces." 2014. www.justice.gov/usao/human-trafficking-task-forces. Accessed September 10, 2015.

———. Office of Justice Programs. "Office for Victims of Crime: Announcements." September 25, 2015. http://ovc.ncjrs.gov/humantrafficking/announcements.html. Accessed February 13, 2016.

United States. Department of State. "Trafficking in Persons Report: June 2014." 2014. www.state.gov/j/tip/rls/tiprpt/2014. Accessed July 18, 2014.

United States. Federal Bureau of Investigation. "Innocence Lost." 2013. https://www.fbi.gov/about-us/investigate/vc_majorthefts/cac/innocencelost. Accessed September 10, 2015.

———. "Sixteen Juveniles Recovered in Joint Super Bowl Operation Targeting Underage Prostitution." 2014. www.fbi.gov/newark/press-releases/2014

/sixteen-juveniles-recovered-in-joint-super-bowl-operation-targeting-under-age-prostitution. Accessed February 20, 2014.

United States. Supreme Court. *Riley v. California,* 134 S.Ct. 999 (2014). www
.google.com/url?sa=t&rct=j&q=&esrc=s&source=web&cd=1&cad=rja&u
act=8&ved=0ahUKEwiT2ufD8PfKAhWByj4KHRaZACoQFgggMAA&url
=http%3A%2F%2Fwww.supremecourt.gov%2Fopinions%2F13pdf%
2F13-132_8l9c.pdf&usg=AFQjCNGTGJru73wutQeeDaYb6nGfjau6bQ.
Accessed February 12, 2016

Vance, Carole S. "Innocence and Experience: Melodramatic Narratives of Sex
Trafficking and Their Consequences for Law and Policy." *History of the
Present* 2, no. 2 (2012): 200–218.

———. "States of Contradiction: Twelve Ways to Do Nothing about Trafficking While Pretending To." *Social Research* 78, no. 3 (2011): 933–48.

———. "Thinking Trafficking, Thinking Sex." *GLQ: A Journal of Lesbian and
Gay Studies* 17, no. 1 (2011): 135–43. doi:10.1215/10642684-2010-024.

Vuolajarvi, Niina, and Carole Vance. "Letter to the Editor: Has Sweden's Prostitution Law Lived Up to Its Promise?" *New York Times,* March 23, 2015.
www.nytimes.com/2015/03/23/opinion/has-swedens-prostitution-law-lived-
up-to-its-promise.html?_r=0. Accessed September 23, 2015.

Wacquant, Loïc. "Deadly Symbiosis: When Ghetto and Prison Meet and
Mesh." *Punishment and Society* 3, no. 1 (2001): 95–133. doi:10.1177/
14624740122228276.

———. "Ordering Insecurity: Social Polarization and the Punitive Upsurge."
Radical Philosophy Review 11 (2008): 9–27.

———. *Punishing the Poor: The Neoliberal Government of Social Insecurity.*
Durham, NC: Duke University Press, 2009.

Washington (State). Supreme Court. "J.S., S.L., and L.C., Respondents, v. Village Voice Media Holdings, L.L.C., d/b/a/ Backpage.com and Backpage.
com, L.L.C., Petitioners, Baruti Hopson and New Times Media, L.L.C.,
d/b/a/ Backpage.com, Defendants." No. 90510-0.

Wayne, Logan Danielle. "Data-Broker Threat: Proposing Federal Legislation to
Protect Post-expungement Privacy." *Journal of Criminal Law and Criminology* 102 (2012): 253–82. http://heinonline.org/HOL/LandingPage?handle=
hein.journals/jclc102&div=12&id=&page=.

Weaver, Vesla M., and Amy E. Lerman. "Political Consequences of the Carceral State." *American Political Science Review* 104, no. 4 (2010): 817–33.
http://journals.cambridge.org/action/displayAbstract?fromPage=online&aid
=7947625&fileId=S0003055410000456.

Weitzer, Ronald. "Miscounting Human Trafficking and Slavery." *OpenDemocracy,* October 8, 2014. https://www.opendemocracy.net/beyondslavery
/ronald-weitzer/miscounting-human-trafficking-and-slavery. Accessed August
26, 2015.

———. "The Social Construction of Sex Trafficking: Ideology and Institution-
alization of a Moral Crusade." *Politics and Society* 35, no. 3 (2007): 447–75.

"What Happened in Ferguson?" *New York Times,* August 10, 2015. www
.nytimes.com/interactive/2014/08/13/us/ferguson-missouri-town-under-
siege-after-police-shooting.html. Accessed January 3, 2016.

Wijers, Marjan. "Women, Labor, and Migration: The Position of Trafficked Women and Strategies for Support." In *Global Sex Workers: Rights, Resistance and Redefinition,* edited by Kamala Kempadoo and Jo Doezema, 69–78. London: Routledge, 1998.

Wijers, Marjan, Lin Lap-Chew, Stichting Tegen Vrouwenhandel, and the Global Alliance Against Traffic in Women. *Trafficking in Women, Forced Labour and Slavery-Like Practices in Marriage, Domestic Labour and Prostitution.* Utrecht, Netherlands: Foundation against Trafficking in Women; Bangkok: Global Alliance against Traffic in Women, 1997.

Williams, Katianne. "Untangling the Dark Web: Taking on the Human Sex Trafficking Industry." *IEEE Women in Engineering Magazine* 7, no. 2 (2013): 23–26. doi:10.1109/MWIE.2013.2280387.

Williams, Linda M. "Harm and Resilience among Prostituted Teens: Broadening Our Understanding of Victimisation and Survival." *Social Policy & Society* 9, no. 2 (2010): 243–54.

———. "Provide Justice for Prostituted Teens: Stop Arresting and Prosecuting Girls." In *Contemporary Issues in Criminal Justice Policy: Proposals from the American Society of Criminology Conference,* edited by Natasha A. Frost, J. Freilich, and Todd R. Clear, 227–306. Belmont, CA: Wadsworth, Cengage Learning, 2010.

Wolch, Jennifer. "The Shadow State: Transformations in the Voluntary Sector." In *The Power of Geography: How Territory Shapes Social Life,* edited by Jennifer R. Wolch and Michael Dear, 197–221. Boston: Unwin Hyman, 1989.

Wolf, Stephanie. "FBI: 16 Teens Rescued, 45 Arrested in Super Bowl Sex-Trafficking Bust." http://kdvr.com/2014/02/04/law-enforcement-rescues-16-teens-arrests-45-in-super-bowl-sex-trafficking-bust/. Accessed February 10, 2014.

Wurth, Margaret H., Rebecca Schleifer, Megan McLemore, Katherine W. Todrys, and Joseph J. Amon. "Condoms as Evidence of Prostitution in the United States and the Criminalization of Sex Work." *Journal of the International AIDS Society* 16 (2013): article 18626.

Young, Robin (host). "Researchers Say Super Bowl Sex Trafficking Included Minors." *Here and Now,* March 6, 2014. http://hereandnow.wbur.org/2014/03/06/superbowl-sex-trafficking. Accessed February 10, 2016.

Young Women's Empowerment Project. *Girls Do What They Have to Do to Survive: Illuminating Methods Used by Girls in the Sex Trade and Street Economy to Fight Back and Heal.* Chicago: Young Women's Empowerment Project, 2009. http://ywepchicago.files.wordpress.com/2011/06/girls-do-what-they-have-to-do-to-survive-a-study-of-resilience-and-resistance.pdf.

———. *Please Support Our Staff, Leadership and Membership.* Chicago: Young Women's Empowerment Project, 2013. http://ywepchicago.wordpress.com/2013/06/18/please-support-our-staff-leadership-and-membership.

Index